Understanding

SALMON
& TROUT

Contributions by Sir Hugh Mackenzie
Edmund de Rothschild, Anthony Netboy
and George Mortimer

Understanding

SALMON
& TROUT

by Tom Ravensdale

JOHN GIFFORD PUBLISHERS

Acknowledgements

The author and publishers would like to thank the Seafield Estate, for supplying some really first class fishing – the best in Scotland, The House of Hardy and Shakespeare Noris for equipment details and pictures. Abu Svangsta, for pictures and tackle details; the Scottish Tourist Association and the Highlands and Islands Development Board for information, Dr. S. S. Chissick, for special photography, and The Anglers' Mail for pictures of fishes.

We also wish to thank the British Tourist Board, and the Ministry of Agriculture of Northern Ireland for details of area fishing, Mr. and Mrs. Birchall, for good company on fishing expeditions, Mr. and Mrs. Farringdon, for wit, and a special acknowledgement to Jim Hardy for corrections and comments throughout the book and Anthony Netboy, who corrected the natural history section, their help was invaluable. Lastly a special thank you to Cliff Purvey for photography and equipment, the best of both.

copyright © 1972 T. Ravensdale
First published in Great Britain by
John Gifford Ltd.
125 Charing Cross Road,
London WC2H 0EB.

ISBN 07071 0343 6

Text set and printed in Great Britain by
C. Tinlings & Co. Ltd., Prescot and London.
Colour printed by Tindall Press, Chelmsford.

Foreword

Salmon fishing is one of the most exhilarating forms of relaxation that I know. It is hard to imagine a more enjoyable day than one spent fishing beside a beautiful river, and one of these, probably my favourite, is deep in the heart of the Scottish Highlands – the lovely River Spey. For there is no river in the world quite like the Spey; there is some magic in it which can bring back to you something of every great river that you have ever known. It may be at a time when its waters wander through flat fields, or it quickens its pace to wind among wooded slopes where the trees crowd down to the water's edge, or it reverberates raging over the rocks like a Norwegian torrent. It will always seem to be most truly itself when it races along paths between high walls which imprison the roar of its rapids. You look up at rocks and screes above you on which ragged larches grip as if their roots were talons of gaunt birds, and you can imagine yourself beside one of many Canadian rivers. But, in a moment, will be voices raised to remind you, once and for all, that you are in Scotland. For a blink of sun lights up a patch of heather high up on the slope above you, and cock grouse starts to scold in the warmth of it. And a pair of oyster catchers pipe to each other as they pass over your head, slow and serious in their search for a safe shingle beach for their nests. And when they find some spit clear of the floods they will shriek at the shy little sandpiper.

This is a river that you must treat with real respect for it runs strong even when it runs low. And you know that strength in the stream when you wade and feel for your footing on its bed of uneven rocks.

A lifetime of sport gives you a wealth of happy hours on which to look back. But there will be very few days, for that is the order of things.

My greatest memory is of a day in early May on the Castle Grant beat, with sky so blue that you could see half-way to heaven. Fishing a fly in the Polwyck pool, I

5

hooked a fish, fresh-run, a twenty-eight pounder, and I had thirty tearing minutes of battle, of kicking rod and screaming reel, before I got him to the gaff and lifted him clear of the tug of that torrent. In the afternoon the sky clouded over, the wind rose and set the branches of the trees rocking and ripples running over the dark waters. I was fishing with a bait on No. 1 burn when I hooked another big salmon, and for one solid hour we fought. I seemed to be playing not only a fighting fish but the race of the rapids as well. Slipping and sliding I followed him downstream and it was two pools further down and a long sixty minutes of my life before I got him ashore. He was but twenty-two pounds, yet so superbly shaped that my triumph was tinged with more than a touch of sadness that he was no longer living to leap and scatter the spray and show his silver sides.

If the sound of the Spey is now in your ears, it will be there as long as you live to listen.

Edmund de Rothschild

Contents

Introduction

BY

ANTHONY NETBOY

The Atlantic salmon alas has reached the stage where in some countries it is an endangered species and in others a vanishing species. In the United States it was officially placed on the Endangered Species list by the Secretary of the Interior in 1966, and in England it has for over a century been a vanishing species. In the last couple of decades the catches of salmon on the remaining rivers in England and Wales have been from 40,000 to 50,000 fish, while on the river Tyne alone a century ago the annual catch sometimes went above 100,000.

Like other valuable natural resources, the scarcer the salmon the more expensive they are, and this axiom holds true for angling possibilities. The prices at which salmon water have sold recently in England (and Scotland) are incredible: up to £1,000 per rod, per week!

The British people have always cherished their salmon and from the time of King Malcom in Scotland in the 11th century, passed laws to regulate and protect it. But the advent of the industrial revolution caused enormous devastation on the rivers of England and Wales and a few Scottish streams.

Weirs and mill dams multiplied; and regulation of catches did not work well. The result is the situation we have today where many once noble rivers are empty of these fishes, such as the Thames, and others which have greatly diminished runs (like the Wye, which is now the premier salmon angling river south of the Scottish border).

While this book by Tom Ravensdale is basically a handbook, readers need not be reminded that opportunities for fishing for salmon or trout are in direct proportion to the effort spent to conserve the resources. Artificial production, is an increasing tool of management and invaluable in the sustainment of the runs but so far as salmon are concerned, England so far has done little to make use of this tool. There is little artificial breeding of salmon, and so far as I can see, not much interest in undertaking such programmes. They are expensive, to be sure, but the expense is returned manyfold by all countries that have undertaken large-scale hatchery work.

The biggest threat to the further existence of *Salmo salar* in the British Isles is the large scale slaughter of fish emanating from British rivers in the waters around Greenland. While no real measure of the impact of this unconscionable fishery, mostly by the Danes and Norwegians, is possible, we know that in recent years, or since the feeding grounds of the salmon in the ocean were discovered, returns of fish to many British rivers have declined, and many an angler has come home with little to show for his effort and expenditures. Another supporting fact for this conclusion is that the catches of grilse have been rising in proportion to the catches of mature salmon and this is probably due to the fact that the Greenland fishery takes only salmon that have been in the sea one winter or more. We do not know as yet where the grilse feed, although there are suspicions it is somewhere in the North Atlantic east of Greenland.

What is clearly needed, and most urgently, is to put a stop to the Greenland fishery, or curb it sharply. International Commissions have struggled with this problem but have failed to make any headway except to get the predator nations to agree not to take any more fish than the record 1969 levels!

The United States, which has only a minimal stake in the Greenland fishery, has just enacted a law which gives the President authority to embargo imports of fish and fish products from any nation that does not adhere to good fishery conservation practices in international waters. The law is aimed squarely at the Danes and Norwegians, from whom the United States imports considerable amounts of fish products. There is no sign yet that the President will use the power but the mere existence of the law has given a profound psychological shock to the Danish and Norwegian governments. It illustrates an ancient theory about national predation on other nation's resources: hit the offender at the pocketbook nerve.

It is to be hoped that the British government will take notice of the so-called 'Atlantic Salmon bill' signed on January 3rd, 1972 by the American President and put forth more effort to get the Danes and others to diminish and eventually stop killing their salmon (which ironically they buy back by importing the fish from Denmark).

9

1 *Salmonidae*

The *Salmonid* family includes Salmon, Trout and Char, all of which are slim, bony predators found in the seas and inland waters of the Northern hemisphere. Technically speaking the family tree begins with the *Osteichthyes* class, from which the sub-class *Neopterygii* is branched. From this spring the *Isopondyli* and *Coregonus* orders.

However, we shall deal only with the well known 'game fish' in these pages, notably the *Salmonids*. Fish such as the *Thymallus vulgaris* (grayling) are of more interest to the coarse fisherman (although some fly men may disagree with this); in any case the Grayling is no longer classified with *Salmonidæ* so the problem resolves itself.

Our specific interest in this book will be centred on *Salmo salar* (the Atlantic salmon); *Salmo trutta* (the wary sea trout); *Salmo irrideus* (the beautiful rainbow trout); and *Salmo fario* (the brown trout or brownie), the latter being the only non-migratory species in the group. From now on we shall call these fishes by their common names.

The fabulous rainbow trout is a relative newcomer to British waters, being introduced from the United States in the late 19th century. It is more voracious than the brown trout and, being a hungrier eater, (it consumes roughly double the daily intake of a brown trout) is a little easier to catch. It is, however, unlikely that rainbows will become natural inhabitants of British waters for they object most strongly to captivity (a small loch is the only safe place to stock rainbows and this is where they are usually found) and will seek means of escape when introduced to new fishing grounds. The brown trout has no such eccentricities; on the contrary, it is a territorial creature and will fight fin and barb to protect its domain. Salmon and sea trout are remarkable wanderers but more of their peculiarities later.

Recognising or differentiating between these four fishes is not always easy and although the rainbows and brownies may be seen in trolley tanks in the best hotels and

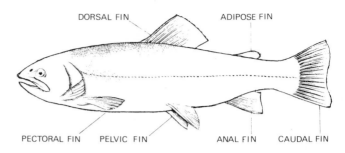

DORSAL FIN   ADIPOSE FIN

PECTORAL FIN   PELVIC FIN   ANAL FIN   CAUDAL FIN

A TYPICAL SALMONID

Fig. 1 Note the typical adipose
fin and complete lateral line

restaurants, it is unlikely that you will find the sea trout or salmon in anything but the finest of public aquariums. Considering the 'natural conditions' the curator has to provide this is not surprising. The salmon and sea trout spend part of their lives in the sea with a water density of roughly 1·025 and a salinity of around 0·34%. Fresh water contains 20% more oxygen than salt water so any change is pretty abrupt even though brackish estuary water is 'run through' first. They also spend a number of years in a river with a water density of approximately 1·0 and a total lack of salinity. Sometimes the mighty salmon will waggle its way into tiny streams little deeper than the breadth of its own body! If these conditions were provided there would still be the problem of providing a roof to each tank or every single specimen would be found on the floor before long, such prodigious jumpers are they. Lastly, the biological peculiarities and mysteries surrounding the salmon, which are far too complex – and poorly understood – to be considered here, would need to be overcome before the aquarist could offer the angler live specimens for examination at will. Suffice to say, if you want to examine a salmon, you must go and catch one!

IDENTIFICATION

All members of the salmonidae family have a long torpedo shaped body and *two* dorsal fins.

The small fin on the back of the fish is called the adipose and the position it occupies helps to indicate the identity of the fish. For example the salmon has 11 or 12

12

scales between the rear of the adipose and the medial line (see fig. 1), which runs the length of the body horizontally; on the other hand trout have 14 scales in the same position. This applies only to adult fish, younger specimens are quite different.

Salmon

In the adult, the jaw bone or mouth ends dead in line with an imaginary perpendicular dropped from the centre of the eye. When they first enter fresh water after a year or more at sea, salmon are a shimmering silver colour with reddish pink spots along the flank *above* the medial line, although an older fish, which has spawned before, may have a few below. This irridescence gradually fades as the months go by until the whole fish goes pink, brownish, and finally cherry red when breeding time arrives. As already explained, there are 11 or 12 scales between the adipose fin and the medial line.

Sea Trout

This fish changes colour with size and it is not always easy to distinguish one from a brown trout. Up to approximately 18 ins., the tail is usually forked but the end tends to square off thereafter until the body length reaches at least 24 ins at which time the tail tends to become rounded.

The adult sea trout has more spots on its side than a salmon and they are quite blackish, but the main difference

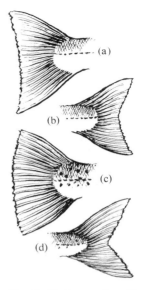

Fig. 2 Various *salmonid* tails.
a. salmon
b. grilse
c. trout
d. sea trout

Fig. 3 A kelt, (bottom) has a much slimmer body than the healthy salmon (above).

13

Fig. 4 A fresh run sea trout.

is that the spots extend *below* the lateral line as well as above. Even more distinct is the apparent size of the mouth. The jaw bone or mouth of the sea trout extends well beyond an imaginary line dropped vertically from the eye, which gives the appearance of a large mouth compared to the salmon. Another, more subtle difference, is the yellow tip which can sometimes be seen on the adipose of a sea trout. Lastly, handling the fishes can sometimes tell a story; the scales of a sea trout tend to come off and stick to the hands whereas salmon or brown trout scales are glued on to the fish much tighter. So is the tail! The salmon may be 'tailed' by hand (which means literally grabbing the fish by the tail after playing him to exhaustion) but a sea trout may slip away. Indeed, any salmon can be held up by grasping just before the tail no matter how wet and slippery he may be but a sea trout will slip from the grasp quite readily.

Brown Trout

In adult form the 'Brownie' is quite similar to the sea trout. The adipose does, however, sport a red tip and

14

spots, which are reddish in colour and scattered *all over* the body. The scales are generally firmer than the sea trout. Colouring depends on the water, foods and even surrounding countryside. The back is usually olive-green to brown with a green to silver sheen on the flanks. The red body spots have a blue edging and the adipose fin often has red spots too. The average maximum length of the brown trout is 30 cms although it will grow much larger occasionally.

Rainbow Trout

There is seldom any difficulty in identifying this colourful beauty and, as they are usually found only in stocked lakes, an identification problem does not often occur. They have the same shape, jaw bone and scale peculiarities as brown trout and although colours vary considerably the back is generally green, turning to brown on the sides and yellow under the belly. A wide rainbow coloured band runs along the flanks and the fish is covered with star shaped black spots.

Fig. 5 A rainbow trout of almost 3 lbs.

15

Young Fishes

To distinguish between trout and salmon parr (baby fishes) is not difficult. The trout jaw bone, as in the adult, extends well beyond the vertical level of the eye and the adipose has a reddish tip. The tail is blunt and the gill-plate spots are gathered together in one group. On the other hand, the salmon jaw bone ends in line with the eye; it has an almost transparent anal fin (see fig. 1); the tail is forked and there is a curious set of eight vertical black bars, commonly called 'finger prints', on its side; trout markings are not very pronounced and are fewer in number. The salmon parr scales are very delicate and only two or three spots decorate the gill cover.

Sexes

To distinguish between male and female is seldom necessary other than for reasons of interest to the angler (or couseinier) and the fish is usually landed before the sexing can take place (although most experienced anglers will sex a salmon on its first leap). Once on the bank the differences become plain. The cock salmon has a much longer 'nose' than the hen and his gill cover is more pointed. As breeding time approaches the cock develops a large 'blister' on his lower jaw. This blister gradually grows into a large 'hook'. It is thought that this curved hook, called a Kype, is an exceedingly efficient 'tailer' and is used to haul competitors off his 'nest' when breeding occurs, but more of this later. The hook does of course provide the fisherman with a means of instant recognition with experience and it is not at all difficult to catch a glimpse of the 'beak' when the cock leaps as he is played or when he surmounts rapids.

The male trout also differs from his opposite sex by

Fig. 6 A tagged parr.

virtue of head size and shape, being much larger and more pointed. The gill cover of the cock is less rounded but his body is more torpedo shaped than the full, deep, narrow shape of the hen. Cocks in general are also a little more colourful.

SALMONIDÆ NATURAL HISTORY

Salmon

The mighty salmon begins life in crude underwater trenches known as *redds*. The story begins far out at sea when some strange undefinable instinct urges the adult salmon to seek fresh clean water in which to propagate. The story is not even as simple as that for he does not seek just any old fresh water – it must come from the river of his birth! This extraordinary side of the salmon has given zoologists, ichthyologists and biologists a whole mass of problems to solve yet for some reason the call of the salmon at sea interests very few scientists and little is known of his range and habits other than the occasional stomach content examination at sea which suggests virtual surface or 'upper layer' feeding on small crustacea, herring fry, sand eels, prawns and so on. A salmon needs clean, oxygenated water and will not enter 'his' breeding river if it is polluted, preferring to die at sea. Anthony Netboy's 'The Atlantic Salmon – A Vanishing Species' describes many salmon problems in this light.

To return to a chronological narrative however, some of the eager salmon, gathering in the shallow upper reaches and river sources of sparkling fresh water have come a long way for their instinctive needs. They have

Fig. 7 The hook or 'kype' of a cock salmon *after* spawning when teeth re-appear.

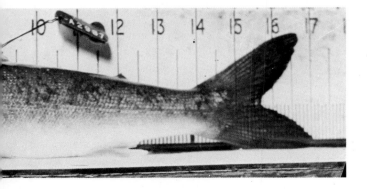

survived the ever increasing number of estuary nets and the shock of moving from salt to fresh water – a truly remarkable biological wonder. After a year or so at sea and a long, long wait at the river mouth for correct water height and temperature (salmon will not enter a river much colder than 10°C) they have dodged and ducked many nets and eager fishing rods with incredibly beautiful and tempting baits; of rubber sand eels and multi-coloured flies; poachers' hooks, deadly low water, 'dry' pools and mysterious water ladders. They have patiently waited for flood waters to raise the water level on low stretches; they have watched innumerable fish whisked miraculously out of the water by invisible nylon threads; fought every rapid the river could offer, the Otter and the Cormorant, and now at last they seek their reward in a fashion which will leave them virtually exhausted, for very few will survive the act of procreation.

In Great Britain November is usually the month chosen for spawning although the season can extend well into February. It is interesting to note that the greatest danger to eggs, the bottom feeders and 'snout' scavengers of the river, are mostly out of action during the spawning period. The eel, which is the most voracious bottom scavenger of all, is hibernating at this time.

The actual spawning commences at dusk and continues well into late evening. The hen moves into a current, closely followed by an extremely excited and deeply coloured cock. The hen selects a suitable length of gravel covered flat bed and commences to waggle her body violently. This action stirs up the gravel and small stones so much that a deep pit is excavated. These pits are called *redds* and are usually about one length of the fish and four times the width. When she is satisfied with the size and shape of her excavation, the hen deposits a stream of eggs into the centre. The cock has been assisting by 'siddling' alongside the hen throughout and generally keeping the hen (and himself) in a state of extreme excitement by shivering against her flanks and touching her *lateral line* (see fig. 1). The blood vessels of both fish, especially the cock as his deep red colour attests, have become greatly distended by this time and the lateral line, which is a highly sensitive 'extra sense' consisting of a complete 'chemical' nervous system (beyond the bounds of this book) is even more 'tuned' than usual. Furthermore its normal function of receiving vibratory waves in water is completely overmasked as the high hormone content blood floods to the skin surface. Each quivering touch of these super-sensitive areas appears to send waves of ecstasy surging through the fish and only very severe interruptions from outside will affect their activities.

When the hen has deposited a batch of eggs she moves upstream a few feet and the cock assumes her previous position in order to expel his sperm. This free swimming substance is then able to fertilise the ova and each time the cock 'comes', a cloud of minute spermatozoa bleaches the water seeking ova to invade. He then returns to the hen's side a few feet upstream and the whole procedure is repeated. Very often the cock ejaculates simultaneously with the female. The stones and gravel thrown up as the hen threshes and waggles her body to dig her pit are re-deposited *onto the last pile of fertilised eggs* and they are then safe from the force of the water current or hungry predators until hatching time, (theoretically at least).

Whilst all these dramatic events are taking place a 3rd, 4th or even 5th salmon may be taking a very active part indeed. These unwanted intruders are young salmon parr who become almost as excited as their big brothers, darting in and out between the two adults *depositing their own milt*! The milt of these young fish is just as effective as that of the larger fish and indeed is often more accurately placed. This fact has no influence on the attitude of the larger cock who is constantly harrassed from all directions by these bothersome miniatures and, in chasing them off, very often returns to find a full grown male in his place and a short sharp scuffle may take place. This is usually restricted to grabbing the tail with the hooked beak (kype) – especially grown for just this purpose – and hauling the stranger off the nest. What with the parr slipping in and out of mating pairs and redds overlapping – occupants and all, a general free for all is nature's way of ensuring that most of the ova laid by the hen are fertilised. Yet still the eggs have a massive fatality percentage; even as the salmon spawn, local residents, such as trout or grayling, are feeding themselves on the eggs! The number of eggs produced by the hen depends on her size but in general an average of 1000 eggs per kilo of body weight can be expected.

Spawning lasts from 3 to 10 days, depending upon the right temperatures. If there is a severe frost during the night, the spawning will be short lived but warm nights will allow a full week or even longer for the salmon to reproduce its kind. The eggs which survive the first devastating days of existence gradually build themselves into sturdy pink circles of life wedged between chunks of rock or small stones. The fresh clear water constantly throbbing past is rich in oxygen and the firm yet gentle action of the stream sustains the embryonic salmon.

Weather now plays its part; stones which anchor the ova may be washed away; a lack of rain will reduce the water height and ova may be left high and dry; temperature also plays a part, for the colder it is, the longer incubation will last, and risks are increased with time. Yet another danger is the possibility of a second run of salmon, which would of course tear up the redds as new fish perform their dramatic spawning activities, and many of the original ova will be washed away.

Incubation lasts from 5–8 weeks, although a severe winter may even delay hatching for another month. The tiny fish, which emerge from the ova, appear to have most of the egg still attached to their bodies and this is not very far from the truth, it is in fact a 'yolk sac' and is nothing more elaborate than a complete food supply to set the young salmon, or *alevin* as it is known at this stage, off to a good start. The alevin is only $\frac{1}{2}$ in. long now but, as the yolk sac is absorbed and the belly retains more natural looking dimensions, the fry is easily recognised as a true blue blooded member of the *salmonidæ* family. Growth is rather slow at first and almost four months pass before the fry reaches 1 in. in body length. Growth then accelerates to a nice healthy level, although weaker fry may hold onto their yolk sac food for twice as long as normal.

The fry emerge nearly all at once, or at least within a few days of each other, and they instinctively group together. Food must now be obtained from the water and life becomes a never ending search for minute aquatic organisms called plankton. Chances of survival have become a matter of speed and agility for these tiddlers are fair game and jolly good eating for every predator in the river. This soon selects the fittest and the weak quickly succumb.

When the young salmon reach 3–4 ins. in length they have developed the characteristic bars (see fig. 6) which identify them as *parr*. Growth will depend on the availability of food and the weather. The parr eat very little, if anything, when the temperature drops and winter is

20

passed in almost total abstinence. Development is again rather slow at this stage in the life of the salmon and maturity may take 2, 3 or even 4 years to reach.

A 2 year old salmon should be 6 ins in length. At this time it seems to receive some strange magic call from the very depths of the far off ocean and in late spring huge shoals begin to drop down the river as the water height permits. It is usual to expect the first May floods to start the exodus and practically all the little salmon make a bee line for the estuary. The brownish blue stripes on their sides have now disappeared and silver flashing flanks take their place. The fish is now called a *smolt*. At the most opportune tidal moment the smolts enter the sea and there ends our narrative for a while.

He travels far and wide, usually in shoals, just like mackerel. Fish on the west coast of Britain are greatly affected by the Gulf Stream and usually drift along leisurely with North Atlantic currents bringing much food, such as herring fry, which cannot help but drift with the currents, and are excellent food for such predators as salmon. The Arctic also offers good feeding grounds and so the salmon can be found in both areas.

Eventually, after 1, 2 or 3 years, it will return to fresh water. If the salmon has been at sea only 1 year it is called a *grilse* and will weigh from 1 to 2 kilos or more. A fish which spends 3 or 4 years at sea may weigh up to 10 kilos or more. A large grilse can be distinguished from a small salmon (which has been at sea, say, 2 years) in a number of ways. A grilse has a small tail and a pronounced taper to its body; this ends in a slim tail body and a vee shaped tail fin. Its head is quite small and it is usually in perfect condition but the scales are very loosely attached.

There are three periods during the year when the salmon (or grilse) 'run' up river; January to May, usually called the spring run; June to August; and September to October. Some areas have heavy grilse runs and it is hard to understand the mechanics of a salmon 'run' up river but physical conditions are undoubtedly the most important deciders. Whilst at sea the salmon, in common with most similar feeders, swim 'with' the sea and wind but in fresh water they move 'against' both current and wind. Provided the temperature in the estuary does not differ from that of the sea more than one or two degrees and is not lower than 15°C *and the wind sweeps to the sea,* there is a good chance of a salmon run. Rivers which have melted

Fig. 8 A fine catch of fresh run salmon.

21

snow water sources seldom have an early run as they tend to 'fill' later than soil or rock fed rivers.

Once in the river, which must be clean and non-polluted, the salmon needs a good rest and a little time to overcome the colossal biological differences between salt and fresh water; they 'weigh' more for one thing but to confuse matters the pressure is less, in fact the whole chemical and physical surroundings, which the salmon has become used to, changes considerably. Once the fish has overcome these differences it starts to move upstream, moving at anything from 10–20 miles a day, depending upon temperature. The salmon will move mainly at night and preferably when the river is in flood. When the water is high and fast, the fish swims out of the force stream but in low water it prefers the centre. The journey is quite leisurely and will be controlled again by weather, especially water height and river characteristics. They cannot of course swim in water much less than their own body depth, although they will occasionally wriggle through shallow water with their backs high and dry when the end is near and their goal is in sight. Dry periods usually force the salmon to stay where they are – usually in deep slow streams known as 'pools' – until the rains come and a 'spate', or flood, allows them to 'run' upstream a little further. Small waterfalls and weirs provide sight-seers with the delightful sight of fresh run salmon gleaming silver as they leap anything up to 3 m. in height.

During the run up river, salmon do not feed but live on body fat accumulated at sea. This remark may well prompt the reader to ask "Why on earth do they take the bait then?" and the answer is not an easy one, but each type of lure which catches the wary salmon has its own story to tell; the pros and cons of baits are discussed in chapter 4.

Salmon spend a great deal of their time leaping even though there is no apparent obstacle or reason for such acrobatics and again it is difficult to place a finger on *the* reason but a number of possibilities seem likely. Firstly the fresh run salmon has usually managed to collect a number of mites or bugs which cling to the skin and cause discomfort and irritation (these parasites are discussed later). The unfortunate fish has no way to scratch himself and a general thrashing around, followed by fast bursts of speed, which result in the fish leaving the water, may perhaps dislodge a mite or two. Underwater studies of fish

22

by the author have indicated a peculiar diving procedure adopted by many parasite infested fishes in which they dive straight for the bottom of the river and scrape their sides along the gravel, dislodging the pests in the process. Sometimes these dives are so strong the sheer momentum of the run sends the fish clean out of the water. Parasite infested fish are not of course the only ones to leap around in a crowded pool and many jumps are undoubtedly caused by sheer excitement as the mating urge nears fever pitch. Battles or minor skirmishes between males often lead to a fleeing fish who swims upwards in an effort to escape a tail bite and swims clean out of the water. There are some who believe that salmon actually jump in order to see obstacles, such as waterfalls, so they can estimate the necessary 'run in' but this seems a little far fetched. Restriction in a small pool will cause most fishes to jump, regardless of their race but one thing is sure – leaping salmon are no more likely to be caught than non-leaping varieties! It is interesting to note that good healthy salmon leap on an even keel whereas kelts, which are worn out emaciated fish, jump unevenly and on their sides.

The salmon finally reach the spawning area in late September. If the river has an early spring run of fish the season is usually closed on September 1st but, if not, the Autumn run may continue well into October. Spawning, takes place in the tiny burns (streams) where the bed is suitably stoned and gravelled. Few salmon survive the spawning act to return to the sea and very few indeed manage a third run. They leave the spawning grounds in a desperate condition with little body fat left for metabolism to function properly. They have winter dead ahead and the cocks have the added difficulty of a huge hooked mouth, which makes feeding very difficult indeed. The unfortunate salmon is now called a *kelt* and is a mere shadow of its former self. Its body becomes emaciated and slim, the tail frays and collects fungus, the head seems huge and grotesque and the gills fill with 'maggots', which feed off their living host. The kelt soon grows very sharp teeth if it survives and eventually begins to feed. The once glorious silver body sheen is now a dull white. Many salmon die during the act of spawning – especially the cocks. In the spawning areas numerous fish can be found on the bank in the early morning and most of them are cocks. One short stretch of the river Spey in Scotland gave up over three hundred fish in one month in this way.

23

The kelts fortunate enough to survive the winter gradually drop down to deeper water and, with a little luck and a lot of determination, may even return to the sea one day and perhaps live to spawn again.

Sea Trout

The natural history of the sea trout is not so very different from that of the salmon but its character is far less extrovert; in fact the sea trout is downright nervous and it takes a great deal of cunning and care to land one. The sea trout usually enters a river for breeding purposes in April or May. Unlike the salmon, the sea trout feeds whilst making its way up-stream although it seldom moves around or eats during day-light. The horn, which grows on the lower jaw in the same way as a salmon, does not grow so large and does not seem an impediment to feeding. Eggs are laid and fertilised in October but in shallower water than salmon although they have been known to lay eggs in the same redds and thus tear up the salmon eggs. The hatching eggs, some months later, are particularly susceptible to being eaten by other fishes and, even worse, dragon fly larvae.

The sea trout will live in the river for 2–4 years whereupon the first May floods to entice them will result in the long trip to sea. The sea trout tends to spend much of its visit to the sea in estuary waters and brackish tidal basins. The following summer sees a return to the river and, if doing so after only one winter the trout are known as *finnock*. After spawning, the sea trout kelts return to the estuary (if they have survived the winter) although they do not seem to suffer so severely from the act of breeding as the salmon, and as elvins are pouring into the rivers in spring, a grand feast usually saves the trout from starvation. Sea trout are generally better fighters than salmon and, at the risk of disagreeing with some anglers, can offer a more sporting and exciting battle for the fisherman. Considering the comparatively few mortalities after spawning it seems reasonable to assume the sea trout is a tougher, stronger fish. The sea trout also lives for twice as long as the salmon – 15 years or so, whereas a 7 year old salmon is quite an old boy.

Brown Trout

This member of the salmon family is the only non-migratory one and although it does not have the romantic

24

1 A brown trout parr.

2 Large trout will live peacefully in an aquarium—not so in the wild!

3 A fine, fresh-run hen salmon.

4 A salmon kelt—note the enlarged head and teeth.

5 A beautifully coloured trout and a tasty breakfast.

6 This dissection of a hen salmon shows clearly the internal organs and their sad condition after spawning. The flesh left on the body is hardly sufficient to maintain metabolism, the reason for such appalling losses when breeding is over.

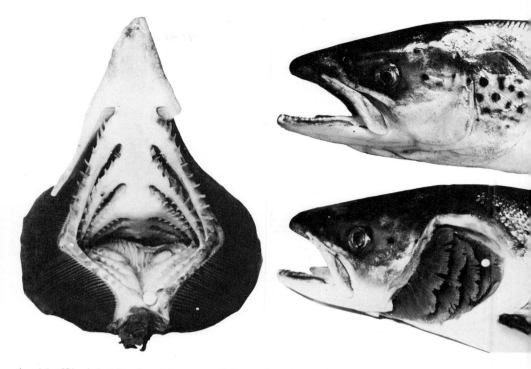

(and baffling) habit of rushing to and from the sea as the feeling takes it, the brownie is nevertheless interesting and will know his section of the river far better than any wandering nomad would. Unlike the others, the brownie is a territorial fish and a large rock, undercut banking or deep cleft will be adopted as a home and fought for with great tenacity. The brown trout will live either in a river, stream or lake and spawning usually takes place after their big brothers have finished, sometime in January or February. This is a difficult time, for food is scarce and ice is forming everywhere. Lake trout also have to contend with the highly dangerous pike, which sometimes spawn at the same time. As with salmon and sea trout, the brownie runs upstream when the urge takes them, usually on dark nights and seldom on a full moon or bright night.

They select shallower burns and side streams than the sea trout and dig out their redds in a similar manner. The operation lasts for about 3 days and almost twice as many ova are laid by the trout than with salmon. Incubation lasts 1–3 months. Lake trout move to the inlet where water enters, if stream fed, to lay their eggs as fast moving water is essential to the ova.

Fig. 9 (left) A complete, dissected gill chamber: note the one way 'filters'.

Fig. 10 (above) The kelt: note the new teeth and lean throat.

Fig. 11 (below) Here the operculum has been removed to show the gills which have been infested by gill 'maggots'.

29

Rainbow Trout

These fishes are usually farm bred and then taken to lakes for stocking when necessary. They are rather short lived, seldom exceeding 7 years of age. A lake is usually cleared of unwanted predators, such as pike, by electric charges sent through the water before young rainbows are set loose and new fish are tipped in every year. Male rainbows are very aggressive and indeed the females are not particularly sociable. Age and size does tend to mellow temperment and large fish can usually be kept together without trouble.

SALMON AND TROUT ENEMIES

These are varied and numerous. Man is of course the Number One criminal with his pollutive ways. Predators, from pike to otters are fairly dangerous, but excessive spates, dry spells, rats and insects account for many dead fish. Perhaps the biggest single cause of death is the sheer act of breeding, which accounts for the greatest depletion of numbers altogether.

Diseases

Diseases claim a large toll too. The worst of all Salmon family ailments is undoubtedly Ulcerative Dermal Necrosis *Fig. 12* The brown trout. (U.D.N.), an ulcerous skin disease, which very quickly

reaches epidemic proportions. The early symptoms of this disease is a slight bleaching of small skin areas, smaller in appearance than ringworm, which usually appear on the head, dorsal fin, along the back and on the tail. Extensive areas of grey or white slimy growth build up over the bleached patches so that the fish can be clearly seen in the water. At this stage the symptoms have been described as being of a white, woolly appearance and likened to fungus, but on closer inspection the lesions show a lack of the fuzzy appearance characteristic of a fungus infection. Eventually, however, a fungus may overgrow the bacterial lesion and cause even more confusion.

Fig. 13 A beautiful 6 lb rainbow trout.

Once out of the water, the slimy matter resembles sodden white or grey filter paper. This can be easily peeled off to reveal an underlying inflamation of shallow ulceration of the skin, with loose scale pockets which may fall out.

18–24 hours after removal of the fish from water, the slimy material dries out to show the underlying haemorrhage and, as this material is so easily rubbed off, it is essential that care is taken to prevent this during packing and transit to the laboratory.

Any fish caught or seen with any of these symptoms should be reported to the gillie and returned to the land owner immediately.

The following advice has been offered by the Spey District Fishery Board regarding this disease:

1. Net or rod and line fishing may proceed as usual and should be neither increased nor decreased in intensity.

2. Fish can be sold provided they are not unsightly and do not have lesions or sores on their bodies, which are symptomatic of this disease. The water bailiffs can identify fish carrying the disease.

3. There is no present restriction on the movement of healthy fish.

4. All infected fish and dead or moribund fish should be removed and buried deeply away from the river.

5. All fishing gear, tackle and clothing of anglers, particularly boots and waders, should be disinfected after fishing by using a strong solution of any good domestic disinfectant, e.g. Jeyes or Dettol.

A fungus (*Bacillus salmonis pestis*) is peculiar to salmon and the *Bacterium salmonicida,* tumour or boil also becomes confused with the aforementioned diseases. The vent enlarges, the fish darkens with patches on the body. Sometimes there are no external signs.

Parasites are common to all animals but the fish is unable to relieve the annoyance of his pests by the common 'scratch'. The pests are therefore able to dig and burrow at will into the skin causing damage which may develop into more serious ailments later. Some parasites are internal and there is no way the angler can detect such cases. But the well known sea louse and gill 'maggots' are easily recognised. The lice are often seen (gleefully) on fresh run fish.

Although most fishermen believe there are two main kinds of louse, called the long-tailed and the short-tailed, they have probably only seen two versions of the same louse. (In fact, there are many kinds of louse but we are referring here to the 'sea louse'.) The usual kind is about $\frac{1}{4}$ in. long. It clings to the skin of the fish by suckers. The 'so-called' long tailed kind are really the same parasites with very long egg sacs hanging from their sides. These sacs fall off after a while, leaving the normal (short-tailed) kind still on the skin. This parasite can only live for 48 hours or so in fresh water; the eggs can live for much longer and may even hatch.

Ospreys, otters etc., do very little damage to salmon or trout stocks. The Osprey tends to go for the more sluggish fish, such as pike, which lie in the shallows of lakes or lochs. In any case, the Osprey is very nearly extinct in Gt.

Britain and the Loch Garten nest is a great centre of attraction for tourists. The otter is another much maligned animal so often blamed for salmon and trout shortage. In fact, the otter feeds mostly on eels, not salmon, and on the rare occasions when a kelt is taken by an otter the remains left on the bank are a very important part of the environmental balance, they serve to feed many other creatures of the riverside. The pike, however, is a very serious threat indeed and can probably account for the greater part of trout and salmon fry losses. The trout eats most of its own fry too, given the chance.

Pollution is now at its greatest danger level – not only for fishes but for man himself. Sewage effluent, industrial and agricultural wastes – even the casual riverside visitor (including the angler!) may damage the water with a little carelessness. There are a number of unwritten rules and regulations the riverside walker should adhere to and the fisherman's code is a good one.

'When in the country, guard against fires. Lock all gates after you. Keep dogs under control. Stay on the path in fields. Do not damage fences or hedges. Take your litter home. Protect wildlife, plants and trees, respect the life of the countryside and . . . think country.'

BREEDING AND FISH FARMING

Not all people destroy everything in sight by the river and the angler, although often accused of depleting fish stocks, probably does more to keep certain species of fish flourishing than any other branch of the public. The hatcheries, which spring up all over the country, are paid for in many cases by angling clubs (or hydro boards who are pestered by the anglers). Much work is done to improve rivers; tons of gravel are tipped into breeding stretches; natural barriers are removed and stream flows over eggs are ensured. The Highlands and Islands Board is directing much research into the fish farming programmes and there are many schemes now under way. These range from rainbow trout hatcheries to the Loch Creran, Argyll, project for an oyster farm costing over £100,000.

An important aspect of fish farming, not often noticed is that fish subjected to inoculation from such diseases as furunculosis in the hatcheries may well become immune to the disease and pass this immunity on to their young and subsequently to wild fishes through normal gene routes.

33

2   *Rods and Reels*

One of the most exciting aspects of salmon and trout fishing is surely the fiddling around with all the vast tackle paraphernalia which fishermen seem to accumulate over the years. The grate of a ratchet as a new line is wound onto a fine reel sends goose pimples up the spine of a true angler and he who can handle the lengths of a fresh lacquered split cane rod without desperately wishing he could fit them together and 'test the whip' is no true sportsman. The fly boxes and battered hat; the hanging waders and the array of last year's lures; the new flies and the unwrapped nylon – all go to make fishing the most exciting and wonderful sport ever devised.

But the right tackle is undoubtedly the key to happy days by the river, it is absolutely vital that correct gear is purchased from the very beginning.

Disregarding poachers and belly ticklers, a rod is the angler's most important – and expensive – tool. Correct selection from the start is vital and selection is the key word here for the variety of salmon rods on the market today is staggering. The type of fishing envisaged is of course of paramount importance and the serious salmon and trout man will probably have half a dozen different rods in his shed.

There are two basic ways to fish – with a fly or with a live/artificial bait; each demands a special rod. A tough overhung Scottish mountain river requires a different technique, and rod, to a flat, open Cornish water and so on. Whatever waters you fish the absolute necessities are: one salmon fly rod, one salmon spinning rod and a trout fly rod. The salmon spinner *can* be used for trout although much of the sport will be lost, but fly rods are not interchangeable. Finance will of course determine type and quality of equipment but the budget conscious angler would do well to purchase one really good rod sooner than three mediocre 'sticks'.

The great dispute between cane or fibre-glass rods has

Fig. 1 Abu fibre-glass rods.

Fig. 15 Single and double handed rods.

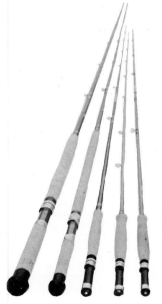

long since died down although there are countless die-hards who 'wouldn't even try a glass rod as a gift' and when one feels the sheer magic in the craftsmanship of say a £65 Hardy Wye split cane rod it is easy to understand. However, the object of a rod is to place the fish enticement precisely where it is required and, if this is done success-fully, bring back the fish. A good fibre-glass rod will do the job just as well as a greenheart or a fine split cane. There is no 'better' type; the best of each are equal to one another in their own way. Frankly the newcomer can virtually forget the subtle differences between high class rods for it takes a great deal of experience to differentiate between them. A glass rod gives its own peculiar brand of handling quality and lightness, which can, on occasion, out-balance the rather heavy feel of a wooden rod. On the other hand a good wooden rod gives the owner a pride and satisfaction which tends to bring an edge of care and craftsmanship into the fisherman just as the Rolls driver handles his car with a little more precision, with full knowledge of the workmanship beneath his fingers – a solid gold pen always writes better than a plastic one! The subtleties between glass and wood are obviously a matter of personal preference – with the pocket in mind. One thing is, however, paramount – quality comes first and be it fibre-glass or steel, greenheart or split cane, it should be the best of its kind.

When selecting a rod, examine the rings to see if they are firmly fixed and straight; ensure that no part of the rod is unvarnished (or coated as the modern glass rods are). Check the butt for grip and length – especially if you are left handed.

Salmon Fly Rods

The purpose built salmon fly rod in best quality split cane is a pretty expensive luxury and the hollow or stagger built job is virtually priceless but it would not be much good if it were too long for the river, such as an overhung chalk stream, so decide where and how you intend to fish first. Nowadays the salmon fly rod is from 12–14 ft in length with popularity perhaps tending towards 12 ft 6 ins. Each and every rod of this class will have its own peculiarities and there are numerous points to look for. A rod of such length should be in three pieces and joints must fit well. It will be a double handed casting rod and if your hands are exceptionally large you should check for ample grip

36

although most rods do tend to have plenty of handle. Equally important are the rings, which should be of the coated metal type and not 'grommetted' with anything, except the tip. The tip of the rod takes most of the strain in action and a sintox or agate ring, which does not shatter so readily when dropped, is preferred – tungsten carbide is excellent. Glass top rod rings are not advisable. Good quality rings often denote a well built rod but not always, so examine the way they are put on; the top ring should be visible in the centre of the bottom or butt ring when the rod is put together and laid on a flat surface.

Correct spacing is also vital and on a 12 ft 6 in. rod there would generally be one large ring only on the butt section, four on the second and six on the top piece – the final ring being agate and the rest plain wire. Slight variations on the second two lengths will depend on bindings and wood type or glass thickness, the object of correctly spaced rings is to ensure a friction free cast and a no tangle retrieve.

In general there are a great number of 'action' choices.

Fig. 16 **Rod making at** Hardy Brothers of Alnwick.

37

There are fast rods and slow rods; stiff rods and supple rods; in fact it is doubtful whether any six experienced fishermen would suggest the same type of action between them when helping you select a rod so the decision is unfortunately one you must make alone. An overstiff rod can be a terrible burden and although it may be the only possible weapon to wield in the teeth of a strong wind it will very soon wear you – and the fish – down. The whip, when (as all anglers love to test) the rod is shaken up and down until it whistles, should be steady and equal in all directions. If not it is almost certainly built with odd joints or lopsided fibre-glass spin. A stiff rod will of course tire out fish very quickly as it will be constantly fighting against the spring of the rod but if you prefer this stiffness then make sure there is a suppleness in the top section at least. One point to remember is that the best rods usually have a spare top joint in case of accidents; when choosing this type of rod make sure *both* tops suit your needs. Put a strip of tape around one top so you can differentiate between them.

A rod, which has a long whippy feeling or softness about it, usually takes a while to return to stability when 'whipped', which means a slow recovery and slow pick up when fishing and is best used with very light lines.

Fig. 17 Abu fly rods.

At the base of a salmon fly rod there should be inscribed the manufacturer's recommended fly line 'weight' i.e. #9; these numbers are explained further on in the section dealing with lines but it is worth remembering that the heavier (higher numbered) lines usually suit heavier and sometimes cumbersome rods.

There is often a lot said about balance of a rod and it is not uncommon to see an otherwise perfectly sensible fisherman testing the balance of a rod in the showrooms by laying the rod on one finger and pronouncing very seriously 'Hmm, not bad' or even sharply drawing in air between his teeth with a hiss and shaking his head in disapproval. Well of course a rod which 'balances' with no reel or line offers no information whatsoever and it is the author's opinion that one which does, even when suitably set up, doesn't offer very much more. However, a badly, *really* badly, balanced outfit is a different story and when the rod and line, complete with reel, is loaded for action the balance will depend on how much line is out at any given time. But, as rod grip is largely a matter of personal choice, it doesn't matter what a rod does as long as it balances for *you* and doesn't give you a sore wrist at the

38

Fig. 18 Spinning rods for single and double handed casting.

end of the day. *Outfit* balance, however, is quite another matter and is exceedingly important.

Salmon Spinning Rods

Ideal lengths for spinning rods depend on the size of the river or lake to be fished. If there is plenty of room for overhead or back-casting a fair length – up to 10 ft – is acceptable, but thickly bushed, narrow rivers will not allow such liberties and 8 ft 6 ins may be the absolute limit – even for side casting. The ideal average spinner is 9 ft long, sturdy and with very strong rings. It is a two handed rod with a subsequently long butt or handle. It is usually a two piece rod and the bottom length will have only one ring – an outsize job – with an agate type insert to lessen friction. Make sure the ring is large enough to allow the

39

Fig. 19

line a free curve when a full fixed spool reel is being used or the line will not slip off easily when casting a light bait. A 10 ft spinner will have up to six rings on the top section and all will have sintox or agate inserts. The top ring should be especially sturdy and free from splits or cracks. The rod can of course be in cane although glass is more common nowadays and can usually be expected. The rod should be quite flexible and have the very best fittings – especially the butt ring. Solid glass rods should be avoided where finances allow as the hollow rod is much lighter and easier to handle on a long day's fishing. If extremely long

40

casting is desirable, the glass rod tends to be slightly stiff in the butt; a cheap glass rod certainly would be, but this is compensated by a sweetness at the tip – where it is needed. Below 9 ft 6 ins, say 8 ft 6 ins, the tip action becomes more apparent. Most of the rod play should be in the thick end or butt half, but if a three section rod is considered, the top joint should be stiff and not sloppy or whippy, like some fly rods. The swing of the rod in general does of course depend on the weight of the bait. Any bait exceeding 1oz. needs a stiffish rod. The rod should curve downwards from the top and rings must not be seen through each other when the rod is not supported.

Sea Trout Fly Rods
The sea trout is similar in many ways to the salmon, and rods do not differ to a great extent except that sheer body weight tends to require slightly heavier equipment for salmon than sea trout. The fly rod used for salmon can of course be used for sea trout but ideally the sea trout fly rod should be from 10–11 ft, that is of course for river fishing, boat rods are usually longer.

Sea trout Spinning Rods
These vanishing rods are probably completely redundant now the fibre-glass rods have reached their peak of quality (although some sea trout men may disagree with this) and a shortish salmon spinner of around 8 ft 6 ins to 9 ft, built in two pieces, with play through the whole length of the rod, will kill plenty of sea trout. Baits should not exceed 1oz. with this type of rod; the salmon rod being better for heavier baits.

Trout Fly Rods
Trout are found in so many different kinds of water it is not surprising to find a large variety of rods. They range from 5 ft solid glass or steel single piece 'toothpicks', to three piece split cane 10 ft lake rods and of course each circumstance calls for the right rod for the job.

To start at the short end, anything much longer than a light six footer would be so much excess baggage on a steep moorland burn of 3 ft or so. On the other hand, the river Spey for example, with its broad flat stretches, warrants a three piece, 10 ft rod. When fishing lakes, from boat or bank a 10 ft two piece rod is advisable. A two piece trout fly rod is far sweeter than a three piece and makes casting over longer distances easier. The ten footer can also be used for salmon fishing. A 9 ft or 9 ft 6 in. rod will have a crisper action and is quite useful for fast water fly work. They are also a little more accurate than the 10 ft jobs. The 8 ft fly rod is best for medium stream work, although Americans and Canadians seem to prefer the shorter 6 ft rod. Reservoir men, who need a relatively long cast, should select a stiffish, two piece 9 ft 3 in. rod – preferably in hollow glass.

Trout Spinning Rods

These are shorter, sturdier rods, seldom exceeding 8 ft 6 ins in length but never less than 5 ft. A trout spinner is usually built in glass, preferably hollow glass rather than solid. Solid rods are much heavier than hollow ones and if a long day's fishing is envisaged, then the hollow rod will prove worthy of the job with less energy use if properly handled. Rings are very important and are often lined with agate or sintox and should be examined from time to time for cracks, especially if the rod has been dropped.

Telescopic Rods

Although still a relative novelty here, telescopic rods have become increasingly popular on the Continent (particularly in West Germany) in recent years.

There has also been a clear rise in interest over the past year or so in telescopic dapping rods, which an increasing number of holidaying anglers have taken over to Ireland with them.

The big point, after all, is convenience – especially for the man who fishes only occasionally. Some of these telescopics are only 3 ft long or so, in the collapsed position, so you could easily slip one into the boot of a Mini without taking up precious space.

The Shakespeare telescopics are:–

The four-joint dapping rod in fibre-glass at 13 ft. It has large chromed rings on collars, chromed screw-reel fitting, and black rubber grips.

A five-joint job extending to 15 ft 6 ins. Other specifications as above.

The 'Telspin', a three-joint, hollow fibre-glass spinning rod (for trout, sea trout etc.). It has a cork handle and screw-reel fitting. The extended length is 7 ft.

There is a three-joint, 10 ft hollow fibre-glass bottom rod, with semi-standoff rings, cork handle, screw winch fitting. It is light and stiff, with tip action.

There is also a longer version with specifications as above, but five-joint and 12 ft 6 ins length.

Rod Maintenance

All rods must be most carefully stored. The best way to store rods is in a stiff, round container of the type used for document carriage. Alternatively, a good rod storage tube can be made from a length of polythene gutter piping or, for a single rod, a length of plastic sink waste piping. A rod bag is of course ideal and can be used to carry rods about in too. Any rod container should be kept absolutely dry. Make sure there is a hole or two for the rods to 'breathe' or they will sweat and deteriorate very rapidly. Rods *must* be gently wiped over after use or they will dampen their containers. If rods are stored in soft bags then do hang them up and *insert the rod with the thin end first* so the heavy ends will strike the floor first if the bag falls. Never lean a rod against a radiator and do not store one in an airing cupboard or warping may occur. The rod itself, if varnished, will need careful handling and examination periodically for cracks in the varnish. To open a stiff joint twist, don't pull the two pieces apart. Although the rod itself may be oiled occasionally ensure that the joints are not oiled or they will stick together; use deer fat on metal joints. Should joints stick, warm the female ferrule gently and twist both sections in different directions. Rings are delicate so check them for binding damage, loosening and, most of all, for insert damage. A cracked porcelain ring can strip long lengths of line and will weaken it to say nothing of the loss of a fish if the line is in use when it breaks. *Never* leave a cane rod on the back window shelf of a car. If you go on a long fishing vacation it may be worth while carrying a few rod spares. Most useful is a small jar of varnish, a reel of ring binding thread, a spare top ring and an intermediate ring.

REELS

There is a correct reel for all kinds of fishing. Spinning will require one type, bait fishing another and fly fishing yet another. It is not only important to use the correct reel but the best reel you can afford.

The cheaper reels may not look very different from the outside, but the important precision parts, such as bearings, cannot be seen easily and the only safeguard against second rate performance – and lost fish as a result, is to purchase the best reels available.

FLY REELS

Trout reels need to be light but large enough for whichever line is to be used. For fly fishing the fly line size should be marked on the butt of the rod and this number will correspond to a specific reel size. The fly reel is of the revolving drum type and must be fixed almost to the very end of the butt *behind* the hand. Should the rod not have a specific fixing point then the reel can be attached to the rod in a manner best suited to the angler's method of casting – a fly reel should never be in front of the hand. The reel should of course be very firmly attached; there is nothing more annoying than a reel sailing through the air with a particularly vigorous cast – especially if it is for the benefit of spectators! Reels do occasionally drop off into the water because of poor fixing and, if a fish is on at the time. . . . also ensure the line is firmly tied to the reel when winding it on.

A 3 or $3\frac{1}{2}$ in. reel will suffice for a line up to $\#6$ and the fly line itself can be 'backed' with 50–100 yds of backing. A salmon fly reel will have a diameter of $3\frac{1}{4}$–$4\frac{1}{2}$ ins, again dependant upon the number on the rod butt. The reel should accept the correct line plus at least 100 yds of backing line. This will give almost 130 yds of line to play the fish with. With all centre pin, revolving drum (Nottingham type), reels some considerable force must be used if the inertia of the drum is to be overcome to remove the added drag of the line, plus a drag if incorporated. Most anglers overcome this initial force acting against their cast by coiling a long length of line in the spare hand. If the river flow is correct the line may be allowed to float in line with the cast; both methods are best suited to small waters, but this is covered in a later section.

Reels can be purchased with optional left or right hand winds: they may even be reversible. Whether the angler is left handed or not, it is well to train the left hand to do the winding if spinning.

It is vital not to overfill the reel and this means not

taking the line up to its limit. It is all very well setting up a reel the night beforehand and filling it nice and parallel to $\frac{1}{8}$ in. of the edge, but if a fish is tugging at the end of the line and running in all directions it is an unusual angler who can think of keeping his line parallel on the reel when winding in. 'Banks' of line building up on one side are inevitable under these conditions and if no room for this is allowed, a jam will occur. Alternatively, a badly filled reel means slow recovery; the pulley laws will explain why, but even to the leanest physics student it is obvious that a line winding in on a 2 in. (poorly filled) drum will retrieve more slowly than a filled spool, and if the fish decides to run towards the angler he will need to wind like mad if his reel is low.

The check should also be light when fishing. A fierce ratchet may sound like heavenly music to the angler but,

Fig. 20 George Mortimer demonstrates trout fly casting.

believe it or not, this noise may be transmitted through the line, into the river bed and picked up by the delicate nervous system of the fish – especially if the quarry is a trout. The whole point of the check, or ratchet, is to cause a slight drag on the line and prevent the reel from overrunning. Imagine pulling the thread on a loosely held cotton reel. When you stop pulling, the reel continues for a while and a tangle results. A ratchet will prevent this, it will also slow down a cast if used against it as well as help tire out the fish. Some reels have an adjustable ratchet, which can be brought into heavy play when a fish is 'on'. Although the drag of such a ratchet may seem very small, it is indeed very heavy to the fish and is much like adding a weight on the line for the fish to drag along.

Some fly reels are equipped with a brake. This is a very useful addition, especially for use with salmon, although the 'rim brake' reel is currently attaining popularity. The brake is merely a thumb on the exposed rim of the reel but it is very efficient and allows the fisherman to retain a personal 'feel' and he can keep in close touch with his catch. Less interesting to the old school but exceedingly efficient was the 'Fish Hawk' system. There are still plenty of these beautiful little reels around. The 'Fish Hawk' 'multiplies' the wind-in rate with an elaborate gear system, it has an exceedingly good clutch. The clutch can be adjusted while a fish is being played.

Speedex Fly Reel

This reel was developed from the earlier 'Fish Hawk' fly reel – a lighter, simplified version, including the geared retrieve and the exposed rim, but without the slipping clutch. It is made from an ultra-lightweight magnesium alloy. Despite the extreme volatility of pure magnesium the metal in the reel is completely non-inflammable once it has gone through the manufacturing process. It is exceptionally strong and resilient.

Because of its lightness, it has been possible to give the Speedex an increased line capacity. The $3\frac{1}{2}$ in. standard model weighs $5\frac{1}{2}$ ozs and takes a D.T. 6F line plus 20 yds of 20 lb. terylene backing. The $3\frac{1}{2}$ in. model weighs 6 ozs and takes a D.T. 7F line.

The Beaulite and the Supercondex are also made with special magnesium alloy which, by reducing their weight, allows them to have greater line capacities compared with previous models. The weight reduction is roughly 30%.

Fig. 21 The Shakespeare 'Speedex'.

Both have an exposed rim for finger-tip control. In addition they have a 180° line-guard, precision-ground spindle, and reversible check tongue for left or right hand wind.

The Beaulite has adjustable tension and a quick release to take-apart. It is available in three sizes; $3\frac{1}{2}$ in. regular width, weighing 5 ozs, with a capacity of AFTM 6D.T. floating fly line, plus 25 yds of 20 lb. terylene 'Gliderback': $3\frac{1}{2}$ in. extra wide, weighing $5\frac{1}{4}$ ozs with a capacity of AFTM 7D.T., plus 100 yds of backing; and a $4\frac{1}{4}$ in. diameter for salmon fishing weighing $8\frac{1}{4}$ ozs taking AFTM 10D.T., plus 200 yds of backing.

The Supercondex, in gun-metal finish and with a screw take-apart, comes in the same sizes – the $3\frac{1}{2}$ in. models each being a $\frac{1}{4}$ oz. lighter than those of the Beaulite – and the same line capacities (all the backing, again, being calculated on Shakespeare's twenty pound 'Gliderback').

Abu 'Deltas' have centred their attack around the line wear problem of some reels. This is caused by the frequent drawing out and reeling in of line against one or more of the reel construction pillows holding the side plates together. The design is simple but effective; the Delta has three wide oval pillows with extra large, friction free surface areas. Some Deltas have an outside control lever which can be used whilst playing the fish.

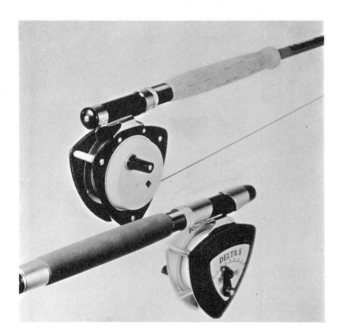

Fig. 22 The Supercondex reel (top).

Fig. 23 The Beaulite (centre).

Fig. 24 Abu 'Delta' fly reels (left).

The Delta 3 Fly Reels

The spool of the Delta has a flange shaped braking drum conveniently placed for easy finger control when the fish runs. No finger is needed on the line and there is little risk of the fingers being struck by the circular handle. The Delta 3 has an adjustable brake operated by turning a screw at the base of the housing. It is easily converted to left or right hand wind. The spool takes fly line up to #8 plus about 100 yds of 18 lb. (0·45mm) backing line. It weighs 8 ozs and gives excellent balance with the majority of fly rods of 8–10ft.

The Abu Delta 5

The Abu Delta 5 is similar to the Delta 3. The main difference between the two is that the tension of Delta 5 is by an outside finger control lever. which can be used while actually playing a fish. The tension can be quickly and easily altered during active fishing and the brake scale is graduated. The spool accepts #8 fly line plus about 100 yds of 18 lb. (0·45mm) backing line. It weighs $8\frac{1}{2}$ ozs and balances with most 8–10 ft rods.

The 'Marquis' rim control fly reels are among the best in the world for fly fishing. There are six sizes available: from the tiny $1\frac{3}{4}$ in.#4 trout reel, to the incredibly light $3\frac{3}{4}$ in. #10 salmon reel. An adjustable click-check is featured and the line spool has an exposed polished rim, which overlaps the frame, to form a large braking surface for instant and sensitive finger control. The drum can be released quickly and sits on a precision ground spindle of carbon steel. An adjustable compensating check allows rapid change over from left to right hand wind and the check can be adjusted by a regulator button on the back of the reel frame.

Perhaps the acme of fly reel perfection are the fabulous Hardy 'Lightweight' and 'Featherweights'. The 'Featherweight' is a super-light (3 ozs) $2\frac{3}{8}$ in. diameter trout reel with compensated check, regulator and optional left or right hand wind. The guard is stainless steel; the spindle is cast steel and the body is aluminum. The 'Lightweight' has a 3 oz, $3\frac{3}{16}$ in. diameter body, the 'Princess' is $3\frac{1}{2}$ in. × $4\frac{3}{4}$ ozs and there is a $3\frac{3}{4}$ in. × 6 ozs sea trout version. Machining on these reels is to an incredible spindle tolerance of $\pm$ 0·00025 in!

FLY REEL CAPACITIES

Marquis Reel

#4 ($2\frac{3}{4}''$ dia.)
D.T.4 AirCel and no backing.
W.F.4 AirCel and 75 yds
W.F.5 AirCel and 50 yds
W.F.6 AirCel and 25 yds

#5 ($3''$ dia.)
D.T.4 AirCel and 75 yds
W.T.4 AirCel and 120 yds
D.T.5 AirCel and no backing
W.F.5 AirCel and 100 yds
W.F.6 AirCel and 75 yds
W.F.7 AirCel and 60 yds
W.F.8 AirCel and 50 yds

#6 ($3\frac{1}{4}''$ dia.)
D.T.5 AirCel and 75 yds
W.F.5 AirCel and 125 yds
D.T.6 AirCel and 40 yds
W.F.6 AirCel and 110 yds
W.F.7 AirCel and 100 yds
W.F.8 AirCel and 80 yds
W.F.9 AirCel and 60 yds

#7 ($3\frac{7}{16}''$ dia.)
D.T.6 AirCel and 75 yds
W.F.6 AirCel and 150 yds
D.T.7 AirCel and 40 yds
W.F.7 AirCel and 125 yds
W.F.8 AirCel and 110 yds
W.F.9 AirCel and 100 yds
W.F.10 AirCel and 75 yds

#8/9 ($3\frac{5}{8}''$ dia.)
D.T.7 AirCel and 100 yds
W.F.7 AirCel and 200 yds
D.T.8 AirCel and 65 yds
W.F.8 AirCel and 175 yds
D.T.9 AirCel and no backing
W.F.9 AirCel and 150 yds
W.F.10 AirCel and 125 yds

#10 ($3''$ dia.)
W.F.8 AirCel and 200 yds
D.T.9 AirCel and 50 yds
W.F.9 AirCel and 175 yds
W.F.10 AirCel and 150 yds

Marquis Salmon Reel

No. 1 ($3\frac{7}{8}''$ dia.)
D.T.8 AirCel and 142 yds
D.T.9 AirCel and 109 yds
W.F.9 AirCel and 219 yds
D.T.10 AirCel and 55 yds
W.F.10 AirCel and 186 yds

No. 2 ($4\frac{1}{8}''$ dia.)
D.T.9 AirCel and 219 yds
D.T.10 AirCel and 186 yds
W.F.10 AirCel and 300 yds
D.T.11 AirCel and 110 yds

Viscount Reel

'130' ($3\frac{1}{4}''$ dia.)
D.T.4 AirCel and 75 yds
D.T.5 AirCel and 50 yds
W.F.5 AirCel and 100 yds
D.T.6 AirCel and 20 yds
W.F.6 AirCel and 100 yds
W.F.7 AirCel and 75 yds
W.F.8 AirCel and 50 yds
W.F.9 AirCel and 25 yds

'140' ($3\frac{5}{8}''$ dia.)
D.T.5 AirCel and 100 yds
W.F.5 AirCel and 175 yds
D.T.6 AirCel and 70 yds
W.F.6 AirCel and 15 yds
D.T.7 AirCel and 50 yds
W.F.7 AirCel and 150 yds
W.F.8 AirCel and 125 yds
W.F.9 AirCel and 100 yds
W.F.10 AirCel and 75 yds

'150' ($3\frac{7}{8}''$ dia.)
D.T.7 AirCel and 225 yds
W.F.7 AirCel and 350 yds
D.T.8 AirCel and 200 yds
W.F.8 AirCel and 325 yds
D.T.9 AirCel and 175 yds
W.F.9 AirCel and 300 yds
D.T.10 AirCel and 50 yds
W.F.10 AirCel and 275 yds

49

Featherweight Reel

D.T.4 AirCel and 20 yds. 20 lbs. Dacron
D.T.5 AirCel and no backing

L.R.H. Lightweight Reel

D.T.4 AirCel and 40 yds. 20 lbs. Dacron
D.T.5 AirCel and 30 yds. 20 lbs. Dacron
D.T.5 AirCel and 50 yds. 15 lbs. Dacron
D.T.6 AirCel and 20 yds. 15 lbs. Dacron
W.F.6 AirCel and 40 yds. 20 lbs. Dacron
W.F.7 AirCel and 30 yds. 15 lbs. Dacron

Princess Reel

D.T.5 AirCel and 80 yds. 15 lbs. Dacron
D.T.6 AirCel and 50 yds. 20 lbs. Dacron
D.T.6 AirCel and 80 yds. 15 lbs. Dacron
W.F.6 AirCel and 100 yds. 20 lbs. Dacron
D.T.7 AirCel and 50 yds. 15 lbs. Dacron
W.F.7 AirCel and 85 yds. 25 lbs. Dacron

St. Aidan Reel

W.F.7 AirCel and 100 yds. 30 lbs. Dacron
D.T.7 AirCel and 100 yds. 20 lbs. Dacron
D.T.6 AirCel and 130 yds. 20 lbs. Dacron
W.F.7 WetCel and 200 yds. 25 lbs. Dacron

St. John Reel

D.T.8 AirCel and 100 yds. 20 lbs. Dacron
W.F.7 AirCel and 150 yds. 25 lbs. Dacron
D.T.9 AirCel and 100 yds. 20 lbs. Dacron
D.T.7 AirCel and 100 yds. 25 lbs. Dacron
W.F.7 WetCel and 200 yds. 20 lbs. Dacron
W.F.8 AirCel and 120 yds. 25 lbs. Dacron

St. George Reel

D.T.6 AirCel and 100 yds. 25 lbs. Dacron
D.T.7 AirCel and 50 yds. 25 lbs. Dacron
W.F.7 AirCel and 100 yds. 25 lbs. Dacron

NOTE:

Backing requirements in yards for 'Marquis' reels are based on 18 lbs B.S. 'Dacron' (0·014 in.) and 'Scientific Anglers' AirCel and WetCel lines.

Backing requirements in yards for 'Marquis Salmon' reels are based on 25 lbs B.S. 'Dacron' (0·020 in.) and 'Scientific Anglers' AirCel and WetCel lines. Those for 'Viscount' reels are based on 18 lbs B.S. 'Dacron' (0·014 in.) and 'Scientific Anglers' AirCel and WetCel lines.

SPINNING REELS

There are basically three types of spinning reel: the revolving drum (Nottingham) reel already described; the multiplier; and the fixed spool reel.

Multiplying Reels

Multiplying reels are usually fitted with an adjustable drag and a strong ratchet check. The multiplying action is in fact a geared retrieve, which operates at about 3:1; that is the drum will revolve three times to one turn of the winder – a very useful fast rewind or 'anti-slack' device. If a fish runs towards the angler at any speed a slack (and consequently broken) line may result. The fast retrieve helps to prevent this to a considerable extent for the angler is able to keep up with the fish's speed. A clutch is usually incorporated and a centrifugal governor deters overruns. The drag is different to the governor; drag is needed when casting into the wind. The overrun is the curse of the multiplier, especially if a light bait is used and one is unable to determine the precise moment of thrust cessation. The drag must be such that the cast is not slowed by too much drag yet not too fast to prevent an overrun and a subsequent 'birds nest' of tangled nylon. Braided nylon tends to be a little less springy than monofilament and doesn't overrun quite so badly although care and

Fig. 25 Abu and cardinal fixed spool reels.

Fig. 26 Ambassadeur multipliers.

Fig. 27 Ambassadeur 5000 series reels.

attention is the best method of trouble avoidance. A correctly used multiplier is unbeatable for long distance casting but a wary thumb should always be poised over the spinning drum, ready to stop it the moment the bait stops tugging on the line in the air and begins to drop. The multiplier is fitted to the rod in an upside position or 'on the top' of the rod instead of being slung underneath.

The Ambassadeur series of multiplying reels are splendid examples of precision instruments. They incorporate a centrifugal brake, drag tension and, most useful, a carriage pawl which winds the line on evenly as it is wound in. When casting, the spool runs free; a double synchronised braking system obviates backlash – a centrifugal brake has the effect of slowing down and smoothing out the fast revolutions of the spool during the initial surge of the cast. The mechanical brake is adjustable to different bait sizes and smooths payout of line at low speeds. There is an automatic tensioning system and a slipping, adjustable clutch. An emergency spare parts kit is also supplied.

THE 5000 MODEL features a single arm crank handle. It has a line capacity of 200 yds × 9 lbs (0·30mm), 140 yds of 12 lbs (0·35mm), or 110 yds of 15 lbs (0·40mm) nylon. A special spool is available which takes 185 yds of 12 lbs (0·35mm), 140 yds of 15 lbs (0·40mm), or 110 yds of 18 lbs (0·45mm) nylon. It weighs 9½ ozs. You may of course wish to use lighter lines and there is no reason not to, but do ensure the reel is correctly filled.

THE 5000B MODEL is fitted with an optional check. The large spool accepts 185 yds of 12 lbs (0·35mm), 140 yds of 15 lb. (0·40mm) or 110 yds of 18 lb. (0·45mm) line. It weighs $9\frac{1}{2}$ ozs and extra spools are available. Where the 5000 is best suited for trout fishing the 5000B is more useful when salmon fishing.

THE 5000C MODEL is a more luxurious reel fitted with stainless steel ever-lasting ball bearings, which give exceedingly smooth running. The crank handle has a balanced single arm. A ball bearing brake affords long casts free of vibration. Two spools are supplied; the smaller spool takes 200 yds of 9 lb. (0·30mm), 140 yds of 12 lb. (0·35mm) or 110 yds of 15 lbs. (0·40mm) line. The larger spool accepts 185 yds of 12 lb. (0.35mm), 140 yds of 15 lb. (0·40mm) or 110 yds of 18 lb. (0·45mm) line. It weighs 11 ozs.

THE 6000 MODEL has an optional check and a balanced, single-arm crank handle. The spool takes 185 yds of 15 lb. (0·40mm), 150 yds of 18 lb. (0·45mm) or 120 yds of 22 lb. (0·50mm) line. It weighs $10\frac{1}{2}$ ozs.

THE 6000C MODEL has an optional check, stainless steel ball bearings and a balanced single arm crank handle. It also has a ball bearing braking system, which helps long distance casting free of backlash. It weighs 12 ozs. and accepts the same lines sizes as the 6000.

THE ABU 3000 has a free running spool, centrifugal brake and a finely adjustable mechanical brake helps to give long, accurate and backlash free casts It is saltwater resistant. The spool takes 175 yds of 12 lb. (0·35mm) or 145 yds of 15 lb. (0·40mm) (without arbor), 175 yds of 9 lb. (0·30mm) or 120 yds of 12 lb. (0·35mm) (with arbor). It is supplied with spare parts, extra brake blocks and removable plastic arbor fitted for varying line capacities. It weighs 9 ozs.

THE ABU 1750A has an adjustable twin braking system, embodying centrifugal and mechanical principles. It has a free running spool, is corrosion proof and the spool takes 145 yds of 9 lb. (0·30mm), 130 yds of 12 lb. (0·35mm) or 100 yds of 15 lb. (0·40mm) line. It weighs $6\frac{1}{2}$ ozs.

THE RECORD SPORT 2100 is fitted with centrifugal and mechanical brakes. The spool is readily freed and re-engaged. It automatically engages when reeling in and has a reel capacity of 250 yds of 9 lb. (0·30mm) or 190 yds of 12 lb. (0·35mm) line. A special competition spool is available; made from chromed magnesium alloy; it weighs only $\frac{1}{2}$ oz. and is conical in section; it takes 170 yds of 9 lb. line. The reel weighs $7\frac{1}{2}$ ozs.

The Pflueger Supreme Salmon Spinning Reel

This has been hailed as 'The finest salmon reel in the world' – and game fishermen willing to spend that kind of money (almost £30) must feel it is worth it.

The reel incorporates a unique 'Hydro-thumb' control, a hydraulically operated device, which helps the angler to avoid overruns. It is adjustable for a wide range of casting weights. Besides the 'Hydro-thumb' anti-backlash control, special features of the Pflueger Supreme include an automatic push-button free spool mechanism located in the centre of the star drag. This means longer casts with lighter weights. The winding mechanism re-engages instantly as the handle is turned forwards.

A $1\frac{3}{4}$ in. solid aluminium spool is resistant to cushion-pressures and gives a high capacity. The reel takes 150 yds of 20 lb. test Terylene.

A self-lubricating, disc-type star drag, provides a smooth and even line yield to a running fish (particularly important when playing a lightly hooked salmon).

There is a push-button auto-reverse, conveniently situated on the rim of the frame, giving the angler a choice of playing the fish from the handle or through the slipping clutch mechanism.

The gears have a 4:1 retrieve ratio. The double-threaded level wind is easily removable for cleaning, and the reel also has convenient oil-ports for easy maintenance.

Fig. 28 The Pflueger Supreme salmon spinning reel.

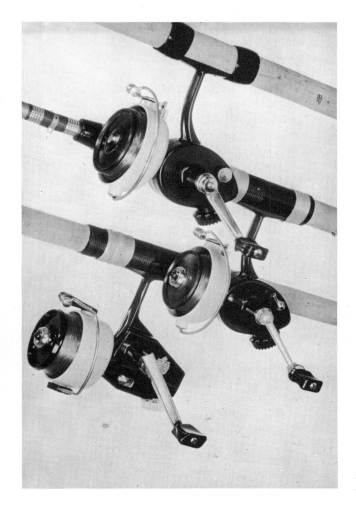

Fig. 29 The Cardinals.

Fixed Spool Reels

Fixed spool styles are perhaps the most popular of all reels. Their popularity undoubtedly stems from the ease with which they can be used. For spinning, the fixed spool is a very useful reel indeed. They are absolutely ideal for ultra light fishing with very light lures of between $\frac{1}{16}$ and $\frac{1}{8}$ ounce. They thrive on 'into the wind' casting and most anglers have one or two in their kits. The fixed spool reel usually incorporates a slipping clutch, has an anti-reverse lever and an automatic or manual pickup bale or hoop; the automatic pickup being operated by winding in the line. The centre spool goes in and out as the line is wound in, this ensures an even distribution of line and, most useful of all, the spools are usually quickly detachable. This means spare spools can very easily be fitted – a useful way of changing line thickness for all types of fishing.

It is important to ensure the best kind of fixed spool reel is purchased for there are many cheap and nasty jobs on the market. The reel should be quiet, for silence in mechanical devices usually means good engineering – and fish are timid. The clutch should be smooth, the bale should be tight and crisp and the handle should be where you want – *on the rod.* It is so easy, especially with big hands, to crack knuckles on a short armed reel. The arm should also be stout and the fitting reliable. If ball bearings are incorporated so much the better. The gearing ratio should be around 3:1 and the ratchet check must be the kind which can be turned off. When filled, the reel should have $\frac{1}{4}$ in. left to prevent line slipping off but be high enough to allow a free peeling off of line.

THE 'MITCHELL 300' is a most reliable reel for general all round use. It incorporates a 'constant cycle' gearing system which lays line in a special way across the wide spool, fitting to an equal sized reel. This results in a long, smooth cast with little effort. The line guide is tungsten carbide and the bale is of mono-block construction. It will accept two different capacity spools with a push-button release. Capacities are: regular spool – 200 yds of 10 lb. B.S.; fine line spool 100 yds of 6 lb. B.S. Left or right hand winders are available and the right handed angler should have a left hand wind.

THE MITCHELL 406 is for early salmon fishing and is slightly larger than the 300. It will handle the heavier lines so often necessary when fishing big waters early in the season and because it is sometimes preferable to use a fixed spool reel in cold weather. The 406 also has a high rate of retrieve (32 ins of line per turn of the handle). It has an anti-reverse and push button spool change. Capacity 200 yds, 17 lb. B.S.

THE 330 has an absolutely beautiful 'self opening' bale. Finger pressure on the bale at casting releases the bale. You do not need to reach across with the off-rod hand to open the bale which means completely one handed casting. For trout the 324 or 320 or 410 are recommendable. Line capacities are shown in the following table:

Mitchell Reel Capacities

Model	Regular Spool	Fine Line Spool
300	200 yds × 10 lb.	100 yds × 6 lb.
406	200 yds × 17 lb.	
330	200 yds × 10 lb.	100 yds × 6 lb.
324	200 yds × 8 lb.	100 yds × 6 lb.
320	150 yds × 8 lb.	
410	200 yds × 10 lb.	100 yds × 6 lb.
408	175 yds × 6 lb.	100 yds × 4 lb.
308	175 yds × 6 lb.	100 yds × 4 lb.

Cardinal fixed spool reels are built to an extreme degree of accuracy. On the Cardinal, the entire bale system is built extra-strong and with twin bale springs, ensuring a safe and reliable operation and eliminating complete loss due to failure of one spring. With the unique rear positioned tension control the fingers are able to operate it easily, quickly and without danger whilst playing a fish. An anti-reverse control is fitted in a most convenient position – near the crank handle. The bale pick-up system is extra strong and can be released so that it rests against the reel housing for safe transportation. It also takes up less room in the bag and prevents unwinding at the same time.

The 'works' include steel wormgear, ball bearings and shaft which add up to smooth, silent operation. The spool is made of Delrin and the entire reel is completely corrosion-proof. The pick-up rotating roller, set in Delrin, 'lubricates' itself automatically using the water as it comes off the line on reel-in. To change spools – say for a lighter (or heavier) line, all that is necessary is a thumb in the centre of the reel and it clicks neatly off. On models 503/504 and 506 the bale is replaced by a press-button. The Abu 503/505 and speed version 506 models are open faced fixed spool reels with a difference. The spool cover makes casting in wind and rain easier. The push-button line release offers cast control for good accuracy and a sensitive finger hold of a fish at the net. The synchro drag is another feature which allows pre-set drag tension to be reduced whilst playing a fish simply by moving the handle backwards. On the 506, minimum drag is achieved automatically simply by letting go of the handle. 503, 505 and 506 all have true fixed spools – the spool does not rotate so there is positively no line twist provided the trace and swivels are correctly positioned.

THE ABU 503 has synchro tension built in but it is adjustable with a coin. The spool takes 250 yds of 7 lb., or 175 yds of 9 lb. line. It is suitable for lines ranging from 2–9 lb. and weighs $10\frac{1}{2}$ ozs.

THE ABU 506 is a fast retrieve – nearly 25 ins of line is recovered per crank revolution. It is suitable for lines ranging from 2–9 lb. and weighs $10\frac{1}{2}$ ozs.

THE CARDINAL 44 retrieves at the rate of 27·7 ins of line per crank revolution and its line capacity without arbor is 220 yds of 7 lb. line. An extra spool with arbor is available giving a capacity of 110 yds of 7 lb. line. It is suitable for lines ranging from 3 lbs to 9 lbs. The gear ratio is 5:1 and the weight is $10\frac{1}{2}$ ozs. The Abu 333 has rear positioned drag control and an anti-reverse button within finger reach. The spool takes 300 yds of 7 lb, 220 yds of 9 lb, 165 yds of 12 lb., or 100 yds of 15 lb. line. It is suitable for 4–5 lb. lines and weighs 11 ozs.

THE ABU 444A is basically the same reel as the 333 but with a rotating line roller mounted in the 'Delrin'. It has a press button spool change and a collapsible crank handle for easy transport. The spool takes 300 yds of 7 lb., 220 yds of 9 lb., 165 yds of 12 lb. or 110 yds of 15 lb. line. It weighs 11 ozs. The Abu Cardinal 66 has a rear mounted tension control, drive gear in ball bearings and an extra strong double spring bale. Without the arbor the spool will accept 220 yds of 12 lb. line, with the extra spool and two reel arbors 220 yds of 9 lb. and 220 yds of 7 lb. line is possible. The reel ratio is 1:3·3 or 21 ins per crank turn. It weighs $13\frac{1}{2}$ ozs.

THE CARDINAL 77 is the largest Cardinal reel, with a spool capacity, without arbor, of 220 yds of 15 lb. line. It has extra spool arbors for 220 yds of 12 lb. and 220 yds of 9 lb. line. The gear ratio is 1:3·3 or 23 ins per crank turn. It weighs $13\frac{1}{2}$ ozs.

Fig. 30 The Abumatic.

Yet another style of fixed spool reel is the Abumatic. The Abumatic is a closed face fixed spool reel. That is to say, the line pulls freely off the stationary spool. But when in use the reel is positioned exactly as is a multiplier reel – on top of the rod. Because the spool is stationary, line twist is avoided. Line wear is also reduced to a minimum because the rotating line pick-up pin and the inner winding cup are both designed of hard-chromed stainless steel, (on the 380, the pick-up is of polished carbide steel).

THE ABUMATIC 110 is a beginner's reel. It has an adjustable friction brake, takes 165 yds of 7 lb. line and weighs 9 ozs. The 120 introduces Synchro-drag and has a tension mechanism located in the crank. The spool accepts 165 yds of 7 lb. line and it weighs 9 ozs. The 160 has a star wheel drag tensioner, an automatic anti-reverse and two rotating pick-up line pins. The spool takes 165 yds of 7 lb. line and the reel weighs $9\frac{1}{2}$ ozs. The 145 has direct drive, which gives direct and positive contact with the fish. The fish is pumped by raising the rod tip then lowering it while reeling in. The adjustable friction drag comes into operation when the fish runs and the crank handle goes into reverse. The spool takes 175 yds of 9 lb. nylon and the reel weighs 11 ozs.

For bigger fish the 290, with auto synchro, is excellent. It is designed so that when the fish runs, the crank is released and the reel takes care of the drag itself. It has an anti-reverse and soft winding cup. The spool takes 220 yds of 9 lb. line and the reel weighs 12 ozs.

THE 'SILEX SUPERBA' is a Nottingham type spinning reel suitable wherever spinning or trolling. It is of sound construction, simple to use and easily kept clean and free from trouble.

THE 'LONGSTONE' is a reel of special interest to the angler who wishes to troll or spin for the heavier salmon. It is fitted with a strong optional check and a stainless steel line guard. The drum can be adjusted for pressure by operating the control nut fitted to the centre of the drum. This nut will give any pressure required for casting and for holding the drum when fishing in a strong current or braking a heavy fish. The drum has a broad rounded rim for hand control. It has a diameter of $4\frac{1}{2}$ ins and a line capacity of 400 yds of 20 lb. braided 'Dacron' or 200 yds of 25 lb. monofilament nylon.

Reels should be very carefully wiped with a slightly oily rag after each day's fishing. Grease should not be used and tightly wound lines should be wound off, dried and re-wound or pressure may build up and crack the drum. Never put a wet reel in a bag and do not store for the winter with nylon line wound on – use a line drier for storage of line. Sand and grit should be avoided like the plague and salt water treated as poison. All parts of the reel must be washed and oiled after an estuary sea trout expedition. Be proud of your reels, they are precision instruments and observe pride of ownership, this in turn will result in reliable service.

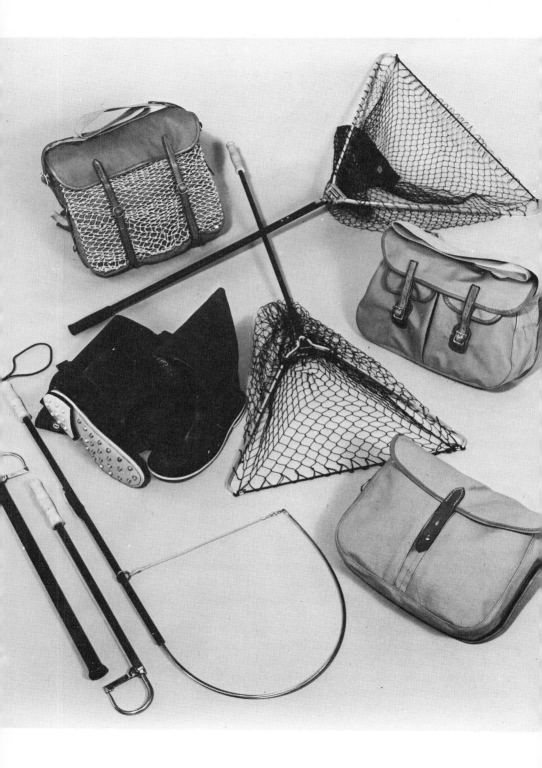

3 *General Tackle*

Landing Aids

The bank landing net, usually wielded by the gillie, can and should be the largest one manageable. It should have a sturdy ring, a good strong handle and a deep wide bottom. If the angler wishes to carry a net with him then again it should be the largest he can cope with. If the handle is to be in one piece then it should be used as a wading staff too and an ideal length would be a 5 ft handle on an 18–36 in. diameter ring. The mesh should be small enough to keep small trout and to avoid net marks on a large salmon. A lead weight can be attached to the middle of the net to ensure instant sinking. A sling will prove useful for looping the staff over the neck to trail behind when casting.

A folding net can be very useful (especially if tele-scopic) and there are plenty of lightweight jobs on the market nowadays. Do make sure the folding net locks in *both* directions otherwise it may well fold the wrong way when a fish enters it. The staff of a net handle is worth measuring off and marking in inches, feet or mm., for use when a fish is landed. For boat use, a larger net handle is necessary – say 6 ft or over depending upon the boat size; always attach such accessories to a length of string and then to the boat – not the oar!

Another landing device, mainly for salmon, is the fisher-man's 'gaff'. A gaff is just a large hook (2 ins in diameter) with a handle. It is sunk into the side of a fish when play is over and the fish is brought out with little fear of loss. The only fault with a gaff is that once hooked, the fish is as good as dead and if a kelt has been hooked it is lost. For this reason gaffing is not usually permitted before April 1st. The gaff should be 4–5 ft long (longer if for boat use) and its point should be kept razor sharp. Needless to say it should also be protected when not in use with a cork or binding. It can be slung on the back as a staff – and indeed used as one. Telescopic safety gaffs can also be purchased.

61

Grant Mortimer, well known tackle dealer and angler of Grantown-On-Spey, Scotland, has designed a very neat gaff come wading staff, with a cunningly arranged curtain wire loop which hangs across the back whilst wading. A flick of the wrist and the gaff is free for use, see fig. 32.

A tailer is perhaps the best – and certainly the most sporting way of landing a fish, especially if there are kelts around. A tailer is simply a running wire noose on the end of a pole. The same applies to other landing devices but when using always draw the noose *towards the head* of the fish. Once the noose is slipped over the tail of a salmon (it is not usual to 'tail' trout due to the fact that they will wriggle away), it cannot free itself but, if the angler wishes to return the fish, be it a kelt or other unwanted fish, it can be held reasonably still with the tailer until de-hooked, then released easily.

A wading staff is vital for the deeper, faster waters and is often quite useful for reaching the river! A good walking stick is considered a trade tool to the highland shepherd and a stout wading stick does the job quite well. A long leash must be fixed to the stick and it should be hung by this to the back when not in use. The staff can of course have a net, tailer or gaff attached to the end but do ensure the latter is protected or a 'strike' could end in a badly gashed back. Never keep a wading stick in front of you or it may trip you up underwater.

A strong rubber cap must be fixed to the bottom of the wader. The sharpened steel tips seen on some staffs may well grip the tricky bottom of a mountain stream quite nicely but unfortunately fish can detect the harsh scraping

Fig. 32 Grant Mortimer demonstrates his gaff-wading stick with quick release cable he designed himself.

of a steel tipped wading staff at considerable distances. A rubber cap is essential unless the angler prefers to give his quarry a better chance!

Waders

This necessary item of the salmon or trout fisherman's gear is often the most neglected. Firstly, the right choice must be made at the beginning. Socks will be worn underneath them – perhaps very thick socks – and these should be worn when trying on the waders in the first place. Special 'socklets' are also available for wear inside the waders. They are virtually soft slippers and will keep the feet extremely warm and comfortable. Needless to say they should be worn when trying on the new waders. Tight waders should be avoided at all costs for when wading in deep water the pressure causes the waders to crush inwards against the legs; if they are tight to begin with they will be unbearable in the water.

The colour of waders does not seem to have much effect on the fish although it would seem prudent to wear relatively dull, flat coloured boots and not the gaudy, bright green jobs offered by some dealers. These are obviously made for wading, but for fishermen?

The length of waders varies considerably. They may come up to the knees or to the chin. Ideally, of course, would be thigh waders for shallow waters and chest waders for deeper stretches but the pocket (and carrying companion) may not stretch to two sets. The choice must be yours but, if you can afford the best, go for a good, soft chest wader – the new all rubber 'stretch ons' are quite light and one never knows when the fish are lying in the deeper areas and it can be most frustrating if you just cannot quite reach the other side of the river when necessary.

A most popular type of wader is the 'brogue' style. This is a pair of long rubber pants and a pair of tough leather 'brogue' shoes. Patching is easy with a common tyre outfit and a good grip is possible with the iron hard shoes.

The type of sole is the choice of the angler but it would be advisable to beware of too many sharp studs on the sole; a fierce trampling along the river bed crushing smaller pieces of rubble and scraping across the larger rocks must alert just about every living thing around. An alternative to studs is felt bottoms or rubber grooves on

Fig. 33 Chest and thigh waders.

63

Fig. 34 The ideal fly waistcoat.

the sole. Felt bottoms are absolutely silent and grip the rocks like suckers under water. Unfortunately walking on grass with felt soles is like walking on ice with skis and acrobatic agility would be a necessity. Rubber grooves do of course grip both under and out of water but can be pretty smooth and slippery when worn out. An alternative is felt soles and studded heels.

Perhaps the biggest single fault in anglers is their masochistic desire to ruin their waders. They do this by chucking them into the car boot and transferring them, in one heap, to the garage floor or cupboard when the day ends. It is absolutely essential that waders are hung up after a day's fishing. One only needs to feel the cold wetness of perspiration, which soaks the socks and trousers through after a few hours fishing, to realise that the inside of the waders are wet through too; furthermore they are wet with *urea*! Perspiration is a secondary means of removing waste from the body, and waders, after a day's fishing, are soaked in sweat. If this is not allowed to dry out the boots will rot. Unless they are hung up pockets of sweat soaked material will occur and the rot will set in.

Clothing

Correct clothing for the day's weather will ensure a happy day's fishing. Poor clothing will almost certainly spoil the day – rain for the unprepared is absolute misery. Clothing should be light yet windproof, strong yet rainproof and warm without discomfort. Good thick socks under the waders or water proofed boots should be worn and a spare pair for mishaps may be left in the car boot. Wader sox are excellent if the weather is sharp but do keep ordinary socks handy for perspiration inside the waders is inevitable and clean, dry socks will be most welcome come going home time.

Jeans are as good as any other form of trouser although the breeches worn by gillies north of the border are extremely comfortable inside waders. Overtrousers of the light plastic type, which can fold into ridiculously small proportions, are handy. Even better are Barbour style oil-skins, which not only keep rain out but resist wind – a useful bonus for spring fishing.

A highland weave jumper under a tough tweed jacket in cold weather will keep the body warm while standing mid-stream for any length of time and the more pockets it has the better. A good, tough hacking jacket or blouse

64

type ex-army jacket, which is wind and rain resistant, may not be so heavy as a tweed and leaves the arms more room to breathe, but if your top garment is not water-proof then for goodness sake take a water-proof barbour style jacket too. These excellent oilproofed coats can be worn over an ordinary coat or with their own heavy lining. Some have a hood and these are perhaps the best top coats of all. Special fly fisherman's waist-coats, arrayed with pockets, zips, fish nets and fly catchers are on the market now and they are excellent value for money although the poachers pocket is not always as waterproof as the makers suggest!

An old battered hat is almost essential to the successful angler and the hoard of flies one often sees stuck in the brim may look very nice and professional but don't expect to remove the flies when needed for they are usually in for good. Seriously though, a hat is very useful for keeping the sun glare down and preventing water from running straight into the eyes during rain.

Polaroid sun glasses will keep glare down but as the lenses tend to remove the reflective effect of surface water it is not considered gentlemanly to wear them when fishing because one can see the bottom of the river very often. Half the fun of fishing is finding the fish and polaroids will allow the angler to see *them* as well as the bottom!

All clothing, when fishing, should of course be non-reflective; shiny chrome buttons for example are fatal for obvious reasons. Top clothing should also be dark green or blackish and blend in generally with the surroundings. Above all you must be water-proof and warm when setting out.

Fig. 35 Some Handy gadgets for the fly man.

Accessories

A most important accessory is of course the tackle bag. For mid-stream trout 'wandering' a small half round basket will carry all your needs. It will swing around and hang behind the back out of the way and, when a fish is netted it can be dropped into the basket quite easily. The flat, hard top of the basket makes an excellent table for fly fixing or bait changing and allows one handed operations.

For heavier gear a salmon bag is more useful. There are so many on the market nowadays it is almost impossible to recommend any particular one. The answer is to obtain the best you can afford, perhaps one with a fish carrying net attached and one or two buckles to hold a net or gaff. Separate pockets for flies, knives and lunch are useful as is

Date	Where Killed	Salmon		Trout				Weight
		Hen	Cock	Hen	Cock	Sea	Rainbow	

Fig. 36 The angler's log book.

a waterproofed top flap. Strangely, most salmon and game bags are not waterproof at all, and this is because game will very quickly deteriorate if enclosed in a near air tight bag. The gadget pockets are, however, often water-proofed from the inside. This is normally vital for the fish pocket and is to prevent fish slime oozing onto the other contents of the bag. The bag must be big enough to hold all your gear without being packed too tightly. Overpacked bags end up with splits, broken zips and sharp edges. The tightly jammed boxes dig into the angler's back and small objects soon find a way out through holes and, as the bag is carried over the shoulder mid-stream, they are lost in the water.

Among the array of goodies to be found in the salmon and trout fisherman's bag is a 'priest'. This is in fact any blunt instrument capable of delivering the last rites to the catch. It is all very well using a local rock or piece of wood whilst bank fishing, but in mid-stream a long piece of shaped club is vital or your catch may find its way back into the water again. A heavy handled knife is a useful tool and if the handle is big enough it may serve as a priest too.

Most of the smaller accessories, baits, spoons, flies etc., are best kept in transparent boxes so they can be seen without opening the lids. A decent one-handed fly box is very useful too although they can be pretty expensive.

An 'otter' can be made up from a piece of dry wood and a few swivels quite easily. An otter is in fact a 'float' used

| Water | | Pool | Temperature | | Fly | Hook | Lure | Bait | Size | Weather | Time |
Height	Colour		Water	Air		Size					

to loosen lines when the line gets itself tangled up on a rock or weed bed. The otter has loose swivels which fit into the rod line. The wood floats and so takes the line downstream – or in the opposite way to the angler's pull if he raises the rod – and thus loosens the hook (hopefully).

As it is quite likely that hooks will get caught now and then, a hook sharpener should be carried at all times; a small piece of grind stone will suffice but correctly shaped hook grinders are available from ABU.

A record book will prove most useful as time goes by. If it lists all the vital information of how and where each catch is landed a picture will emerge in due time and patterns will appear quite regularly; weather, moon phase, temperature etc., all may indicate fish possibilities. Unfortunately a river changes of the years and perfectly good 'lies', indicated perhaps by a map in your record book, may be washed away in the very next spate. Bank erosion occurs all the time and overhangs are made and broken in a night so don't be too surprised when a faithful old corner suddenly stops producing fish – it may not be there any more! A good layout is suggested in fig. 36 – the blank opposite page may be used for photographs.

If you travel by car a roof rod rack, made from two small clips, will prove useful as rods may be carried when fitted up. If you need to move from spot to spot – as is most likely – the complete fitted rod may be slipped onto the roof of the car and is ready for use upon arrival at the new venue. Face the butt forwards when fitting it on the roof so that the reel is in view from the driving seat in case of accidents and *mind the tip* when opening the boot!

Incidentally, rods should always be carried *butt first*, especially among trees. If the rod stubs against a shoot or catches in a tree then the butt will bend but the rod tip would almost certainly break. Car boots are treacherous places to keep rods for other gear is usually stowed on top and the rings get damaged, to say nothing of the strain on the rod as it bends under the weight.

Anti-midge cream, in the form of a paste, spray or soap bar, is very useful, especially for evening fishing. A few dabs on exposed skin parts presents no discomfort to the angler but does ensure a midge-free hour or so. Abu 'Stopp' aerosol and 'skeet-o-stick' are both excellent repellants and very easy to apply. Some of the older more experienced anglers recommend Eucalyptus and olive oil to deter mosquitos and the angler is welcome to try it out – at his own risk.

A good balance is the first thing a lucky fisherman looks for as he proudly holds his catch for all to see and the modern scales are light enough to slip into the gadget bag without being noticed. An excellent tool is the 'puma' priest knife. It is a heavy handled knife with a ball on the end – to donk fish – and markings along the knife blade. A leather cord hangs in the middle and when the knife is hung by this cord it can be used to weigh a fish; a very useful tool. A knife, of any description, is of course essential. One with scissors included is a really useful tool and very few experienced anglers would be without this scissor-knife. Anglers' pliers, such as the Abu job, which has a disgorger, scaler, lead trimmer, tin and bottle opener, are good but rather cumbersome.

Pieces of lead, bits of spare line and plastic boxes all go into the bag along with a thermometer, fish scaler, fly pouch, spare hooks, swivels, traces: in fact there is very little one can leave out of the bag pack when it comes down to it. The angler usually carries twice as much as he needs but, after all, that's the fun of fishing.

One other item is always welcome in the angler's hold-all – especially on his first salmon outing – that is a flask of highland cream! The first enquiry from the successful fisherman's gillie will be, 'Where is the Scotch?' and woe betide the sportsman without it! It can also get pretty chilly standing waist deep in a fast flowing river.

LINES

Fishing lines have changed dramatically over the years. Smothering long lengths of silk or gut with grease, although still practised (probably in conjunction with green heart rods) by many experienced and adept anglers, is virtually a dying art. Thanks to modern technology, all the work has been done on the lines before the fisherman ever sees them. His problem is now one of selection: he must choose from many brands and types.

Fly Lines

The obvious line to commence this section with is of course the fly line. This is because the fly line is the most complex of all lines to describe. This should not deter the would be angler for there is a special line just for beginners and, considering the high cost of good fly lines, it would seem foolhardy to practice with an expensive line in any case. There are plenty of more experienced fishermen around quite willing to pass on their advice and most tackle dealers are fairly knowledgeable fellows, quite happy to recommend a suitable fly line.

The first thing a newcomer shows his surprise with, is the thickness of a fly line. It is as thick as a thin piece of string and one would think the fish would be scared out of the pool when it glides past, but in fact they cannot see the line at all – or if they do they pay no attention to it, at least not in coloured water. The thickness and weight is carefully planned. A floating line needs to be thick in order to incorporate air bubbles which give it buoyancy. The weight is essential to casting; after all the fly at the tip isn't heavy enough to take a line out and if it was 'leaded' it would sink when it reached the water and that is not always desirable. The level at which the fly is pulled through the water is also very important. And so the weight necessary for casting is placed in the length of line which will be sent out. The floating fly line is in fact made with a centre core around which is a coating of special supple plastic material. This plastic is baked in a highly scientific and precise way and millions of tiny air bubbles are formed throughout the length of the line. The degree of buoyancy is predetermined and designed into the line. A floating line would have a specific gravity slightly lower than that of water – say 0·95. A sinking line may be

Fig. 36a Combination knife and pliers are extremely useful when in midstream at times.

greased for some of its length to give an accurate fishing depth if required.

In order to standardise fly lines Jim Hardy, of Hardy Bros., introduced a standard set of fly line sizes to the U.K. The Association of Fishing Tackle manufacturers have agreed to the system and 'AFTM' standards are usually stamped on the handle of fly rods. Corresponding lines and reels may be purchased as matching sets. This gives an excellently balanced outfit with all the thinking done by the experts – the manufacturers. The AFTM numbers classify line by the actual weight of the first 30 ft of taper. Most fly lines are tapered at one or both ends. This taper is designed in order to 'shoot' the line easily through the air just as a rocket is tapered – a matter of streamlining. In the weight classification the level point is not counted and an average casting length of 30 ft is generally accepted. The weights are classed as follows:

Fly Line Weights

No.	Wt. in grains	Range	No.	Wt. in grains	Range
#1	60	54–66	#7	185	177–193
#2	80	74–86	#8	210	202–218
#3	100	94–106	#9	240	230–250
#4	120	114–126	#10	280	270–290
#5	140	134–146	#11	330	318–342
#6	160	152–168	#12	380	368–392

The range allows for acceptable manufacturing tolerances. Each range is a 'workable' range i.e. a rod suitable for any one category can handle this range. With this system one may simply match the AFTM number, signified with the symbol #, throughout the fishing outfit, and a correctly balanced set will result.

There are numerous line styles but only four basic kinds of shape.

a THE DOUBLE TAPERED LINE, usually denoted as 'D.T.'. This line has a uniform length diameter throughout its middle and a taper at each end. This gives a soft, rather delicate line delivery and is best suited for fine fishing. As the taper becomes worn and ragged it can be reversed and a whole new tapered length can be used.

b THE WEIGHT FORWARD LINE, usually referred to with the letters 'W.F.'. This line is shaped just as it says – with

70

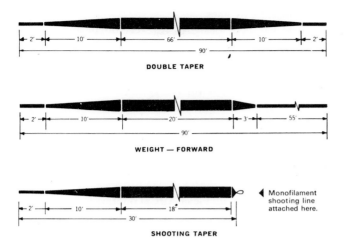

Fig. 37 Fly line types.

the weightiest part of the line to the front. The front taper is in fact heavier than the small diametered line length. It is more of a 'shooting' line and gives longer casts than the D.T. It is very useful when casting into a head wind but is not for the beginner.

c THE LEVEL LINE, briefly written as 'L', is not a good line to learn with. It is parallel throughout its length and consequently doesn't cost as much as the other lines. It is useful only when casting is not necessary.

d THE SHOOTING TAPER LINE, often reduced to 'S.T.' for convenience but sometimes confused with 'single taper', another beginner's line, is in fact a very special line of more interest to the real expert. It corresponds to the front taper and belly of the weight forward line but attaches to a special nylon monofilament shooting line, which is itself tapered too. The S.T. line can be cast over extremely long distances in the right hands.

These basic lines are designed in a number of patterns and are given further letters of specification as they are specialised. 'F' for example refers to a floating line; 'S' means a sinking or wet fly line; the intermediate is what it says – an intermediate weight – marked 'I'; the sinking tip line is designated by 'F/S' or synchro taper. This may all sound very confusing but is really a very good way of simplifying an otherwise complex system. A line marked D.T. 5F for example would mean a double tapered, size 5 floating line and if you wished to fish a wet fly with a rod marked #7 you would choose perhaps a D.T. 7S line or a double tapered #7 sinking line.

AirCel floating fly lines

This line has been designed to exceedingly fine scientifically precise limits and has an accurate buoyancy matched with the correct casting weight to match the # number of the rod, reel and line. It is available in mahogany or white. White is a good choice if night fishing is envisaged and even in daylight a mahogany line may be hard to follow in turbulent peat coloured water – remember, the fish cannot see the line at all except perhaps in crystal clear low pools so colour is really almost irrelevant as far as the fish are concerned.

Sizes available in AirCel floating line

double taper	shooting taper	single taper	weight forward taper
length 30 yds	length 30 ft	length 15 yds (available in white only)	length 30 yds
D.T. 5F	S.T. 5F	S.T. 5F	W.F. 6F
D.T. 6F	S.T. 6F	W.F. 7F	W.F. 7F
D.T. 7F	S.T. 7F		W.F. 8F
D.T. 8F	S.T. 8F		
	S.T. 9F		
	S.T. 10F		

AirCel supreme floating line

This is a cleverly designed line. Made to standards of extreme accuracy, it will lie just below the surface of the water for the length of the tapered tip but the rest of the line stays high on the surface and will lift off upon retrieve with little effort. An excellent and precise line, it is available in dark mahogany or ivory and is 30 yds in length.

Sizes available in AirCel supreme floating line

Double taper	Weight forward taper
D.T. 4F	W.F. 5F
D.T. 5F	W.F. 6F
W.F. 6F	W.F. 7F
D.T. 7F	W.F. 8F
D.T. 8F	W.F. 9F
D.T. 9F	W.F. 10F
D.T. 10F	
D.T. 11F (Ivory only)	

Of course not all fly fishing is with dry flies. Some fish lie in very deep waters and the fly must sink to attract them. After all, a fly is supposed to be imitating the real thing and hatching flies, rising from the bottom of the river will 'con' trout over and over but your imitation must get to the bottom of the river first.

WetCel fly lines have been developed after many years of research, for fishing below the water surface with the fly. There are three types of sinking line: slow, fast and extra fast. The fly can be fished at any depth and WetCel lines can be used for estuary fishing as they are resistant to salt water.

THE WETCEL 1 SINKING FLY LINE has the largest diameter and lowest density of the three and is designed to sink very slowly. It is most useful in shallow waters, lakes or slow rivers and will not tangle in weeds or the bottom before retrieve. It can of course be retrieved slowly if required. It is medium green in colour.

WetCel 1 sinking fly line sizes

Double taper	length	weight forward	length	shooting taper	length
D.T. 6S	30 yds	W.F. 7S	30 yds	S.T. 7S	30 ft
D.T. 7S	30 yds	W.F. 8S	37 yds	S.T. 8S	30 ft
D.T. 8S	30 yds	W.F. 9S	37 yds	S.T. 9S	30 ft
D.T. 10S	30 yds			S.T. 10S	30 ft

THE WETCEL 11 is a fast sinking line very useful for cutting through heavy currents. It will stay under the surface even when a fast retrieve is needed. It is most useful for fishing deep or turbid waters or when a fast under-water retrieve is required. It is dark green in colour.

WetCel II line sizes

Double taper	length	weight taper	length	level	length	shooting taper	length
D.T. 5S	30 yds	W.F. 6S	30 yds	L 5S	25 yds	S.T. 7S	30 ft
D.T. 6S	30 yds	W.F. 7S	30 yds	L 6S	25 yds	S.T. 8S	30 ft
D.T. 7S	30 yds	W.F. 8S	37 yds	L 7S	25 yds	S.T. 9S	30 ft
D.T. 8S	30 yds			L 8S	25 yds	S.T. 10S	30 ft
D.T. 9S	30 yds			L 9S	25 yds		
D.T. 10S	30 yds						

THE WETCEL HI-D is an extra fast shooting taper fly line designed especially for very deep water lake fishing. It is also most useful for deep rivers with very fast currents and its high density allows a rapid sinking action even though the water is flowing with great turbulence. It is salt water repellent although, like all lines, it should be washed in fresh water after a day in the estuary. It comes in a greenish black colour. Sizes available range from S.T. 7S to S.T. 10S; all are 30 ft long.

THE FISHERMAN INTERMEDIATE DENSITY FLY LINE sinks, but only very slowly. This allows the fisherman to fish at whatever depth he wishes, dependant upon the speed of his retrieve. A slow retrieve will obviously give the line more time to sink and a fast retrieve will keep the fly nearer the surface. The line can be made to float if it is 'dressed' – given a coating of floatation dressing. The 'Fisherman' has a very similar density to silk line, is green in colour, 30 yds in length and is available from #5–#10.

THE SYNCHRO-TAPER wet tip and wet head floating-sinking fly line is a controlled kind of intermediate line. There is a specific length of 10 ft at the tip of the line which sinks, the rest floats and allows a gentle lift-off. The synchro is available in a clever two-tone green design. Double taper sizes range from #6–#10 and the weight forward line ranges from #7–#10. The letter designation is F/S.

Other WetCel lines include the 'wet head float/sink' fly line, which has a fast sinking head with a floating running line. It is two-tone green, 30 yds long and ranges from W.F. 7F/S to W.F. 10F/S. The AirCel shooting line is a small diametered floating line for use with shooting taper lines. Its diameter is 0.029 in. and it is 100 ft long.

THE ABULON SINKING LINE is a rapid sinker designed for use in deep or fast waters. It is green in colour. Double taper sizes range from #6–#12. They are 30 yds long. The weight forward sizes range from #7 (30 yds long) to #12; all lines over #7 being 37 yds in length.

THE ABULON TOURIST FLOATING is a light green, 25 yd double tapered line available from #6–#9. As its name suggests, it is an economy line and is most useful for beginners although none the less efficient at its job.

THE ABULON FLOATING WHITE line comes in 30 yd double taper sizes of #5–#9 and in weight forward sizes of #5–#8.

THE ABULON SINK FLOAT comes with a light green 16 ft

sinking tip with a dark grey body or with an ivory body and a mahogany tip. The 30 yd lines comes in sizes from #6- #10.

Fly lines are expensive and great care should be taken with them at all times. It is not necessary to strip off the line and dry it after a day's fishing but if a fish was landed on the last reel in then the line will be wound too tightly on the reel spool and is best removed and re-wound without the stress. If estuary fishing the line should be rinsed in fresh water. As the reel should also have a flushing it may be best to soak the line and reel at one go in the same bucket. Line driers are very simple to make and are a good way to store lines without stress. No fly line should be left on the reel over long periods, such as the winter, and a metal coat hanger can be easily converted to line storage hooks.

Lastly, it is worth keeping lines in sealed plastic bags, looped in large coils when not in use in order to keep foreign substances, such as gnat spray or anti-midge cream, off the line.

NYLON LINE. This ingenious gift from the technologists to the angler has revolutionised fishing from top to bottom. It has allowed a thickness, strength and length of line previously unheard of; has permitted rods to shorten appreciably and has opened whole new fields for reels, baits, flies and so forth. Needless to say, the effect of nylon upon the world's industry and economics is phenomenal. From changing the face of world war II (by shielding low level radar interference) to causing a possible world pollution problem (nylon is as yet biologically indestructible and nylon product containers are increasing daily). However, from the fisherman's point of view, nylon is a wonderful discovery.

Nylon lines come in two ways: monofilament, (or one stranded), and braided (many stranded). It is exceedingly tough and comes from water, air and coal! Braided nylon is best for saline water areas and for use with multiplying reels. It is quite thick and 30–50 pound strain is not unusual. Monofilament is by far the most popular form of nylon. It comes in two forms originally: hard nylon, from Germany, and soft nylon, from France, although latest techniques have resulted in a general fishing monofilament strand which is available in almost any length. The best monofilament line comes from the United States.

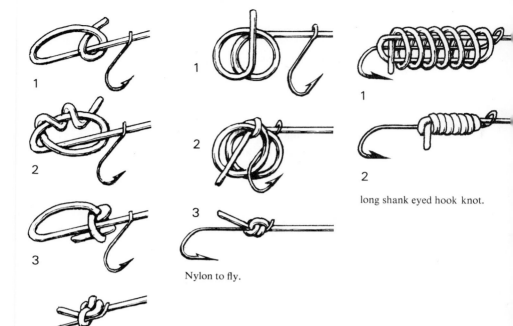

1

2

3

4

Nylon to eyed bait hook.

1

2

3

Nylon to fly.

1

2

long shank eyed hook knot.

Fig. 38 Some nylon knots.

The stiffish German line is more popular for dry fly fishing in chalk streams whereas soft, French line is mainly used for wet fly fishing. Monofilament is exceedingly good for spinning, is colourless, doesn't reflect the sunlight or flash in the water, needs no extra care, will not fray if rod rings are kept in good order and never rots. On the other hand it can become brittle with time and will stretch if wound onto the reel too tightly. Subsequent shrinkage under these circumstances leads to terrific pressure on the drum and possible fracture.

Most casts and traces, fly terminals etc., are made from monofilament nylon but special knots are essential at all times (see fig. 38). The weakest point in any nylon is the knot so never undo a knot; cut off that section and dispose of it. Although nylon has many assets, it can become worn with constant casting and being whipped through the rod rings throughout the day – especially if one of the rings is worn – so renew nylon line frequently, it is cheap enough.

Always dispose of the last few yards – especially from the swivel downwards – after a day's fishing and *every time a fish is landed. NEVER* throw these unwanted pieces of nylon away; they may be caught up in the thicket and end

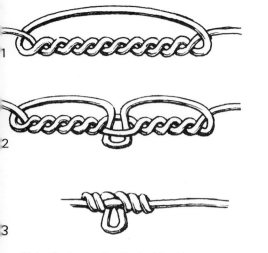

Nylon fly dropper knot using blood knot.

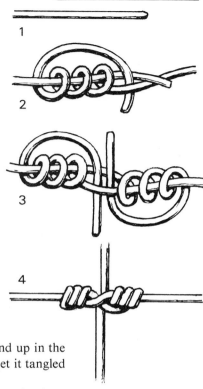

up strangling some poor animal or they can end up in the river where some angler – maybe you – will get it tangled around his fishing line.

Nylon line should be removed from the reel during long periods of non-use. The fly line drier and storer can be put to use here too.

Joining two lines, blood knot fashion.

Do not use light baits with a heavy line or the casting length will be shortened considerably; conversely a heavy bait should not be used on a light line or it may break. A light line may be used for heavy baits if the leader beyond the swivel is heavy. Suggested line breaking strain to bait weight ratios are as follows:

Line Strengths

Line breaking strain	Maximum bait
3–5 lbs	$\frac{1}{4}$ oz.
5–10 lbs	$\frac{1}{2}$ oz.
10–15 lbs	1 oz.
15–22 lbs	2 oz.
22–35 lbs	8 oz.

Abulon fishing line

Abulon is available in sizes ranging from 0·12–0·50mm. in continuous lengths of 220 yds in Great Britain.

Abulon Sizes

mm	ins	lbs
0·12	0·005	2
0·15	0·006	3
0·20	0·008	4
0·25	0·010	7
0·30	0·012	9
0·35	0·014	12
0·40	0·016	15
0·45	0·018	18
0·50	0·020	22

It is of course much more economical to purchase line in longer lengths and Abulon is available in 1000 m. spools in the following sizes:–

ins	mm	lbs
0·008	0·20	4
0·010	0·25	7
0·012	0·30	9
0·014	0·35	12

500 m. spools are available in the following sizes:–

ins	mm	lbs
0·016	0·40	15
0·018	0·45	18
0·020	0·50	22
0·024	0·60	29

Abulon can also be obtained in thicknesses of 0·15–0·45 mm. on spools holding $27\frac{1}{2}$ yds and 0·50–0·90 mm. on spools holding 55 yds. Both are available on 10 connected spools.

mm	ins	lbs
0·15	0·006	$2\frac{1}{2}$
0·20	0·008	4
0·25	0·010	7
0·30	0·012	9
0·35	0·014	12
0·40	0·016	15
0·45	0·018	18
0·50	0·020	22
0·60	0·024	29

0·70	0·028	39
0·80	0·032	50
0·90	0·036	60

Silk worm gut

This rather outdated fishing line is seldom used nowadays, but, as there are still a few diehards left (usually the best anglers), a few words here may not be amiss.

Gut sizes are quite simple when you can remember the conversion sizes; they are shown in fig. 39.

Fig. 39. Gut Sizes

Size	Class	Actual dimensions
4X	fine	0·006 ins
3X	medium	0·007 ins
2X	heavy	0·008 ins
1X	very heavy	0·009 ins

Undrawn gut is 1X. Fine trout is 0·010 in. Medium is 0·012 in. Stout is 0·013 in. Sea trout gut is 0·014 in. Light salmon is 0·016 in. Strong salmon is 0·018 in. and Hebra is 0·020 in. Drawn gut has the number before the X and is mainly used for trout or very light salmon fishing. It is called drawn because it actually *is* drawn through fine holes in a special grid in order to shave off all the edge fibres and make a smooth line. It does smooth out the line of course, but only at the cost of strength and drawn gut should not be used if big fish are about.

Silk worm gut must be kept cool and should not be left in sunlight, which, due to ultra violet radiation, destroys its molecular interlacing framework. To prevent brittleness in gut, soak overnight in a solution of glycerine and water.

Whether you use nylon or gut, braided silk or plastic fly line it is essential that the reel is full, to within $\frac{1}{4}$ in. before casting. This can be ensured if 'backing line' is used to fill up the spool. Incidentally, when attaching the fly line to the backing line – or indeed any line but especially the thick fly lines, it is important that the knot is smaller than the top ring of the rod! Fluency of a joint can be obtained if the two lines are spliced together.

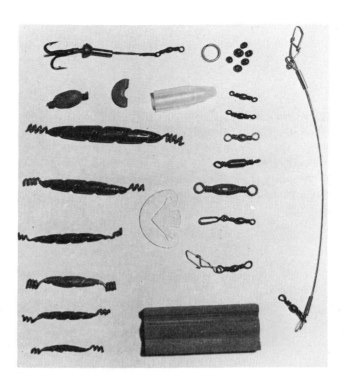

Fig. 40 Weights, swivels, anti-kinks, trace and hook sharpener.

Traces

If, when spinning, the line was connected directly to the spinner it seems fairly obvious that the line would end up badly twisted. To prevent this happening to any serious degree a 'trace' is made up. A trace is a length of line, say 30–40 ins long, connected to the actual fishing line by a swivel. The swivel then allows the bait to spin but not the line. Another swivel is used to connect the bottom end of the cast to the spinner. Some swivels even have a safety pin type slip added so that various baits may be tried out without tying new knots every time. The best swivels are the ball bearing type and, as most swivels are much stronger than the thickest line, an over large one is quite unnecessary.

An even more certain way to avoid line twist is the use of an 'anti-kink' clip, which is a flat perspex 'propeller', designed to deter the line from spinning by allowing only the section of line below the swivel to turn.

However, it is an exceptional angler who can spend a day spinning without putting a few turns in his main line and a good way to straighten out a 'kinked' line is to send a few casts downstream whilst winding in as fast as possible. Another method is to use left and right handed spinners alternatively. The direction of spin is of course decided by the position of the fins of the minnow or the shape of the spoon.

Weights

It is not often that lead weights are needed when salmon or trout fishing but when rough water keeps the bait high, or the fish are deep at the bottom of the pool, the only way to get the lure down is to add lead. If a fly will not go down then use a double hook or add a pinched, split shot 2 ft in front of the fly. When spinning, the best place to add the weight is around the wire which runs through the minnow, this helps the bait to 'swim' on an even keel but, if this is not enough or impractical, do not add lead *below* the swivel. Twisted weights, see fig. 40, can be added just above the swivel: this will not only act as an anti-kink vane but will help pull the bait in a straight line. Furthermore, to the fish, the oval shaped lead bullet looks remarkably as if it is a small fish or insect being hotly pursued by the spinning lure a yard or so behind. Lead wire is part and parcel of every angler's kit so always carry a little of the thinnest you can get.

Tapered leaders

Tapered leaders, made in monofilament nylon, are designed with a point suitable for the fly size, most likely to be used with the corresponding outfit. The butt or tail of the leader is of heavy diameter so as to transmit the power during a cast from the point of the line smoothly along the leader.

Hardy tapered leader sizes

4	tapered to	5X		
4	tapered to	4X	}	$2\frac{1}{2}$ yds long
6	tapered to	3X		
7	tapered to	2X		
8	tapered to	1X	}	3 yds long
9/10	tapered to	0X		

81

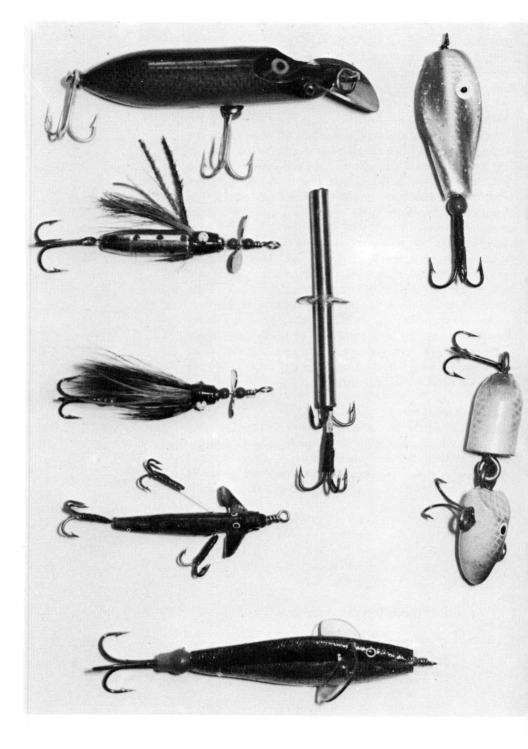

4   *Baits*

The salmon is, as explained in Chapter 1, a migratory fish; it is only in the river for one purpose – to breed. During its trip upstream it has little interest in anything else and so why does the salmon take a bait at all? The answer to this profound question is not simple and much argument over a 'wee dram' has taken place in angling pubs after a day's fishing.

Study of salmon in aquariums and by aqua-lung in Scottish rivers has shown the author a distinct behaviour pattern. The stomachs of numerous salmon have been examined and a series of minor experiments all indicate the same basic reason why a salmon should take a bait. It should be understood that the hypotheses now presented have been noted or formulated by the author and have in no way been scientifically proved – or disproved.

The reason for an adult salmon to be in fresh water at all is due to a deep urge within the biological structure of the fish to procreate. Its desire to mate with another of its species is overwhelming and it heads into the mouth of a river (reputed to be the very one in which it was born, although recent tests have disproved the *absolute* certainty of this theory).

The biological wonder of how the fish is able to cope with such drastic changes of environment as de-salination, higher oxygen rate, pH change, water density change and so on, has proved to be beyond the understanding of the scientists so far.

As food is seldom found in the stomachs of these fishes it is assumed, quite feasibly, that the fish lives off its own body fat during its stay in fresh water just as other animals (such as the dormant bear) do in winter; why then does a salmon take the lure? It is almost certainly not feeding. Underwater observation by Tom Ravensdale has shown that when a salmon arrives in a pool it first looks for somewhere safe to hide; an overhanging rock; a satisfactorily oxygenated current stream or a dark hole may be just what he is looking for. But there is invariably an occupant of such choice spots already in possession and if the newcomer is bigger than the present occupant there is a brief snapping and bumping after which the larger fish takes over the area. He will then guard this lease most jealously and any other arrival must fight him for a surrender of it. The consequence is a continuous array of skirmishes and general bad temperedness throughout the pool. Most of the general activities in a pool when the salmon leap and splash about in a random fashion is due to squabbling and chasing – over-runs, which end up in the fish leaping out of the water through the sheer momentum of their high speed diving and swooping. They flash down to avoid a larger fish, swerve upwards again from the bottom and carry on straight into the air. Regular leaping in the same deep water channel of a pool usually denotes movement into the next pool or a search for oxygen but the whole point is that during this jealous home guarding activity and general snap or be snapped at, any small fish which dares to swim into the arena is liable to a severe nip on the rump, but if the tiddler happens to be connected to a cunning little gillie on the bank it will display a turn of speed and superhuman (or super fish) strength certain to astonish even the most obstreperous of salmon. One can imagine the shock when, after giving the tail of a cheeky little 2 in. fish a quick nip, a ten pound salmon is promptly grabbed by the mouth and dragged halfway across the pool like a torpedo. What it thinks of the little beast's muscles one will never know.

So the theory is that the salmon isn't feeding at all, it is protecting its lie (or has just been thrown out of one) and is bullying any local daredevil silly enough to come within reach.

Other observations under water have shown different forms of activity. The salmon live in shoals at sea and there is good reason to assume that they enter the estuaries in groups or part shoals. They do of course thin out as the long drive upstream begins but fish still enter new pools in small groups and, as they become con-stricted, after the spacious Atlantic, the fun and games begin. They are flushed with the excitement of prospective breeding, light headed with excess oxygen and thrust together in a feverish situation. Any strange creature floating past the exuberant fish will inevitably be snapped at. To add to these two bait taking reasons is yet another 'theory': in Chapter one I described the mating process of

84

7 A cock salmon! They don't come much bigger than this. The Ambassadeur and Abu rod are ideal for such heavy water fishing.

See illustration on page 28

8 Make sure you are well equipped for the job. A good set of waders, gaff, tailer or landing net and a good game bag are essentials for the game fisher.

(See page 103)

11 Make sure the centrifugal brake corks are on when you put your Abu multiplier back together again.

12 Star drag tension on the Ambassadeur multiplier. The complexity of these reels is quite extraordinary.

13 The fabulous Hardy trout and salmon fly reels. For precision, lightness and quality they are supreme.

9 The featherlight fly rods by Hardy. Note the collapsible, telescopic landing net and spacious game bag.

10 Spinner or fly fishing demands quality tackle. These fibreglass rods and lightweight reel are Jim Hardy's design.

salmon and the activities of the young parr. The parr take an active part in the reproductive activities of adult salmon and the poor cock has a very devil of a task in keeping his hen to himself. In between actual breeding spasms he must chase away adult suitors seeking to impress his mate with their vivid red coats and quivering flanks; at the same time he is constantly being buzzed by these troublesome parr. Now, if the salmon is on his second breeding trip he may well have a fair grudge against the small parr and snap at them on his way upstream from sheer annoyance. With youngsters the reaction is probably instinctive. And of course a great deal of 'courting' goes on in the pools on the way up. This often leads to spawning, even in very deep, large rivers.

These theories are all very well for it is quite difficult to disprove them, but the inevitable question always arises; 'They may explain the salmon taking a snap at spinning lures but what about flies? *They* don't represent a danger to the salmon's hiding place nor an interference at breeding time – so why will a salmon take a fly?'. Well, the answer may well be that flies, grubs and insects *do* represent a danger to the salmon; they are a direct and very real threat to his offspring. There is hardly a more juicy tit-bit to offer young fry than fish eggs and very few sub-aquatic predators, be they cray-fish or beetles, will refuse a nice healthy batch of spawn. And so it is quite possible that a salmon snapping at a fly is not feeding at all but protecting its unborn young.

Many fishes will behave in this way; the Siamese fighting fish, *Betta splendens*, for example will kill his own mate if she dares venture too close to 'his' eggs and a shoal of salmon, if provoked or excited are just as spiteful as the Siamese fighter.

A final theory (and all postulations as to the reasons why salmon take baits must be theories only) is that salmon, once in the waters of their birth, or at least water similar to them, remember their days of frantic dashes for tiny morsels of food when young. The free-for-all race to a fallen caterpillar or the hatching nymph as it rose to the surface or the luscious worm washed from a bank during a spate – all the years of living on these dainty morsels may not have been completely wiped from the salmon's mind during its stay at sea and the instinct to race for and snap at *anything* which resembles food in any way may well be too deeply rooted to forget.

F

The familiar fresh water life and layout may well bring back memories of old food habits and the occasional snap at a choice morsel may be almost automatic. Salmon certainly do snap at small insects in the water under scrutiny but every occasion this has been witnessed by the author, the insect has been immediately spat out and forgotten.

Which of these theories is effective at any one time is anyone's guess – it could be one or the other, a part of one or a part of all, but one thing is certain: if we knew precisely why and how a salmon took the lure we would have lost the point and fun of fishing at all. At the moment it is a battle of wits and patience, trial and error – like luck and the weather; may it remain so.

So much for the salmon. Sea trout, on the other hand, most certainly *are* feeding on their way upstream. They are, however, extremely timid fish and, unlike the salmon, do not dash around showing off at any excuse in the middle of the day. They are shy, timid, intelligent creatures, demanding utmost care and cunning to catch. And, once on a line, the sea trout can often show the mighty salmon how to fight for its life, so vigorously does it cling to its own.

The brown trout does, of course, feed non-stop. Being a territorial fish it will sit in its favourite spot waiting for food to come its way and then a quick pounce and Bob may well be your uncle!

Now that 'bait taking' is providing the reader with a suitable reason to wonder how fish are caught at all – and a headache to go with it – we may consider some of the baits which occasionally bring a fish home. There are, of course, countless varieties of bait and just as many makes as types. There is a bait for every single fish – and a fish for every single bait.

When considering which type of bait to use it is important to consider the weather, the air and water temperatures, colour and speed of water and so on. But first and foremost comes the understanding of the anatomical system of a fish in relation to its ability to catch the lure you present. A fish can taste, smell and see. It has no eyelids and is therefore violently and unavoidably dazzled when presented with a shiny lure in bright sunlight. It can in fact see much better in diffused or shaded light. The lesson is clear – a dull bait on a dull day and keep out of the sunlight – he may not see the bait, nor will he care to

88

leave his lie on a sunny day. (In fact he *may* see the lure –
very clearly and it is this clearness which frightens him.
What we mean is that he won't see the bait as an edible or
'killable' object and will actually be afraid of it.) Secondly,
a fish does not have the binocular vision we humans have.
If you place your hand perpendicular to your face and rest
it upon your nose you will see what this means. Now close
one eye – then the other; as you change eyes you seem to
change the *position* of what you are looking at. On top of
this, a number of objects in the field of view of your left
eye cannot be seen with the other eye without moving
and vice versa. You may even find a slight colour change
between each eye. Well fishes suffer the restriction you
would have to endure if you walked around with your
hand in front of your face all day and, like the fish, you
would have some difficulty in judging position and *distance* without binocular vision. Although the fish has
extreme panoramic vision and thus a much larger field of
view than man, it suffers in consequence by not being able
to focus both eyes on the same object. Members of the
salmon family have their eyes placed fairly high up on the
head and tilted slightly forward. This places further
restriction on a salmon's vision, but the end result is that it
cannot see behind or below itself very well. A bait is best
seen, then, from below, which means whilst looking up
into the sky. So colour, it would seem, plays little part in
the desire of fish to take the bait for it only sees the
silhouette (of a surface bait at least), which is black. This
even suggests that a *black* fly is best at night. But flies
cover such a wide field that a whole chapter has been
devoted to them. Night vision is discussed in the sea trout
at night section. On the other hand, salmon *can see* colour.

Hooks

All baits, be they live minnows, flies or worms, must have
a hook, (or hooks) somewhere in their cunning design and
the shape, size or angle of the hook is extremely important. Hook sizes range from veritable cactus hairs to great
meat hooks.

The hook should be measured from the limit of the bend
to the beginning of the eye – do not include the eye in your
measurements. The actual size of the hook depends upon
the length of the shank. While measuring, do not make
any allowance for the various styles of bend or shape.
When selecting hooks, the length of the shank, the amount

89

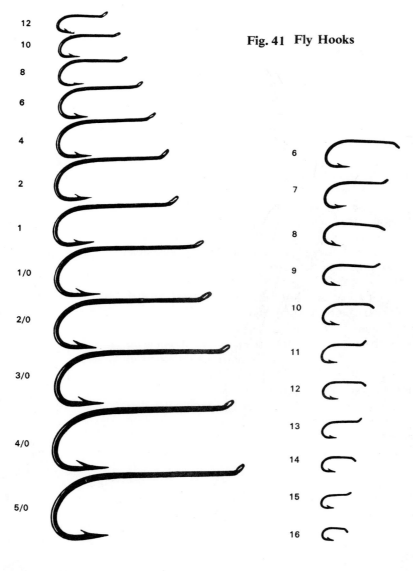

12
10
8
6
4
2
1
1/0
2/0
3/0
4/0
5/0

Fig. 41 Fly Hooks

6
7
8
9
10
11
12
13
14
15
16

**Hardy Wire Salmon
Fly Hooks
Actual Size**

**Hardy Fly Hooks
Examples show up-eyed
and down-eyed hooks
Actual Size**

of curve, or gape and the offset barb angle should be considered. There are four basic types of hook but many different varieties of these types. The starting points are: long shanked, short shanked, up-turned shank and the hog's backed shank. Beware of too severe a hog's back for over-curvature tends to put a wobble or spin onto the bait – unless of course you require a wobble! The eye of the hook is also very important. It can be up-turned, straight, down-turned (mainly on fly hooks – discussed in the next chapter) or gut eyed. Some hooks can be obtained with a gut trace already attached, but most salmon and trout men prefer to attach the hook to the trace themselves.

For salmon and sea trout the gape of the hook should be at least one third of the length of the shank. A long shank has a much more effective pull than a short shank. It will also be driven home easier.

The bend of a hook is very important. There are again numerous shapes, kinks and offset angles, but the three basic standard bends are:– the square bend, the round bend and the Limerick. Most popular is the round bend especially for the smaller fish such as river trout. For larger fish such as lake trout and small sea trout the square bend is a safer hook. For salmon the Limerick is generally accepted as the finer hook.

The colour of a hook will depend upon the type of bait being used. Dull brown or black hooks are usually quite safe but for live bait silver fish or minnows the use of a silver hook is quite acceptable. A red hook is best for shrimp or prawn and even for worm and a gold hook is good for maggots. In fact maggot sized hooks usually come with leader attached and these hooks are invariably gold.

Hooks must be kept absolutely needle sharp at all times. A small piece of oil stone or even a properly shaped Abu fish hook stone doesn't take up much space in the tackle box and more fishes have been lost over blunt hooks – especially when bait fishing with such lures as prawn – than for any other reason. When sharpening coloured hooks or painted hooks such as the black type, remember that if you take the point off you may have a dazzling white tip glinting into the eyes of your prey and he may be warned off, so dirty the hook with a blade of grass before casting or, better still, leave the hook a few days until the atmosphere coats the point again.

For salmon, the Limerick is best. There should be no

Fig. 42 Top to bottom:
Treble Limerick
Round tandem
Double salmon
Cod forged
Wide gape (down-turned eye)
Wide gape (up-turned eye).

bend off or 'sneck' incorporated into the hook design. Alternatively a double hook may be used although these are usually restricted to fly fishing. The point of a double hook is, apart from the obvious fact that there is a double possibility of hooking the fish, that it is heavier than a single hook and will take a light bait deeper without the use of lead. But a word of warning – never use a double hook larger than No. 2.

For trout, a tapered shank with a round bend is best and a down-turned eye will help pull the hook into the mouth of the fish when striking.

For worming, a round bend hook is essential. It should have a wide gape and no sneck. Pennel or Stuart tackles are more effective in holding the worm in a natural position but the worm will not live as long when pierced two or three times.

NATURAL BAITS

It is not always possible to entice fish to bite with the more 'gentile' baits, such as the fly, and other methods are sometimes necessary. One may admire the diehard fly-men who simply refuse to use anything else, but it can be a bit of a bind fishing for days on end with no sign of a fish. If the water is poor, say because of severe flooding, or badly coloured, then only a stubborn angler takes a fly rod to the water at all. Natural baits have accounted for many fish under these sort of conditions and, provided they are used well, a great deal of fun can be had.

Fresh baits are far better than the preserved jobs one can get in most tackle dealers for it is the smell which attracts the fish in the first place and Formalin doesn't smell too nice at all.

Fresh baits can be collected with little effort but there is often a local bait provider who will supply you with a day's bait for a 'wee dram' afterwards. Ideally, use females with roe bulging in their abdomen and if the bait is not mouth mounted, close the lips to prevent water drag. Cut off all fins to stop undesirable (or uncontrollable) wobble and keep the bait in salt sooner than a chemical preservative if they are prepared the night before. Do not keep a mounted bait in salt or the metal parts will corrode.

The bait, whatever it is, will need to be mounted on a special trace. Traces come in all manner of shapes and

92

sizes and of course can be made by the angler himself with a few trebles, a roll of wire and some darning needles.

Manufactured natural bait traces, such as the 'archer' type are basically a leaded needle, which is thrust into the mouth of the bait and sent through the body; it ends with a plastic propeller shaped nose, which spins the bait as it travels through the water (see fig. 48). Lashed to the leaded needle with strong wire is usually a pair of treble hooks. Some traces fairly bristle with hooks but there is seldom a need for more than two. One of the barbs on the treble hook is often bent almost perpendicular to the others, this barb is thrust into the side of the bait in order to prevent it sliding off the trace. The other two are for ensnaring the prospective fish. The second treble hook will lie at the tail – a frequent spot for a 'bully' to snap at. The whole bait can also be lashed onto the trace very firmly with a piece of strong wire. Most fishermen keep a roll of wire in their tackle bag in the form of an old electric motor magnet. The wire coil around the magnet is ideal for this purpose!

If you use a bait of less than 2 ins in length, do not use more than one treble. A baiting needle may not need weighting at all but if it does, wind a little lead wire around the whole length of the needle – not in one bundle or the bait will not 'swim' on an even keel.

Another type of mount is one which has no propeller vanes to spin it. The hooks are simply lashed onto the side and tail of the bait with wire – plus of course the third hook of the treble embedded in the flesh. A wobble is introduced into the bait by curving the abdomen and fixing the two trebles closer together (see fig. 43). This method of bait mounting is usually best for large baits when hunting the 'big 'uns' for example, in the larger lakes, or when seeking Ferox (very large carnivorous trout). The only other time is when the water is really fast and turbulent. For salmon and general river fishing it is very unlikely that a bait exceeding 4 ins will be necessary but half pound trout may well be acceptable when trolling (see Chapter 9) in a large lake.

Remember – as with all such equipment – wash the mounts after use in salt or brackish water and never leave a mount in the salt used for bait preserving or the metal parts will be attacked.

Worms
Worms spring to mind as the most natural of all baits and

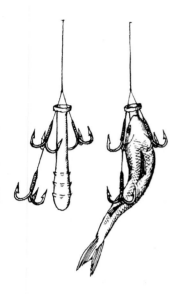

Fig. 43 Wobble bait tackle.

Fig. 44 Stuart tackled worm.

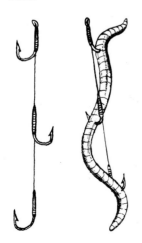

of course very few foods attract a hungry trout more quickly. The type of worm depends very much upon the type of fish you are looking for. The smaller worms, such as brandlings, which are found in dung heaps and can be recognised by their vivid yellow and red stripes, are best for rainbow trout and small brownies. They smell strongly and wriggle violently. They are best on single hooks. Huge earth-worms, such as those found on lawns at night, are called lob-worms and are best for salmon and large trout.

Catching the worms the night before can be almost as much fun as catching the fish! If you are ever in the vicinity of Tomintoul, in the heart of the salmon and trout fishing Highlands, and you see a number of bottoms bobbing up and down in the light of as many torches on the village green at 2 a.m., you can be sure it will be Moe and Vi, Tom and Soraya or Rene and Fred. Each pair will have a cloth bag tied round one neck and a torch held by the other. The idea is that when the worms come out to feed at night they can be seen in the light of the torch and pounced on by the second 'worm hunter'. And we mean *pounce* for there is hardly a faster creature in the world than a worm at night! It is absolute greased lightning and, until you learn which end to pounce on first, you won't catch one single worm. Beware also that the torch light doesn't fall directly on the worm for it is light sensitive and will vanish as if by magic. A red light seems to bother them less, so perhaps they are only affected by one part of the spectrum – an interesting point of study for someone's Ph.D. thesis perhaps. Lastly, the worm is also sensitive to the vibrations of your feet. So do creep stealthily about the lawn in your search and if you find two worms engaged in extra feeding activities such as could only be imagined as a nuptial embrace, don't bother them for they would only die if whipped out of the ground and thrown into the cloth bag around your neck. A little damp moss will keep the worms for a few days but do cover them over at night or they will climb all over the place.

One surprising danger in handling worms is the very strong acid, which is secreted through their skins. Touching the shiny mucous continuously may lead to quite severe burning of the skin at the finger tips. This can be sufficient to cause peeling and will at least wear away the 'finger-prints' in much the same way as pumice stone would. The obvious remedy is to wear gloves when catching worms or rinse the hands every so often.

94

These large worms are best presented on a double hook (Pennel) or even a triple hook (Stuart tackle) and should be affixed in the method shown in fig. 44. Single and double hook positions are shown in fig. 45.

Large lob-worms may be bunched on a single hook in groups of up to six. This bundle of worms may be 'trundled' down-stream occasionally. This method of fishing is not always considered 'gentlemanly' by some angling snobs but is perfectly legal unless your fishing permit states 'No worming'. It is really a spate fishing method.

The writhing mass of worms must look very much like a young squid to the sea going fish and therefore an object to be killed, if not eaten. As the bundle also rushes up (in a cloudy spate water) on the lying fish, frightening the life out of it, this may cause the desired reaction. As for the hook size, this will depend very much upon weather etc., but a general hook size to water condition for worming is shown in fig. 46.

Fig. 45 Correct mounting of worms on a single hook.

Fig. 46   Worming hook sizes

Temp. °C	River height	Current speed	Water colour	Hook size regardless of No.
2	normal	normal	normal	5/0
2	low	normal	normal	3/0
2	high	normal	normal	6/0
2	normal	slow	normal	4/0
2	normal	fast	normal	6/0
2	normal	normal	clear	4/0
2	normal	normal	cloudy	6/0
5	normal	normal	normal	2/0
10	normal	normal	normal	4
15	normal	normal	normal	8
20	normal	normal	normal	12

As you can see from fig. 46 the considerations are temperature, river height, current speed and water colour. When measuring the water temperature, this must be done in fast current and not where there is a slow pool. When the temperature is below 10°C, the worm should be allowed to fall to the bottom and fished generally deeper than when the temperature is higher. The warmer the water, the smaller the hook (and worm) and when the water is really cold the worm should be fished very slowly, but then, worm fishing is described in a later chapter. It is

95

not necessary to use smaller hooks when using a Pennel or Stuart.

For the angler still not convinced of why a *salmon* should go for a worm it is worth considering the effect that young eels (very similar to large worms) have on freshly laid fish eggs. Eels love to dig into the gravel searching for tid-bits and salmon (or trout) eggs are laid in gravel beds!

Maggots

Maggots or gentils are mainly used for stream trout, although a sea trout may occasionally take a bundle. Maggots should only be used with small hooks and fine gear. They will provide the fisherman with an excellent day's sport although a number of strange catches may result. Keep the maggots cool and dry; in fact the fridge is an excellent place to keep them on a hot summers night – but don't tell the wife I said so.

Prawn and Shrimp

Prawn and shrimp baits are perhaps the most controversial of all fish lures. One of two things will happen when a prawn is thrown into a pool; the salmon (for they are seldom taken by trout when whole although numerous tiddlers may nibble at it) will either queue up to take it or they will run for their lives! Why this is so is the subject for much conjecture, but the author feels that the smell of prawns, which is considerable under water as well as above, reminds the salmon of its recent ocean life. The tang of sea foods invariably make one think of the sea and this probably happens to the fish too. A waft of the sea may suddenly produce absolute panic at the thought of possible predators and thorough confusion in the tiny brain of a fish resulting in the startling effect prawns will have sometimes: the fish scatter in panic and rush from one end of the pool to the other.

On the other hand the smell may trigger off in the memory department a desire for food (even though it is spat out once taken) and there is not a more effective bait than prawn or shrimp when the fish *are* taking. Why the salmon will be for or against at any particular moment is beyond comprehension, but one possibility is the population density situation of the pool. Relatively few tests (and therefore inconclusive as evidence) were conducted by Tom Ravensdale in pools of widely varying populations. However, the pools with large numbers of salmon did seem quite upset by the prawn whereas relatively empty pools contained many aggressive fish quite happy to snap at the bait. The conclusions drawn from these observations suggest that when a pool is over-populated, i.e. there are more salmon than hiding places, or lies, the fish are nervous. Those with lies are wary of losing them and those without lies are afraid of predators – or anglers with their terrifying shadows looming over the surface every so often. The smell of salt water and all the dangers that go with it may prove too much for a nervous disposition, and general panic results when a prawn is tossed into the pool. Alternatively, when there is plenty of room for the occupants of a pool. a sense of well being pervades and they are quite fearless. Sea smells *then* present quite a different picture and the result is a good day's salmon fishing.

If this last situation sounds incredible then consider this experiment by the author: An empty aquarium was filled and a 2 in. fish (the type is irrelevant for consideration of the aspects under consideration here) was placed in it. The fish sulked in one corner. Another 2 in. fish was placed in the tank with it. He sulked in the other; both refused food. A 2 in. fish went into the third corner and behaved the same way.

A second aquarium was given a gravel bed and one rock hiding place. A 2 in. fish was put into the tank. It promptly went into the rocks. A second 2 in. fish, when introduced to the tank was chased away from the cave as was the third fish. The smaller fish dominated the tank until the larger one finally ousted him and took over the hole. Even though the large fish was unable to actually enter the sanctuary he displayed the same aggressiveness and fearless attitude that the smaller one did. The interesting part of the experiment came when the fishes were fed – they refused to eat, even the fish with a 'home' would not leave it.

Yet another tank was set up, this time with adequate hiding places for all three fish and the resulting activity, as they dashed happily around the aquarium, rushing up to the surface for food and chasing each other around in general enjoyment, was quite startling.

Analysis of these results seems to confirm the nervous, edgy, situation when housing is short and *could* explain the seemingly haphazard way that shrimp or prawn is taken by the salmon.

Fig. 47 Prawn mounting: note the fine wire to hold the bait.

The feeding of fishes is described in considerable detail by Tom Ravensdale in his book, 'Coral fishes – their care and maintenance', published by Gifford.

A word of warning then; never use prawn or shrimp unless all else has failed, for once the occupants of a pool have been shocked in this way they will stay shocked for some time to come. And *always* enquire whether prawn or shrimp bait is allowed! Very few beats permit the use of such 'ungentlemanly devices'.

Prawns should be fixed to the hook with a special device made for the job, called a 'prawn tackle', or threaded through the line with a needle and a *treble* hook (not a *triple* hook!) can be attached to the end. When the bait is snatched at, it shoots up the line out of the way and the hook can be sunk home. It should be threaded onto the line, or attached to the tackle, so that it pulls through the water *tail first*.

Sand Eels

Sand eels are extremely good bait for sea trout and are best used when the sea trout are just entering the estuary although this is not of paramount importance. The sand eel, incidentally, is not an eel at all, it is a normal, albeit elongated, *fish*. When mounting, cut off the head and remove the innards in order to make room for the leaded mounting spike. If the spike is not leaded there is no need to remove the gut. Affix the hooks firmly – plenty of hooks may be used on a sand eel when sea trout fishing but only two are necessary for salmon or brown trout fishing, although they seldom interest the latter. Tie the bait with wire only if necessary and use a black or dull wire if at all; the eel is usually tough enough to stay on the hooks without wiring.

Minnows

Minnows are next in popularity to worm and prawn. They are offered in preserved form and many colours by most tackle dealers: the most popular being gold and silver. There is no need to buy minnows; they are easy to catch. Simply lie a jam jar with a conical top in water near the

98

river bank in a fair current with a few scraps of bread or worm inside and the jar will fill up rapidly with minnows.

Another method of trapping minnows is to lay your landing net, if suitably fine meshed, on the bottom by the bank and place a flat rock with a few bunches of weed in it. Then go upstream a few dozen yards and stir up the bottom with a stick as you walk back to the net. Most of the disturbed tiddlers, which scurried off as you frightened them, will stop under the rock with a weed and you can lift the whole lot out with your net.

If you catch the minnows in the river you are fishing, make sure they are minnows and not salmon or trout fry.

Once caught, the minnows should be tapped on the head with a stone and mounted in the same way as sand eels. The only difference is that it is not necessary to remove the head unless the bait is too large. The treble hook on the mount should not be lashed too tightly to the bait. This is very important, many fish are lost by tying the treble mount too tightly to the bait. A number of small knife point digs into the skin of the bait will help the smell to float away more efficiently. Well known champion caster and fisherman, Jim Hardy, swears by female minnows full of berry, especially for trout. The male, with his scarlet coat is rarely taken.

Gudgeon

Gudgeon are treated in much the same fashion as minnows and will give similar results. They do however, tend to have a sharp pointed dorsal fin and this is best cut off altogether. If the fish is to be frightened off on its first bite by a sharp pointed object at all it should be your hook and not a fish bone. The gudgeon is described more fully in Tom Ravensdale's companion book, "Understanding coarse fishes".

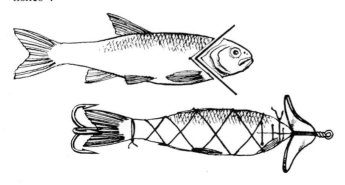

Fig. 48 Live baits should have the head and fins removed for spinning.

Sprats

These are offered by most fishing tackle dealers in neat little polythene packs. They come in gold or silver and really do smell rather bad. If you don't like the smell, it is quite possible the fish won't (although maggots don't send me into raptures!) and the only thing one can do is soak them in salt for the night, but don't mount them first if this is your intention or the mounts will rust.

The sprat can be used with or without a head and gut, depending upon size. It is a fairly good bait, especially in deep rivers or large lakes. It is an early bait and tends to be more effective before April.

ARTIFICIAL BAITS

Sometimes the best baits are not real ones at all. The artificial bait is much easier to control in the water and certainly a lot easier to handle out of water. The precise size required is easily obtained. They last for as long as one can expect for they don't go bad. The hooks are fairly well placed and less fish will be lost on an artificial bait than on a natural one. The artificial bait will also fish at the depth you want in consequence.

Artificial baits, like so many angling accessories, come in every possible shape and size imaginable. The trick is to select the right one for the right fish on the right day – that's all!

Artificial lures should be used only when conditions are not fit for fly fishing, during a spate for example, when the river is too high and dirty. Of paramount importance is the golden rule that spinning ceases when a fly-man comes into sight. He is allowed to fish through your pool and you should wait until he has done so before resuming your attempts to catch a fish. Artificial lures mean almost anything which isn't 'real' – a piece of silver paper or a twist of thread may catch a fish and orange pips, shoe lace eyes or cigarette ends have even been known to kill fish.

The more recognisable lures are grouped into small manufactured fish-like wooden or metallic devices; either imitation fish or spinning spoons, which set up vibrations of interest to the prey.

Minnows or Devons

These are certainly the most popular salmon baits of all

and it is almost certain that more weight of salmon has been hooked on spinning lures of the devon variety than on any other kind of lure – including the fly! The devon is a hollow imitation fish which is threaded onto a small trace. At the tail is a treble hook; there are two fins either half way along the body or near the head; and the whole unit is attached by the wire trace to a swivel. The treble hook should not extend beyond the width of the fins. If the fins are extra large, the hook should be even smaller and in general about the size of a normal fish tail. The eye of the swivel should just show and allow the line to be attached to it. If the swivel sticks out of the mouth of the fish too much it may kink and prevent the body sliding up the line when 'taken'. The devon itself should have a hole big enough for the swivel to slip through so that when the fish does take the devon it is thrown forwards and the hook can take hold. The fins on the body of the devon serve as the propeller blades and are slotted at an angle to give either a left or right hand spin as the lure is pulled through the water. This is to lessen the chances of line twist and kink.

The swivel is attached to the fishing line and roughly 30–60 ins along the line another swivel is attached. Just above this swivel a small piece of lead, or an anti-kink clip will help cut down line twist too. Some devons are solid metal; these cast very well and can be tossed considerable distances with either a fixed spool reel or a multiplier (or even a Nottingham reel although this type is the least popular of all reels for spinning). The drawback of a heavy devon is the need to retrieve it quickly or it will sink to the

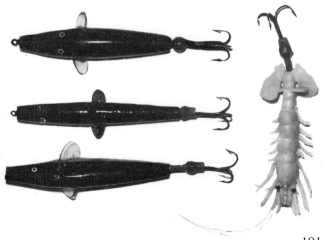

Fig. 49 Metal devons and a nylon prawn.

101

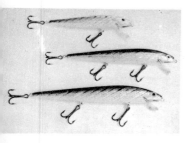

Fig. 50 Abu lures (top).

Fig. 51 Abu spoons (bottom).

bottom and get caught up in rocks or weed. They are best for deep or very fast water and in lakes.

The wooden devons are much more versatile for they can easily be made heavier when necessary. This is usually done by adding lead wire or shot to the line but if possible the lead wire (very thin) can be coiled neatly around the wire *inside* the devon. This ensures the devon still 'swims' on an even plane and is not tilted head down as with the other method, it all depends on how much room is inside the devon for it must be allowed to spin.

The reflex devon is the same as above but the body is flat sided. This gives the bait a slight wobble and sends out different vibrations or waves. It is a rather old fashioned devon and has almost vanished in favour of the modern jobs.

Whichever devon you choose, the basic rule is: dull, matt, drab coloured devons in dirty or cloudy water and, bright, shiny ones on clear water. If the water is peat stained (brown) then use a gold-brown devon or a green-yellow one. In clear chalk streams use a blue-silver or a black-grey. Slim copper tubes with wings make good sea trout lures and they can be home-made to any length.

Keep the treble points sharp at all times and bear in mind the number of times you get snagged at the bottom at the end of the day – you cannot expect the hook to stay sharp after such a pounding.

The size of your minnow is most important and this should be decided even before the colour and style is. Much will depend on temperature and water conditions and a rough chart of bait sizes can be seen in fig. 52.

Fig. 52. Devon minnow sizes

Temp. °C	River height	Current speed	Water colour	Maximum bait length excluding hook
2	normal	normal	normal	4 ins
2	low	normal	normal	3 ins
2	high	normal	normal	$3\frac{1}{2}$ ins
2	normal	slow	normal	$3\frac{1}{4}$ ins
2	normal	fast	normal	$3\frac{3}{4}$ ins
2	normal	normal	clear	3 ins
2	normal	normal	cloudy	$3\frac{1}{2}$ ins
2	normal	normal	normal	$2\frac{3}{4}$ ins
5	normal	normal	normal	$2\frac{1}{2}$ ins
10	normal	normal	normal	2 ins
15	normal	normal	normal	$1\frac{1}{2}$ ins
20	normal	normal	normal	1 in.

102

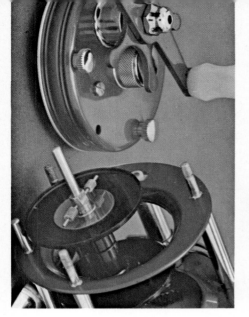

(See captions on page 86)

14 The Abu-Flies. Their extra weight allows long distance casting and 'spinning' on 'fly only' waters!

15 Top: Abu-Fly.
Left: Quill.
Right: Transparent, fixed spinner.
Bottom: Wobbler.

These are of course only guide lines and somewhere to
start from. You will need to try out various sizes and
colours, depending upon the weather. Remember, the
weight of the line will determine its 'swim' speed and rate
of draw so juggle around with weight as well as length –
don't be afraid to try out your hunches, that's what fishing
is all about.

Phantoms

These little fish lures are really rather thin, wobbly
minnows. They come in a variety of colours and can be
twisted to suit the shape desired. They are best in coloured
water and can be filled with lead to get them down. They
have a rather hump-backed appearance and the smaller
ones are quite attractive to trout, especially rainbows.
They do best in lakes but can of course be tried in deep
river pools.

Plugs

The plug is an imitation fish, which is pulled through the
water without spinning. Plugs 'wobble' their way through
the water imitating a fish in trouble. Their erratic movements can be exaggerated by waving the rod from side to
side making the bait change direction. Some plugs are
jointed *in the centre* to give an even more pronounced
wobble.

The Abu killer 'Must-lure' is an excellent hard plastic
lure available in these sizes: $\frac{3}{8}$ oz., $\frac{1}{2}$ oz., and $\frac{3}{4}$ oz. They
are obtainable in blue, gold or silver. The Abu Hi-Lo
wobbler is an excellent and cleverly designed plug with a
cunning 'depth device' affixed to the mouth of the fish.
This is a little plate or lip which enables it to be fixed at
any depth. (see fig. 53).

The lip can be set for the depth required and it is
available in all colours and sizes. An articulated body
gives a wobbling motion if required. The largest Hi-Lo
weighs $1\frac{1}{2}$ ozs and is 6 ins long. A really wicked lure is the
Cello or Cello-dip. It is made of soft plastic, which deters
the fish from instant fear when biting it. Being flexible it is
quite difficult for the fish to disgorge it once he has taken
and the two trebles soon take hold. The Cello, unlike all
other lures so far, is a surface bait and will float no matter
how tough the water is. There are two models; the flat
nosed plug, and the 'lipped' swimmer. A shrimp is also
available, with three treble hooks it is quite hard for a

G   105

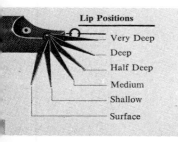

Lip Positions

Very Deep
Deep
Half Deep
Medium
Shallow
Surface

Fig. 53 Abu Hi-Lo.

Fig. 54 (left) An Abu spoon.

Fig. 55 (right) A mepps spinner.

hooked fish to escape once it has taken hold. Most of these Abu lures are best suited to salmon or large lake trout.

Spoons

Spoons come second in popularity to devons for the spinning enthusiasts and a fair handyman can make himself a grand display of different shapes and sizes if he cares to. There are of course many spoons offered by the tackle manufacturers and the most popular group are the 'Mepps' spoons. In the Mepps (see fig. 55) it is the spoon which actually revolves around a solid, straight pulling body whereas in the normal spoon the whole unit spins. The spoon is usually oval in shape and it is the small end of the elipse which pulls through the water first. With the bar spoon the wider end is pulled first.

For trout, the 'Must lure Droppen' is a very successful lure indeed. It has been designed for distance casting with little effort. The spoon revolves around a body, which is entirely covered by the length of the spoon, and new models have saddle shackle, which allows the spoon to rotate at the slightest water pressure. The point of balance at the rear, where the bulbous brass body hangs, stabilises the motion of the whole unit as it is pulled through the water. This helps to cut down line twist. These Droppen lures come in many shapes and sizes. A slightly more elaborate spoon from Abu is the 'Reflex'. These have a fish body, a cunningly designed striped spoon which revolves around it, and the hook is hidden in an attractive bunch of hair. The hair looks incredibly real – like a fish-tail under water and a weedless model is available. Weights range from $\frac{1}{16}$ oz. to $\frac{3}{8}$ oz. Many, many more spoons fill the pages of angling catalogues so we will not waste valuable space here, but one type does stand out above all others – the toby.

Tobys

The toby is perhaps the most famous of all 'spoons'. It is not a true spoon as such, it is a design of its own – and a very successful one indeed. It will be taken by trout and salmon alike. It fishes well in any water and casts in all weather conditions. The toby comes in many colours but the striped black-gold jobs have probably killed more salmon than any other kind.

The toby weedless is a very cleverly designed anti-weed lure. The hook, which is single as against the usual treble

106

type, is capped by a soft, lined bundle of hair. This line is slipped off by the fish's mouth when he takes.

The Toby

Weight (oz.)	Length (in.)	Weight (oz.)	Length (in.)
$\frac{1}{8}$	$1\frac{3}{4}$	$\frac{1}{4}$	$2\frac{1}{2}$
$\frac{3}{8}$	$2\frac{1}{2}$	$\frac{3}{8}$	3
$\frac{5}{8}$	$3\frac{1}{2}$	$\frac{3}{4}$	3
1	$3\frac{1}{2}$	$1\frac{1}{8}$	$3\frac{1}{2}$

These baits do not cover the whole range of possibilities by any means but they are a starting point. If you keep a good log book of your trout and salmon fishing days it will differ for each river; it will differ for each month and it will differ for almost every possible circumstance. And so, all a book of this kind can do is lay out some of the baits used by the author (successfully on occasions); the rest is up to you. I have known fish to fall for frogs, caterpillars and slugs, buttons and pencils, chocolate wrappings and cheese spread; so don't accept the end of this chapter as the end to bait possibilities – there is no end to the baits a member of the *Salmonidae* family will accept – try some.

Fig. 56 Tobys, the most successful of all heavy waters spinning lures.

5   Flies

No salmon and trout book could possibly go to press
without a long section on flies. The fly fisherman is the
aristocrat of the angling world – or so it is said – and there
is certainly a magic in wading thigh deep in a broad
salmon river with a 12 ft 6 in. 'Hardy Wye' whipping out
a whistling stream of fly line in one hand and a gaff-ended
wading staff in the other. The sight of a salmon fly man
from a passing car is enough to tug at the heart strings,
bring memories of personal stories and late night fishing
jokes back and the subtle, creeping, skulking trout man,
with his 'phantom' flicking into the stream, sends thrills of
joy no motor racing fan will ever know, through the veins
of a true blue angler.

To the fly! Why the fly? Well, the reasons vary from
species to species (fish to fish some would say). The
salmon has been fairly well explained – his temperament
has more to do with the reason he accepts flies than
hunger, for he doesn't *eat* flies – at least not in fresh water.
Some anglers will tell you he sucks the juice from the fly
but this probably isn't true; he snaps at the fly and 'kills'
it: it is then spat out with no more thought. We are
constantly referring to 'flies' here but we do not always
mean 'flies' at all; we mean insects of all descriptions; we
mean grubs, nymphs and of course spiders, aquatic
beetles, caterpillars, moths and so on. Now many of these
insects represent a danger to the spawn of salmon. Some
flies (and other insects) are parasitic and will lay eggs in
the spawn, thus killing the host. Others are liable to feed
on the spawn etc., and so the salmon has little reason to be
fond of any insect even if the dislike is only instinctive.

The sea trout *does* feed on flies and provided he is
presented with the kind, size and colour of the one he is
eating, *at any particular moment* you may get a take if
you present the fly at this precise moment in a precise and
acceptable way.

Brown and rainbow trout do of course live all the time

Fig. 57 Silver Wilkinson (top).
Fig. 58 Durham Ranger (bottom).

in a river or lake and 'bugs' are very much part of their natural diet. They are, however, extremely fussy little blighters and will only eat what they want to eat. A trout 'rise' may last only a few minutes in the day. As the differences between each fish group feeding habits are so varied we will split the flies into fish sections.

Salmon flies

If my theories are to be accepted the fly is, to the salmon, a living object which must be destroyed. This means the fly presented by the angler may not necessarily represent a specific fly or beetle but that it should be regarded as an annoying little pest – just as a fly is to the horse. Large flies can, of course, look like small fishes and these have no business near a salmon on its way to the breeding grounds. There is a very definite group of flies more readily accepted by the salmon than any other types, or so it would seem from tackle shop sales. However, it is much more likely that these fly patterns are more acceptable to the fisherman than to the fish! The facts are that a correctly *sized* fly has much more influence with the fish than any one particular colour or pattern. The fun is in the selection of a combination of all three factors. The salmon fly is by no means like anything the salmon has ever seen in its short life at sea; it need not, then, be necessarily an attempt to imitate a specific insect. Even the shrimp fly is pink – hardly a natural colour.

Fig. 59. Fly sizes

Temp. °C	River height	Current	Water colour	Fly size	Fly colour	Dressing
2	normal	normal	normal	5/0	medium	medium
2	low	normal	normal	3/0	bright	light
2	high	normal	normal	6/0	dull	heavy
2	normal	slow	normal	4/0	medium	light
2	normal	fast	normal	6/0	bright	heavy
2	normal	normal	clear	4/0	medium	light
2	normal	normal	cloudy	6/0	dull	heavy
5	normal	normal	normal	2/0	medium	light
10	normal	normal	normal	4/0	medium	light
15	normal	normal	normal	8/0	medium	light
20	normal	normal	normal	12/0	medium	light

110

The size of a fly is, as explained, of paramount importance and finding the right size will be, in the main, a problem of trial and error. There must be a starting point though and fig. 59 will give some indication of correct (starting) sizes for flies, depending upon various factors.

The leader, or cast, should be tapered nylon or gut and must never be longer than the rod, although some trout casts are. An ideal length is 9 ft and, as a little of the tip will be wasted each time a fly is tied (never use a curled nylon tip), it will progressively shorten so keep an eye on its working or sinking length. Unlike a trout cast, the salmon leader should carry a single fly, although some anglers insist on using two. This can prove very difficult and worrying when a fish accepts, for the second hook can (and will) snag on rocks or roots and the fish may be lost.

Once the actual fly size has been decided – and much trial and error will determine this – the colour of the fly can be chosen. When changing an unaccepted fly, you may change the pattern as well as size but if the salmon are rising for your lure and refusing to take it, or are rising short, then the pattern is probably correct but the fly is almost certainly too large. In these circumstances change only the size of your fly. Slight changes are pointless so jump several sizes when changing – a salmon *can* recognise colour.

Always start with the smaller flies (they hook better anyway) and work upwards, changing colour and pattern as you go. Only start with large flies when the water is very high, deeply coloured, very heavy or when fishing a very deep pool. A general starting point is indicated in fig. 60.

Fig. 60. Average salmon fly sizes

Size	Water height	Temperature	Wind
Large Medium Small	High Normal Low	Cold Normal Warm	Moderate Light

The smaller flies are obviously for low, clear water in a light breeze or in shallow, clear water. The colder the weather, the larger the fly. A fly will usually be larger in the spring or in the autumn: Remember the rule: bright day – bright fly; dull day – dull fly, see fig. 61.

111

Black Doctor
5/0

Dusty Miller
1/0

Silver Wilkinson
Ex. Small
10

Thunder and Lightning
Ex. Small
12

Fig. 62 Various salmon flies.

Fig. 61. Some salmon flies

Bright day	Moderate light	Overcast
Dusty Miller	Thunder & lightning	Black doctor
Silver doctor	Torish	Mar lodge
Red sandy	Jock scott	Lady Caroline
Kate	Dunkeld	Stoat's tail
General practitioner	Green Highlander	Raven's tail

This may seem a little illogical but in fact, on a bright day, all manner of things shine and flash under the water's surface. The stones themselves – quartz, flint, mica – all reflect the sunlight with dazzling beams of dancing light and the river bed becomes a jewelled blanket of goodies, some of which move and flash all the time. It follows that a bright lure – be it a fly or a spinner will not be too out of place. In fact it will seem part of an expected pattern. The sides of a small fish will flash very enticingly if its scales are in good fettle. But, on a dull day nothing will shine too brightly at all; certainly not anything which moves. A bright fly would most certainly look very much out of place and quite artificial (and suspicious) to the salmon or trout. Strictly speaking, it is not so much the highly colourful fly which offends on a gloomy day, more the dazzling tinsel bodied jobs with metallic brushes and binding – even a silvered hook can exaggerate brightness in a gloomy pool. The colourful flies are best on a moderate kind of day with patches of sunshine and intermittent cloud, or when it is bright without being *really* sunny. A good indication is the need for sun glasses: this will indeed be a *bright* day.

Salmon flies should not be 'overdressed' or they will refuse to swim in a vertical position and will drag along on their sides rather than being 'fished' as a fly should be.

In the spring – and usually in tidal areas and river estuaries – a large fly may be needed. Artificial shrimps, General practitioner or even 'fly eels', with linked double hooks are useful lures.

In low water, and particularly in sunny weather, dry flies come into their own. The dry fly must float and needs a fine wire hook and a long shank. The dry fly has much less dressing than a normal fly.

Dry flies are usually taken by fresh run salmon. Fish which have been in a pool for some time and have become red seldom take a floating fly.

16 From the black gnat and general practitioner; the bloody butcher to the may fly—all have their use on the right day and the right water.

17 A good fly box which can be used mid-stream with one hand is essential.

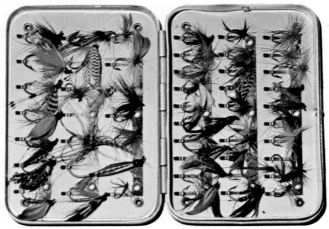

18 A beautifully tied collection of may flies; the double hooks are for fast waters.

19 Prawn and worm flies, especially useful for estuary fishing.

20 Tube flies are useful in their ability to be used on the same hook and trace even at varying lengths.

21 Fully-dressed salmon flies.
22 Some estuary flies, streamers and stoats tails on single, double (pennel) and treble hooks.

26 Estuary fishing demands some pretty powerful beach casting at times. This Abu rod and multiplier is a fine combination in the right hands.

See illustration on page 173

23 Left: The Raven's Tail. Right: The Morty's Mer.

24 Some sea trout flies; butchers and bloody butchers with heavy double hooks for deep waters.

25 Lightly dressed salmon flies with a polystickle (centre).

The size of the dry fly will depend on the same conditions as any other fly and only trial and error will help the angler. Remember, it is the size of the salmon fly which counts first and foremost, the colour and pattern is secondary, but it is usually worth trying a colour which blends in with the surrounding aquatic scenery. If the river is peaty and brown, use a March Brown. If it is yellow and sandy then use a sand coloured fly.

Always start with a small hook and work your way up in size – and brightness. Should your salmon flies have no effect, do not hesitate to use a sea trout fly; but start with double hooks first.

Tube flies are useful in that they use a treble hook. This does of course increase the hooking power of the fly. The tube fly is more of a streamer than a fly and tends to look like a tiny fish sooner than an insect. On strict 'fly only' rivers, even when the water is obviously too big for flies, the tube fly can sometimes overcome the rule of law without upsetting anybody.

Fly hooks have either a turned-up or turned down eye. The more popular kind is the up-eye.

Sea Trout flies

Sea trout flies are just a little smaller than salmon flies. They are also more colourful sometimes and usually have a spot of red in either the tail or the body. Some, such as the Cardinal, even have red wings.

Fig. 63 A standard salmon upturned eye hook.

When fishing the deeper pools it is desirable to get the fly down to the bottom and this means using the heavier double hook. If the pool is dark, a silver body will help but make sure the sun doesn't penetrate the pool deep enough to cause an over-bright flashing.

Sea trout are very shy animals and will often be found sulking on the bottom of deep pools or alternatively hidden in the white foam of very fast water during daylight hours. This means sunken fly fishing and rather vivid lures, or they would never be seen as colour fades with depth but do try to keep the fly 'in blend' just the same. Sea trout are best sought at night or in the late evening.

Fly sizes are not quite so variant with sea trout and it is always advisable to start with a very small single (or even smaller double) hook. The colour of your fly will depend upon the usual river and weather conditions, see fig. 64.

117

Fig. 64. Sea-Trout Flies

Bright day	Moderate light	Overcast	Night
Cardinal	Zulu black	Mallard	Mallard & Green
Bloody Butcher	Wickham	Mallard & Green	Priest
Heckham	Woodcock & Red	Mallard & Black	Heather moth
Professor	Alexandra	March Brown	Hardy's favourite
King Fisher	Butcher	Woodcock	Red Palmer
		Hare's ear	

Sea trout casts can hold up to three flies just as the brown trout cast but, in the author's opinion, it is not really necessary, nor is it always wise to use more than one fly at night or two in the day. In fact one fly at all times is the safest way to fish for sea trout and there is no reason to assume that two or even three flies are beneficial at all. One single 'plop' as the fly drops to the surface may not startle the timid sea trout too much but a rain of flies crashing down on the roof of a quiet pool may well cause a little panic. Secondly the hooked sea trout, as already explained, is quite capable of running the extra hooks into a rocky spot and that's that!

When estuary fishing for sea trout remember to wash the flies after use or rust will very quickly eat into the hooks and rot the tying.

Trout flies

The art of trout fly fishing would itself warrant the production of a whole set of books. Chalk stream stalking, burn bobs, spey casting and trailing; fly trolling and stream walking. All aspects of trout fly fishing demand their own type and style of fly. In this section on trout flies it is obviously impossible to even scratch the surface of the subject, but a general starting point may perhaps emerge. The angler is then on his own and must add experience to his knowledge before being able to gain the full benefit and enjoyment from the gentle art of trout fly fishing.

The variety of trout flies must run into many thousands and when one considers the basic food source of trout as flies, grubs and nymphs – it is not surprising.

Wet Flies

Wet fly fishing usually means the lure is to be presented at various levels under the water surface. It does not neces-

sarily mean that the lure is a fly. Indeed many 'wet flies'
are 'nymphs' or spiders. A nymph is a type of underwater
insect which usually interests the trout a great deal. When
the sun shines brightly the fish needn't come to the surface
and risk his neck for a floating fly – he can now see the
river bed (and these small insects) quite clearly.

Aquatic flies usually lay their eggs in or on the water.
The resulting 'hatched' eggs are the creepy crawly insects
one sees in the water known as nymphs. These nymphs
change their 'shells' as they grow many times. Some live
for as long as two years in this state but all eventually
change into identical copies of their parents and swim to
the surface where they become 'duns'. After the duns leave
the water they rest for a while on pieces of vegetation or
stones on the bank. Then they cast another shuck and, as
they have developed wings by this time, they are able to
fly off to mate with their own kind, often returning to die
in the water eventually. Their airborne life is sometimes
only a few days. It is the interpretation of such moments
and a 'reading' of the river which tells an angler which
type of fly is hatching or moving at any particular time. It
is actually the swarms of spinners flying up and down the
river bank, close to the water which tell an angler the
story.

There are two major differences between artificial
nymphs: those for use in crystal clear water, such as chalk
streams, and the rough stream varieties. The clear type
must be very neatly tied and look as real as possible. In
fact a box of chalk stream flies should be so life-like that
you would be unable to leave the lid open for fear of real
flies trying to mate with them! Seriously though, the dark
water nymphs need not be quite so fussy and very rough
models will catch fish when close inspection is ruled out.
The shrimp fly for example, will seldom fool a clear water
trout, but in fast water the fish must rush out and grab his
food without too great an examination before it is whisked
away with the current. The shrimp fly, incidentally, is best
fished in early spring when the water is still pretty cold
and the fish are not coming to the surface for food.

When nymph fishing, the cast usually carries three flies
(or spiders – or nymphs) and if the tail fly (or spider) is a
dry one, it will indicate a bite on the other hooks apart
from fishing in its own right. These three flies should be
spaced about 3 ft apart. The two wet flies can of course be
hackled or winged.

Fig. 65 Trout flies.

It is always worth studying the river for a while to see which flies are emerging and even which ones are being taken by the trout. Certain nymphs will be seen only at specific times of the year, see fig. 66.

Fig. 66. Some fly periods

Fly	Colour	Period Found
Large olive	dark green	October to May
Medium olive	yellow-grey	April to October
Small olive	dark green	April to October
Iron blue	blue grey	May to September
May fly	yellow green	May

Fig. 67 Dry trout flies.

Dry flies

The dry flies represent either hackled spiders and other insects or flies with or without wings and can be used on rivers and lakes alike. They are usually fished as single flies to a cast (unlike wet flies) but can of course have a dropper or bob-fly on the cast just as the wet fly system does. Spider flies are particularly good in quiet streams although this is not always the easiest way to catch fish.

It is difficult to say when to fish the dry fly and it is usually only when wet flies have failed, but if you see a trout rising slowly or 'nosing' around a pool then he is probably taking surface flies. Find out what he is taking and you may have something like it in your bag. If he doesn't break the surface though he is probably 'nymphing'.

If the rise is for winged flies then use a winged fly, if it is not and you only have the winged variety, cut the wings off!

In March, the famous March browns or dark olives are around and in May the May flies appear. These are very easily recognised with their long streamers and daddy-long-legs style.

The dry fly will be kept afloat if it is sprayed with 'dry fly', an excellent floating chemical, which does not seem to deter fish. Use the spray on all the dry flies you may use but keep it well away from wet flies or they will not sink when required to. Flies are best sprayed an hour or so before use.

The type of trout fly to use at any one particular time is almost impossible to judge without all the material facts, but a general starting point is indicated in fig. 68.

120

Fig. 68. Trout Fly Types

Bright day	Moderate light	Overcast
Cinnamon sedge	Alder	Dark partridge
Red spinner	Cahill dark	Curse
Red tag	Grey hackle/yellow	Little chap
Orange quill	Brown-bi-visible	Dark olive
Parmachenee Belle	Royal coachman	Mole fly
McGinty	Coch-y-bodhu	Hofland's fancy

Flies must be kept in sensible boxes. There are many kinds on the market but those with magnetic bars are very good indeed. The windowed, one handed, salmon fly boxes are beautiful pieces of workmanship but do not always display the fly as well as the open type. Don't fill your hat or lapels with flies – they are the very devil to get out and look rather ostentatious. The origin of putting a fly in a hat is to keep a prized fly which has killed a large fish.

FLY TYING

There is no reason why a fisherman should buy all his flies from a tackle dealer; there are numerous books on fly tying around and the John Veniard fly tying outfits are excellent value for money. Only a few tools are needed and the joy of catching a fish on your own design or make of fly is undeniable. There is nothing to stop you inventing a fly or spider of your own and even less to stop a fish taking it.

The anatomy of a fly will depend on its style but a fairly heavy salmon fly is quite complex.

The tools

The equipment needed for fly tying is surprisingly simple and extremely cheap. All that one could possibly need is obtainable from Veniard dealers. Firstly, is the hook vice; although many fly tiers don't use one at all, a rather silly way to start. There are plenty of hook vices around so get hold of the best you can afford – it will give you pounds worth of flies in the long run.

Next is the very essential hackle pliers. Two pair of these are recommended as one pair can be used to hold the cotton spools, if a hole is drilled through the vertical part of the circumference bars.

Fig. 69 Anatomy of a salmon fly.

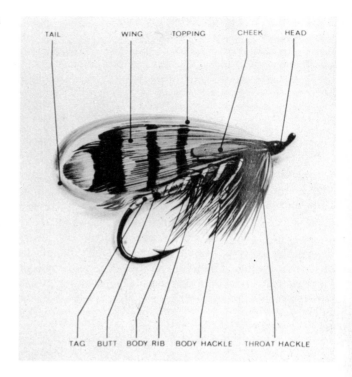

TAIL   WING   TOPPING   CHEEK   HEAD

TAG   BUTT   BODY RIB   BODY HACKLE   THROAT HACKLE

A pair of good quality, pointed tweezers are absolutely essential and small, sharp pointed scissors are just as important. As long as the scissors are kept razor sharp they will prove invaluable. A safety (single edged) razor blade will soon pay for itself and a long darning needle, or even better, a microscope mounting needle, completes the ironmongery.

Tying gear
A whole range of tying silks and tinsels will be needed. Tying spools of various coloured silks do not cost very much, nor do the wide variety of tinsel; serrated, plain gold or silver mottled and shiny or flat or coppered – all go into the fly tying box in neat rows. There are three basic tinsel body ribbon styles: flat, (shiny or non-lustre), oval shaped and round section. A roll of gold wire (brass), a roll of silver and a roll of lacquered wire, (from a dynamo winding) will complete the line needs. A whole range of silk colours in various thicknesses should be collected but the very thinnest strong silks are usually best, such as Gossamer or Naples. The types of silks used can be an

122

interesting experimental aspect of fly tying. The most important colours are black, white, yellow, red, green and brown. To strengthen the silks and make them last a lot longer, wax must be used at all times. The wax is rubbed up and down the thread in swift actions until it melts and runs into the fibre of the yarn. Lastly, a pot of clear varnish and a pot of brown varnish is needed to finish off the thread knots. A dab of varnish over the eye of the hook and spread across the final tied knot will not only prevent the silk from undoing, it will protect it against the rough and tumble of rocks and the action of water.

Fly Hooks

The fly hook is always eyed although occasionally a cast *is* linked on. As explained in chapter four, hooks come in various shapes and sizes. For the fly, there are only half a

Fig. 70 Fly tying materials.

123

dozen really popular shapes: the wide gape, the round bend, sneck, Limerick and low water versions, which are a little lighter and finely wired. Nearly all fly hooks are black enamelled. The eye can, of course, be turned up or down and some even have a barb or two on the heel of the shank. Hook sizes *never* include the eye so, when measuring, do so from the heel or crown of the hook to a point where the eye begins. When tying dry flies it is usual, although not absolutely essential, to use an up-turned eye. On trout flies it is just as usual to use an up-turned eye for dry flies but on salmon flies, the up-turned eye is seen on all flies, wet or dry. Wide gape hooks, especially trout hooks, are very definitely dry fly jobs, although up- and down-turned eyes are available. The tip of the wide gape hook is not parallel with the shank, and turns slightly upwards. The round bend hooks are specifically used for wet flies and worming but the Limerick, probably the most popular, is a general all round hook.

A hook with a deep smooth 'round bend' is physically stronger and less liable to snap than any other form of hook but the quality of hardening and tempering when the hook was made will determine its performance in the river. Don't wait until you lose a good fish with a bad hook, buy the very best hooks available: they are cheap enough. For salmon and sea trout flies, the double hook is very often used.

Fur and feather

Now we come to the heart of fly tying – the feathers and skins. The collection of feathers to be found in the shed of a fly tying angler would astonish the uninitiated. No fly tier could walk past a good partridge feather, nor could he visit the zoo without wanting to whip the tails from half the bird-house exhibits. Only here does the novice see the real side of salmon and trout fishing; the science of the fly.

For fly bodies you will need at least the following: seal's fur, rabbit and hare fur, mole skin, sheep wool and various quills. For wings, you will need: wing quills, grouse tail, and all manner of shoulder and side feathers. For hackles you will need cock and hen hackles (from the throat) and for tails, all kinds of streamer material. It is almost impossible to list all the material one can use for the selection is endless; hare's ear and mole skin, starling wings, cock and hen hackles, partridge parts and seal's

124

fur, ram's wool and bear skin – all have a place and all will be needed in the fly tier's box.

John Veniard's fly dressing guides are to be thoroughly recommended for the more serious fly tier.

Hackled flies

To tie a hackled fly, preferably a large plain trout fly, is perhaps the easiest way to begin fly tying. If you start with a small fly it becomes finicky and is much more difficult to handle. Fix an upturned eyed hook in the vice by the bend and tie the end of a 12–18 in. length of silk (any colour will do for now) to a point just behind the eye. Now rub a piece of wax (or paint on if you are using liquid wax), the whole length of the silk. Wind the silk around the hook shank until you reach a point in line with the hook barb, if you wish to add a tail to the fly, now is the time to do so. Cock hackles – straight of course – are stiffer than hens' and are best for the tail. Alternatively a few strands (no more than four) can be taken from the hair of an animal. The length should not be over 1 in. and can be cut later. Hold the strands along the hook shank and lash them into position with two or three silk turns. If you wish the tail to stand up, pass an extra loop of silk behind the exit strands.

After deciding upon the body colour and type you wish, lay the fur or lining in a twisting motion around the hook shank and wind the silk line around the same way as before until you reach the original position just behind the eye. If you want to incorporate tinsel in order to give the body a striped effect this should be wound at the same time and lashed at each end by the silk thread. The thickness of the body will depend on the number of times the silk is wound back and forth. If you intend using a mole skin or other such body, it will of course be quite broad in any case. For the hackle you must now decide if the fly is to be wet or dry. If dry, use a cock hackle, which is much stiffer and less liable to become waterlogged too soon. If you want a wet fly then use a soft hen hackle.

Once you have decided upon the hackle, strip off the soft fluffy 'down' on the lower part of the feather and pull the rest of the fibres into a right angled position. Trim the edges to make a fairly straight line but don't worry too much as final trimming will ensure a 'real' looking fly if you have tied it well. Tie the hackle by the quill – just where you began stripping off the fluffy feathers – to the same point behind the hook eye as before, with the silk line. Grasp the tip of the hackle in the hackle pliers and commence winding the feather around the hook shaft: one turn of the hackle to one turn of the silk. Do not allow the hackle to overlap. Wind the silk back to the eye without overlapping the feather or disturbing its upright position. Knot the silk as a final end to finish off the joint and the fly is finished.

Wet winged flies

The wet fly is designed for total underwater use and although the silk line must be waxed in the same manner as for any other type of fly, it is advisable to keep oil and grease away from your working area. Wash your hands before commencing work and beware of touching your hair, which may contain natural oils, if not synthetic! A wet fly should be 'rinsed' and saturated before casting on the day of use anyway but prior precautions are not amiss.

Set the hook in the vice (single for normal level or double for deeper fishing and in heavy water) by the curve of the shank and tie your silk on just before the eye as usual. Run the length of the body in a twisting motion and lash on the tail if one is to be used. The body should end at a point parallel with the hook point or barb. Now tie in the body with the design of your choice, using a hare or mole-skin, depending upon the fly or spider you are imitating. Strip a hackle from a hen feather (hen feathers are softer and sink easier than cock's) and tie into position as before, but this time do not cut the silk end off. Now take a pair of quill feathers and cut about $\frac{1}{4}$ in. out of each, half way along their lengths. Strip off the fluffy 'down' and place them in position parallel with the body and as high as you wish the 'wings' to be. Tie in position with the free end of the silk, cut them to the desired shape and finish off with varnish.

There are many hundreds of variations to the above two styles and they are only intended as a starting point for the do-it-yourself fly tier. Anyone interested enough can purchase a fly tying outfit and fill his winter evenings with a very useful and interesting pass-time.

A few of the most popular and successful flies are described briefly below. See fig. 69 for the anatomy details.

126

Some Famous Flies

Fly	Body	Wings	Hackle	Tail
Butcher	Silver	Blue	Black	Red
March brown	Hare	Pheasant wing	Partridge	2 or 3 hairs
May fly (winged)	Red straw	Grey	Brown partridge	3 pheasant tail
May fly (hackled)	Yellow/gold/red silk		,, ,,	3 or hackle
Artful dodger	Purple gold	Pheasant wing	Red	
Coachman	Peacock	White	Beige	
Cochy Bondhu	Bronze peacock gold tinsel		Pink	
Blue dunn	Grey seal	Starling wing	Grey	3
Jungle cock	Black/gold wire	Jungle cock	Black cock	3 or 4 pheasant tail
Black nymph	Black seal		,, ,,	3
Black gnat	Black	Starling wing	Black	
Priest	Silver		Badger	3 red
Zulu	Black seal		Black cock	2 red
Greenwell	Yellow/gold	Dark starling	Furnace cock	
Wickham	Gold	Starling	Red	3 red
Alexandra	Silver	Green	Black	3 red
Peter Ross	Silver-red	Teal breast	Black	tipped
Watson's fancy	Red-seal/black	Black cock	Black	Gold pheasant
Kingfisher	Red-white	Grey	Grey	Gold pheasant
Red tag	Brown-gold		Red	Red

Fully dressed salmon flies are a little more complicated but are sometimes easier to make as they are much larger than trout flies.

Sea Flies

Estuary fishing for sea trout and salmon is a very absorbing and exact science. The art of boating – or even the art of selecting a good boatman – is only learned by the really dedicated angler. If you watch a professional fisherman, who makes his living from estuary salmon, when he uses the fly on a line (or should we say flies) you will learn a great deal, but do not attempt to copy his flies – they will have been chosen to suit the whole season in *that* estuary. The pro' may also be netting, or at least ready to net if the fly doesn't work. For sea or estuary fishing you would do better to tie a set of flies of your own for general use.

Streamers

Streamers are rather 'hairy' flies, used more as a general

127

Some Famous Salmon Flies

Fly	Tag	Tail	Butt	Body	Throat	Wings	Sides	Cheeks	Head
Jock Scott	Silver/ yellow	Crow	Black	Yellow black/ silver	Guinea fowl	Turkey tail pheasant tail Blue/red/brown	Jungle cock	Blue	Black
Dusty Miller	Silver/ yellow	Crow	Black	Silver/ orange	Guinea fowl	Guinea fowl Turkey & pheasant brown	Jungle cock	Black	Black
Mar Lodge	Silver	Jungle cock	Black	Silver/ black	Guinea fowl	Yellow/red/ blue/grey	Jungle cock	Black	Black
Thunder & Lightning	Gold/ yellow	Topping	Black	Black/ gold	Blue	Brown	Jungle cock	Black	Black
Silver Doctor	Silver/ yellow	Topping	Red	Silver	Blue	Yellow/blue/ brown	Pheasant tail	Red	Red
Raven's tail	Silver	Yellow	Silver	Red/ silver/ black	Stoat's hair	Guinea fowl pheasant yellow/red	Long Raven's tail	Jungle cock	Black
Morty's Merlin	Silver	Yellow	Silver	Yellow silver/ black	Guinea fowl	Guinea fowl pheasant yellow/red	Jungle cock	Black	Black

lure than an actual 'fly'. They are quite useful in estuary fishing and will catch fish almost anywhere at the right time. The hooks for streamers are either very long in the shank or are tied double, in pennel fashion; some use treble hooks.

Long hackles and hair are the main materials and the design is merely a matter of taste, although a jungle cock feather is usually used to simulate the eye. When using streamers in brackish water don't forget to wash them well after use.

Although river and lake flies are very often meant to be copies of specific insects, the sea fly is seldom meant to be any particular marine creature. On occasions even a bare hook will be taken and if there are mackerel around you may well be pestered with almost any fly or lure you use.

The sea fly is really only a long feather or streamer with very little scientific thought put into it. A simple silver or gold body with a long white goat hair wing will suffice.

128

Even the tail and hackle may be left out. Cheap domestic fowl feathers are good enough; they can be dyed to any colour although yellow, red and white will be quite sufficient. A hackle may be tied in if a two-tone colour is required. The hackle may even be taken the whole length of the body. A more elaborate model may have a swivel and a small spinning spoon added. Shrimp and prawn flies come into their own in brackish or salt water.

To tie a general sea fly – including estuary lures – the best way is to sketch out your design and tie in the following way.

Body

Fix a long shanked galvanised or stainless steel hook in the fly vice and tie on a 12 in. length of nylon or silk, which has been suitably waxed, close to the eye. Wind the silk along the shank to a point opposite the hook barb. One or two extra winds will tie in the rib material if required; a tail should be whipped in by two or three further turns if one is to be incorporated. If a fat body, tinselled or otherwise, is wanted, appropriate materials should be laid along the hook shank and tied in as the silk is wound back to the eye.

Hackle

Place the hackle onto the hook with the shiny side of the feather outside and bind tightly in position with silk. Affix the end of the hackle to the hackle pliers and turn the whole thing around the hook three or four times, taking great care to keep the strands at a 45° angle to the hook shank. Tie the final knot and seal with dark varnish. Trim off the excess feather and seal again with a thick coat of clear varnish.

Wings

Sea fly wings are very long and must lie parallel to the hook shank. If wings are planned, use an 18 in. length of silk at the beginning and not a 12 in. piece. Quill feathers are best, although straight hackle feathers are usable. Take an even pair of feathers and cut $\frac{1}{4}$ in. segment, from each, close to the quill. Place the two even ends together with the curve of the fibre outwards and lie them along the hook shank. Lash on the wings over and under with silk. Take the silk back to the eye and tie off. Shape the ends of the wings with sharp scissors and strip off the loose silk end.

Fig. 71 Some sea trout flies.

129

Fig 72 Outfit Balance

Jet set classification	Purpose	Suitable 'Jet' Fly rod	Suitable 'Marquis' Fly reel	Suitable 'Jet' Fly line	Suitable 'Jet' Leader
#4 Extra light	Trout-small streams brooks & burns, tiny flies, fine leaders. Also suitable for the very young angler	#4 7″ 215 2¾ oz. 70 gr	#4 2¾″ dia.	D.T. 4F only or W.E. 4F plus 75x backing	#4 Tapered to 5x (0·006″)
#5 Very light	Trout-small streams, where delicate casting is required. Also suitable for the young angler	#5 7½′ 230cm 2¾ oz. 80 gr	#5 3″ dia.	D.T. 5F only or W.F. 5F plus 50x backing	#5 Tapered to 4x (0·007″)
#6 Light	Trout-general purpose for fishing medium sized rivers. Boat fishing on lakes & reservoirs. Comprises 3 different rod lengths to suit individual requirements.	8′ 245cm 3½ oz. 105 gr #6 8½′ 260cm 4¼ oz. 120 gr 9″ 275cm 4¼ oz. 127 gr	#6 3″ dia.	D.T. 6F plus 40x backing or W.F. 6F plus 110x backing	#6 Tapered to 3x (0·008″)
#7 Medium light	Trout-medium sized streams excellent for dry fly & windy conditions. Comprises 2 rod lengths to suit individual requirements.	8½′ 260cm #7 4 oz. 127 gr 9′ 275cm 4½ oz. 130 gr	#7 3″ dia.	D.T. 7F plus 40x backing or W.F. 7F plus 125x backing	#7 Tapered to 2x (0·009″)
#8 Medium	Large trout, sea trout & light salmon, large streams, lakes, all wet & dry flies, lures.	#8 8′9″ 270cm 4½ oz. 130 gr	#8/9 3⅝″ dia.	D.T. 8F plus 65x backing or W.F. 8F plus 175x backing	#8 Tapered to 1x (0·010″)
#9 Medium powerful	Grilse & medium salmon. Medium sized rivers.	#9 9″ 275cm 5 oz. 147 gr	#8/9 3⅝″ dia.	D.T. 9F only or W.F. 9F plus 150x backing	#9/10 Tapered to 0x
#10 Powerful	Large trout, sea trout, grilse & medium salmon. Wherever distance is of utmost importance, reservoirs, large rivers & lakes, large flies, windy conditions, superb for casting a shooting tapered line.	#10 9′3″ 280cm 5½ oz. 163 gr	#10 3¾″ dia.	W.F. 10F plus 150x backing	#9/10 Tapered to 0x (0·011″)

Touch all loose ends with varnish and a final coating all over the hook will finish the fly.

Never be afraid to experiment with flies, especially sea flies. If you come across a nice piece of fur or feather, whip up a fly, use your imagination – the fish won't mind.

Balance

The balance of a fly is of extreme importance at all times. A heavy fly is often, erroneously, thought of being much easier to cast than a light fly on the same principle as bait casting or spinning. The heavier the bait – (up to a point) the longer and easier it is to cast. In fly fishing, however, the heavy fly completely upsets the balance of the whole outfit. It is the line which is cast and not the bait, as you will learn in the next chapter. Although we have described a great deal of equipment already and will be considering presentation method later, the balance of a fly is so vital to the balance of a complete outfit that we are covering outfit balance yet again – but with a variety of rod set-ups to select from.

If your *complete* outfit doesn't balance perfectly from fly to rod butt, you will begin with a disadvantage you may never be able to overcome, even in later days when your fishing experience is added to basic principles. If you start on the wrong foot it is always difficult to correct. The Hardy answer to balance is a really good 'Jet set' system, designed to offer a beginner the experience of a lifetime in a completely balanced set up. The 'Jet set' fly rod is built in two pieces with no metal ferrules to interrupt the power curve of the cast. Instead, the two sections are joined by a specially designed spigot so flexible that it produces virtually a one piece action. The jets are certainly beautiful rods to use, and the other gear needed to get a full correct 'jet set' balance has been described in chapter two. Fig. 72 gives an extremely accurate balance system whatever your choice.

If this section has interested you then make full use of your gillie on a bad day by asking him to teach you his methods of fly tying. Most gillies have a whole range of flies and various techniques only relevant in *their* waters. Never forget that a marvellous fly on one water may be quite useless on another. Fly tying is almost as interesting a hobby as fishing; when you combine the two. . . .

6   *Casting*

At last! You have gathered together your rods and reels, lines and baits, floppy hats and battered jackets and, having read this far, would like to go and catch a fish. But, unfortunately you must now learn how to handle the equipment. Fly fishing involves the presentation of an imitation fly, nymph, spider or lure to the unsuspecting fish and it usually takes a great deal of experience before the angler can perform this seemingly simple operation with any degree of efficiency at all. Much of the following chapter was assembled with the help of well known angler and casting instructor, George Mortimer, who has spent his life on the most famous salmon river in the world, the Spey of Scotland. He caught his first salmon at the age of six and learned the art of fish finding as a gillie on the famous Seafield Estate beats. For the past sixteen years he has taught angling on courses run by the Scottish Council of Physical Recreation. He is also an instructor on courses run by The House of Hardy and is the current president of the Grantown-On-Spey Angling Association. He has taught many well known figures some of his art and will teach many more.

FLY-CASTING

To cast a line is *not* an easy operation but, once learned, it is like riding a bicycle – you will never forget how to do it! The analogy doesn't end there either; just as it would be very difficult to explain how to ride a bicycle by the printed word, it is very hard to describe the technique of casting in this way. The answer is to find a good teacher! There are a number of special casting schools in Britain with really excellent instructors most willing (and very patient) to help the newcomer to improve his casting. Abu, for example have a school at Aviemore in Scotland and Hardy's, of Pall Mall, operate 'The London School of

133

Casting'. Both schools supply all the necessary equipment and a complete salmon and trout angling course is offered by the House of Hardy, P.O. Box No. 3, Alnwick, Northumberland. The courses operate in Scotland and Norway. Everyone is welcome (ladies and rank beginners included), so spend a week learning to cast properly; it's well worth it. Notwithstanding the difficulties, however, we will make some sort of attempt to describe the more popular methods of casting here, the rest is up to you. There will be plenty of experienced anglers around to show you *their* methods you may be assured.

The best casting masters are usually the ever useful gillies, so do not sit in the fishing hut on a poor day for fish, go and practice your casting with the gillie – or with this book.

To practice your very first casts it may be better to find a field near the river and get in a few hours before frightening all the fish for miles around when you slash the first few yards of line over the bank. Fly casting is nothing like bait casting at all, so don't rely on any childhood memories of canal side lunges, you must start at the beginning. In bait casting it is the weight of the bait which, when flung into the air with enough force, retains the momentum and power to drag out a deal of line behind it. The heavier the bait, the more easily it will pull out a line. But, this is not the case with fly casting; it is the line itself which does the pulling and throwing, not the bait. It follows that a length of line must be wound off the reel before it can be thrown anywhere in the first place.

The line must be 'cast' or thrown into the air, behind or to the side of the angler. This is called 'back casting' and the accuracy of the back cast will determine the quality of the front cast, so make sure you can throw a good line behind you *first* and the rest will follow more easily. Do not try to throw a long line from the beginning, learn to cast a short line and increase the distance as you gain experience and remember, there is no logical reason to assume fish to be on the other side of the river. If this were so, you would be better off crossing over; or would you then wish to cast to this side of the river? Be satisfied with a good, short cast. If you master that well enough the rest is easy.

Whether you are in the middle of a large field, feeling a complete idiot, waving a rod around with no water in sight (ignoring the anxious little men in white coats), or standing breathlessly before a magnificent salmon pool, we will ask you to imagine you are standing on the south bank of a river which flows from east to west. Make sure there are no trees or bushes within range of your fly and always remember there is up to 9 ft of monofilament line (which you probably cannot see too well) on the end of the clearly visible fly line as it whistles through the air or floats down-stream.

Adopt a comfortable stance, with feet slightly apart, and with the thought that you may be up to your armpits in heavy water trying to do the same thing very shortly. No really tiring effort should go into casting and you certainly do not need to be a superman to cast a fair line. Take pride in your casting and remember you will have an audience more than likely at various times and there is nothing worse than tangling a fly line with a whole bridge full of spectators grinning at you when you do so. We shall assume all readers of this book to be right handed for the purpose of describing fly casting: should you be left handed, simply reverse the instructions (and the river flow).

All fly casting revolves around the one simple basic method described here. The variations are legion but learn this style first and adopt the best variation suited to your own personal taste afterwards.

Place your right elbow comfortably at your side, with the forearm raised in a horizontal, forward position. If the rod is two handed, the right hand should be grasping the rod at a point just where it falls naturally and the left hand should be on the end of the butt. A one handed rod must be held just in front of the reel; in both cases the line is held lightly between the fingers of the right hand. Raise the *forearm* (not the whole arm as one would expect) to a vertical position with increasing velocity until, at a point just before twelve o'clock, a sharp 'flick' ends the lift of the rod and flings the line up and back behind the angler. There is now a slight pause to allow loose line to 'catch up' with the faster moving coil. Do not continue the power of your back cast beyond the vertical or the line will hit the ground. Now chop the hand back to a nine o'clock position with a sharp, 'wrist flick' at ten o'clock. Imagine you are knocking a nail in with a hammer at this last flick. The elbow has not left your side during the action so far. The line should now shoot out over the water and the rod can be lowered to its normal, horizontal position. If you are facing a wind, do not administer the final 'hammer chop' until almost nine o'clock.

Having mastered this simple basic casting method (using a short line at first) you may now consider some of the more exotic casting techniques. There are only two *really* different methods; the continuous motion cast and the double motion cast, all other forms of casting stem from and build around these two. The more popular adaptations of the double motion cast include the overhead cast, the side cast and the false cast. This is used to dry out the fly when dry fly fishing or to get a long length of line out with a smallish rod and can perhaps be considered a multi-motion cast. The continuous motion casting variations are based upon the switch cast, the Spey cast, and the very impressive looking double switch cast. Whichever style you adopt, and it will be necessary to learn more than one if you are going to fish more than one water (it would be hopeless trying to whip up a huge overhead cast on a narrow, bush lined stream), keep your basic teaching in mind all the while. Always try to cast a straight line and this means keeping the line within the length range you and the rod can cope with. If the line is not straight when it lands on the water the fly will not actually 'fish'. It will only move through the water in a satisfactory manner and be 'fishing' or 'swimming' if the line is straight and able to move with the current, instead of being awkwardly tossed and dragged around at unnatural angles when the line is kinked or curved. Try to make the fly drop *gently* into the water and lower the rod the minute it lands. Do not put too much unnecessary energy into the cast – let your rod cast the fly, not the whole of your body – it is a common fault to try exerting the body weight into the cast, and it avails nothing but an aching back. Lengthen the amount of free line in slow, short sections, do not whip off reels of line in long jerks – smoothness is the key word at all times.

In the double motion cast, the two movements are; the back cast ... pause ... and the forward cast. The back cast will be affected by the manner in which the line is lifted off the water. So will the fish, and a snatched lift is almost as bad as throwing a rock in the river. When using a sinking line, which is for fishing with nymphs or deep flies, remember that quite a long length of line (including up to 9 ft of monofilament leader) is under the surface and water will drag heavily on the line. There is little point in

Fig. 73 World champion caster Jim Hardy casts a neat trout fly.

136

trying to use any power in lifting the line to the surface for, apart from frightening the fish, you will not succeed in getting any momentum at all. Draw the sunken line in by the left hand in a smooth, gentle motion and, if using a two handed rod, let the line fall loosely into the water by your feet. If using a one handed rod, the line may be held in the left hand. Indeed, you will eventually learn to hold such loose line even with a two handed rod, but do not attempt to do so at this stage. When the line is on the surface, lift the rod up in a sweeping motion, thus flinging the line into the air and over your head. Always ensure there is room behind when contemplating this type of cast. If you find it necessary to cast into the wind, do not take the rod tip beyond a vertical position, indeed, it should stop at eleven o'clock. For the time being you will need to know exactly what happens to your line when it is thrown up and backwards like this and so it will be necessary to turn the top half of your body from the hips in order to see behind you. For practice purposes it is advisable, pocket permitting, to use a white line when casting against, say, a cliff or a tree lined background. If open space is the casting area, then a dark coloured line would be seen better than a white one.

Having adopted a good stance and back cast viewing position, you can now tell when the line has reached the end of its travel limit. It should not actually stop, but if you can see the precise moment the fly line itself straightens then there is still a few feet of near invisible nylon leader exerting a very vital force on the line and keeping it straight for that last split second as the forward cast commences. There should be no actual 'end' of a backcast, we are simply trying to determine the 'moment of turn' when the line looses its rearward momentum and gains a forward force. We are trying to get a mental picture of this 'moment' as this is the time to turn your line and commence the forward cast. It is this motion estimation which makes casting so difficult – or so simple. It is all a matter of timing. The trouble is that there is *no specific time period* applicable to the motion as each individual cast will differ. The length of line out against the length of the rod and the force or direction of wind etc., plus of course the force used by the caster, the weight of the line and the size of the fly will determine this 'moment of turn' and the only indication you will have of its period is the *time it takes to reach*. In other words, if it

138

takes two seconds to raise the rod to the vertical position it should take another two for the line to extend behind. This is a very broad statement and is not meant to be taken literally but is fairly true for an average cast. Whatever the actual time taken, you will soon learn to 'feel' the moment without looking. However, to return to the cast; once the 'moment' arrives and the line reaches its fullest rearward extension, it should be brought forward (not at an angle, to avoid collision between forward and rearward travelling line, as this is how rod tops are bent) by a downward and forward motion of the rod. If there is no wind, the rod should be brought forcefully to a ten o'clock position, with the 'hammer blow' action during the last few minutes of our imaginary clock. If there is a head-wind, the rod should be brought a little lower down before the 'hammer blow', say, to nine o'clock. The former release point will give the fly a broad entry. A whippy rod tends to give a broader entry than a stiff rod. A later release point gives a correspondingly narrow entry and presents less wind resistance. The 'width' of the entry is measurable visually and is in fact a width comparison between the S loop of the line as the forward travelling curve passes the rearward travelling section. The distance between the 'two' lines is the width of entry.

Double motion overhead cast (single handed)
The desired (manageable) length of line should be allowed to straighten out on the surface of the water for the commencement of a cast of this nature – the current will do this for you although you will need to walk backwards if practicing in a field. Begin with the rod in a horizontal position and the fly line laid out in line with the rod tip; lift the line off the water surface with a sharp 'force pull' between eleven and twelve o'clock. At the same time, pull the line through the bottom ring with the left hand; this imparts even more momentum to the flying line and sends it high and rearwards. Pause just long enough for the line to straighten out. You should by now be able to judge this without looking behind but never be afraid to do so, it will help to improve your technique. The lift off period will be roughly the same length of time as the pause; the more line you have out, the longer the pause will be.

Now cast forward with a short, sharp 'jab' releasing the line in the left hand as the rod reaches the release point (ten o'clock under normal conditions or nine o'clock into

Fig. 74 Using a phantom on Loch Vaa.

the wind). Do not forget to impart a wrist dealt hammer blow at the end of the cast. The loose line, released by the left hand should shoot through the rod rings. The amount of line held in this manner may be gradually increased until you are proficient and are able to 'shoot' a fairly long line. This 'line shooting' is very useful on a small river with no room to keep a long line in the air.

Double motion overhead cast (double handed)

The hand position with this cast is very important. In principle the two hands push and pull respectively, rather like the basic principle of holding a golf club – one hand pulls and the other pushes. The right hand pulls and should be placed above the reel, whereas the left hand, which pushes, should clasp the rod almost at the end of the butt. Begin with the rod in a normal, horizontal position, facing towards the river. The rod point should be lowered to the water at the commencement of the back-cast with double-handed rods. This gives a greater arc of lifting to get the line back more easily. Also at the start of the back-cast, with a double-handed rod, the weight should be on the forward foot, and during the early part of the lift,

140

transfer the weight back onto the back foot. This takes half the effort out of the arms when lifting the bigger rods. When changing direction in casting, the rod point should be moved to the direction required before the line is lifted in the back-cast, then the change in diretion of the line in the air takes place in the back-cast and the line is ready, straight behind the rod point for the forward cast. If direction is changed in the forward cast, a good cast cannot really be made. Hold the reel end of the line by the right hand. As proficiency increases you will learn to hold loose lengths of line in the *left* hand and 'shoot' in the same manner as described in the last section. Lift the line gently off the water surface and back-cast over the right shoulder, flinging the line high into the air. A last hard flick at the end should bring the rod to a vertical position (unless it is windy, in which case the back-cast should end at eleven o'clock). Pause until the line straightens and cast forwards, not forgetting the sharp flick at the end.

The Side Cast (single handed)
This cast is quite useful when wading close to a high bank or in a restricted, tree lined stream. It can be perfomed

with a single or double handed rod but is normally only used with a one handed rod as the Spey cast is better for salmon fishing.

The fisherman should allow his line to drift with the current until it has stopped 'fishing' and is lying parallel with the bank. He then draws the line up and back-casts over his right *arm* instead of his shoulder, parallel to the bank behind. The usual pause is followed by a forward cast, which winds around and takes the line over to the far bank, adjacent to the angler.

The Switch Cast (single motion – one or two handed)
This cast is most useful when a strong wind from behind (or a high cliff face) prevents a good back-cast which determines the effect of the forward cast.

Start when the line is paid out before you on the water surface in a fairly straight line. Lift and back-cast as described but keep to one fluid movement until the line begins to lift from the water. Before the line actually lifts, take the rod to your right shoulder, turn the body slightly to the right and make a normal forward cast from a twelve o'clock position, aiming the line as high as you can. The fly does not become airborne until the forward cast has been made and should not go past the rear of the angler. In fact he should be able to see the fly all the time. The most important aspect of this cast is the circular trajectory of the line; it should be a sweet curve with no jerkiness – no pauses, and no line 'cracking'. If the line is kept moving it will pull itself along. Although the cast can be performed with a one or two handed rod, it is really a salmon rod cast (two handed) but can be very effective when fishing a lake from a tree lined bank for trout. The 'hammer blow' at the end is particularly important in the switch cast and must be delivered somewhat forcefully.

The double switch cast
This very dramatic looking cast is more often used by gillies when they wish to impress their charges than for what it was developed and there is no denying the beautiful designs some fishermen seem able to produce. A well executed double switch sends shivers of appreciation and admiration down the back of any fishing onlooker.

However – to its execution. The *real* point of using the double switch is when there just is not enough space to throw line into the air. It should not be used unless

142

necessary for it is extremely difficult to execute without disturbing the water. Done well, this will be denied by experts, but not everybody who uses this cast *are* experts and a pool can very quickly get 'beaten up' with the double switch cast in wrong hands.

Commence the cast with your line at full extension down-stream (where it has presumably ended up after the last cast). Turn and face the opposite bank and lift the rod in a sharp but smooth action to toss the bulk of floating line across the river and to your right. Now swing the rod to your left shoulder, using this part of the movement as the 'take off'. Do not forget at this stage that the cast is a *single motion operation* and should not be jerky. The last 15–20 ft of your line should, at this point, be just a little down-stream, with the bulk of the line in the air to your centre and right. Now perform a normal overhead cast – or at least continue the cast as if you were performing an overhead cast. Do so from the left shoulder, which is where you ended up from the second part of the lift, and throw the line high in the air. There should be some degree of force used here, with the right hand guiding the rod butt up, as the left hand flicks it down. The fly should enter the water directly ahead and opposite you and at no time must the line go behind. Once you have mastered the double switch cast you will be able to perform variations in which the line does actually go behind – or at least to one side, but do not try this yet awhile.

The Spey Cast

This famous cast need not, of course, be restricted to the Spey. It is again useful on restricted sections although the Spey is a particularly wide river where it is seldom necessary to use restrictive casts.

Adopt a comfortable stance, facing the opposite bank, and allow the line to drift into the nearside with the current. Keeping the legs adjacent to the bank, turn from the hips and face the left. To begin with, and solely whilst learning the cast, it is advisable to return to our original idea of watching the line in the air. In this cast the fly does in fact go a little behind you and so you may have to turn your head to unnatural positions but, once you have mastered the timing, you will be able to cast by memory. Although the cast is a continuous one, performed in a single sweeping action, it does in fact require three specific motions. To begin with, these motions should expend roughly the same amount of time. For example, if you can count to four on the first part, then count to four during the second and third parts of the cast. The three motions can be described as; RAISE; SWING; and CAST. Under no circumstances should these motions be separated – they are fluid aspects of one single movement; I am only separating them here for clarity.

To return to the actual mechanics; raise the rod in the back casting motion until it reaches an eleven o'clock position and the line has almost left the water. This is part one of the cast – both remaining parts should take the same period to complete each. *Swing* the rod and the top half of your body sharply to the right, lifting the bulk of the line towards the opposite bank and taking the tip of the rod to a twelve o'clock position (or even a one o'clock position if you have a long line out). This completes the second part of the cast and should leave the fly *still in the water* just a little to your right. *Cast* by swinging the rod up to the level of your right shoulder and whipping it down with a forceful chop – using the hammer blow all the way. The rod should stop moving at a ten o'clock position and face the opposite bank.

False casting

False casting means just what it says – casting without letting the fly land on the water. The false cast is used for drying out the line or a dry fly. It is also used in order to change the direction of the cast or as a means of paying out more line.

The cast is made as a normal, overhead, one or two handed operation but, on the forward cast, the 'hammer blow' is not delivered, the rod pausing at ten o'clock. If the false cast is simply a fly drying exercise, the rear cast is repeated just before the fly lands. This type of false cast is usually only performed once. If, however, you are false casting in order to bring out a longer line, hold the spare in the left hand. When making the second back-cast, peel off more line – not too much at a time. You will eventually learn how to peel off line when casting forward too. In order to 'shoot' the line effectively and in a straight line, do not let the extra line free until the rod is in a ten o'clock, forward casting position. Never let the line go whilst the rod is actually moving, wait until the rod stops and the loose line carries on shooting with momentum imparted by the line already out. For getting a long line out, the false cast may be 'whipped' through the air as many times as you wish, but if you hear the line cracking like a whip, check that the fly is still on the end of the line – it probably isn't!

The third reason for false casting, to change the position of the cast, is more useful when boat fishing, but it can be used on a large pool just as effectively. It is all a matter of timing. The change of direction is facilitated if you turn your whole body towards the spot you wish to reach, just as the fly is beginning to turn and the rod is immobile at twelve o'clock. The forward cast is then turned at the same angle as you 'chop' downwards.

Lastly, remember which fly line you are using at all times; and why! The floating line is for wet flies and nymphs near the surface or for dry flies. The fly must be delivered gently and the larger the fly, the shorter the leader. You will be fly casting with one of four baits: wet fly, dry fly, nymp or lure. When casting, keep in mind the fly in use and the fish you seek accordingly.

BAIT CASTING

There are three bait casting reels: the Nottingham type revolving drum reel, which is not very popular for long distance casting although very useful for worming or maggoting in the smaller streams; the multiplying reel, which can really throw a long line in the right hands, even with a very short rod; and the ever popular, easy to use, fixed spool reel.

Each style of reel will of course demand its own method of casting and the beginner would do well to stick to a fixed spool reel, at least to start with. One thing worth remembering is the thinner lines usually cast better than thick ones.

Nottingham style reels
Some Nottingham type reels have a multiplying action and retrieve at a very fast rate. Some have a clutch and yet others have both. The casting actions for all reels differ a little. The only reel with a different braking method is a rim control model. In this case, the thumb or finger is placed on the rim and not the line.

A normal overhead cast is usual for distance casting but, this cannot be performed if there is not enough room

Fig. 75 Moe Birchall spinning the Spey in Autumn.

behind. Assuming there *is* plenty of space, the cast commences with the rod held over one shoulder and about one third rod length of line, including the swivel, hanging. For practice purposes it is advisable to use a heavy bait. This is much easier to cast and weights may be progressively lowered as you become more proficient. Whether one or two hands are used, there is no real difference in the method of casting. If one hand is used, hold the rod below the reel with one finger on the line. If using two, keep the left hand above the reel and the right hand just below it with the finger poised over the brake drum. If the reel has rim control or a brake, the finger should of course be applied to one or the other.

Face the direction you wish to cast into and take the ratchet off if possible. Swing the rod back over the shoulder and let the bait take itself back almost level with your head. As it swings back to your side, cast with one smooth action by 'chopping' the rod in the required direction. Release the drum of the reel at roughly nine o'clock. As the bait sails gracefully through the air (we hope), keep the finger poised ready to prevent the reel

146

spool from over-running. The moment to stop the spool (by clamping the finger onto the line) is entirely dependant upon the trajectory, bait weight, line thickness, drum drag, wind, applied force and goodness knows how many more factors. So the brake must be applied at your discretion. *The* moment is when the bait has stopped pulling the line off the reel and is dropping into the water. If the bait was thrown too high, the air will take the bait on an unnecessarily long path, which will give a line length greater than the distance between the two points and *drag* must result. So keep the bait low and do not stop the drum spinning until it really has stopped pulling the line out. If the bait is stopped too early, it may catapult back at a force greater than its forward motion, resulting in a short, tangled cast.

If the bait is heavy, it is not necessary to swing it back as far as you would a light bait. It is easy to visualise this cast if you imagine you are *bowling* a cricket ball, but that your hand is the tip of the rod. Use the top half of the rod for the final surge of power but follow through with the rest of the rod or a jerky cast will result.

The side cast is very similar to the overhead but, instead of commencing with the rod over the shoulder, it is lowered to a point in line with the hip. There are two distinctive side motion casts: if you imagine you are holding a tennis racket instead of a cricket ball, it is easy to see how a forehand sweep or a backhand sweep is possible. With the forehand side cast, the rod is held in the right hand. The cast commences from the right side (or cast with the left hand from the left side). A backhand cast is made by the right hand from the left side and vice versa. Although the forehand cast tends to have a little more power in it, the backhand cast is definitely more accurate and better controlled. The rod is swung away from the bank – left or right – with a sweeping flick and stopped dead, at a slightly off-centre point. The last foot or so will bring the bait centrally in line with the body as the line is delivered by the whip of the rod. When the line reaches the desired direction, it may be released. Do not forget to stop the spool spinning when the line stops surging – or when the bait is over the spot you wish to place it.

The side cast is a very easy way to deliver bait and is far less tiring than any other form of casting. Another advantage is the amount of room needed to deliver the cast; it is only the length of the rod plus 3 or 4 ft. It is therefore ideal for overhung streams, narrow, tree lined

147

rivers and other restricted fishing circumstances. Yet a third advantage is the very low trajectory and the straightness of the path taken by the bait. By staying low there is less of a splash when the bait lands and the rod does all the work if its design is fully utilised.

There is a swing cast for baits just as there is a swing cast for fly fishing but the two are not at all similar. The bait swing cast is a very gentle affair with hardly any real energy used during its execution. It can be an extremely accurate way of placing the bait – be it a worm or a spinner. It is probably used more for worming or high bank fishing than anything else and is very useful indeed at restrictive spots. In fact it is a cast which can be performed within the length of the rod. The rod almost keeps still.

There are three forms of swing cast; the normal, the catapult and the loose coil method. The normal swing cast commences with a line hanging almost the length of the rod. The body faces the direction the bait is required to travel into – usually the opposite bank – and the line is swung back and forth, across the water, past your side, until it reaches a satisfactory momentum. Just when the line reaches the peak of its forward motion, the reel is released and the bait will continue through the air in the direction of the line. It is not a particularly long cast and is completely hopeless in a wind, but even the most sensitive fishes are not disturbed by this form of delivery and you can keep it up all day. It is rather like tossing a cricket ball underhand and is considered rather feminine for just that reason, but it is very effective for overhung streams, and in any case plenty of women fish!

The catapult swing cast is not a method to be used very often and although the Americans place great store in short rod casting by this means, the author does not recommend it, except on very rare occasions when a very long cast is needed and there is no room to use the normal methods. So do not blame anyone if you snap a perfectly good rod – you have been warned.

The cast is commenced with the rod tip pointing downwards or to one side of the body. The bait is held in one hand as the rod is bent very severely into a bow (ouch). The bait is released with a twang and the line whishes outwards, flinging the bait (or snapping the rod) far across the water.

The final swing bait cast is really an adaption of the

148

first normal cast. The only difference is that, instead of letting the forward motion of the bait peel line off the spool, which slows down the line considerably, the line is taken off beforehand and laid in loops on the ground. It is consequently not suitable as a wading cast. The large coils are (supposedly) whipped up and carried out after the bait with the greatest of ease. It is an excellent boat casting method.

The switch cast is quite a popular river bait cast and, although it may present some strain if long distances are aimed at, it gives a long draw-in time for rest.

Point the rod to the left side of your bank, parallel and a little to the rear, keeping your body facing the direction you wish to cast, usually the opposite bank. Lift the rod with one third of its length carrying loose line and swing the bait towards your waist. Allow it to swing back past its original point and, as the swing reaches its maximum, turn the rod with the line straight and parallel with it, across the river and release the line just before it reaches the desired direction. Use force towards the end and don't forget to stop the drum with the brake or finger as it reaches a maximum travel moment.

The Multiplier

This beautiful spinning reel is definitely not for the learner, unless a good casting instructor is around. Miscasting with a multiplier is the easiest fishing manoeuver possible and even the most experienced fly-caster may have trouble with a multiplier at first. But, once the trick has been mastered, well, there is not a sweeter, or easier spinning reel to use.

As explained in chapter 2, the multiplier is fixed to the top side of the rod, or one could say the rod is turned upside down. Precisely; the rod rings stand up instead of hanging down, and the reel is fixed on the same side as the rings. The right thumb lies just over the line guard, ready to arrest spool action and the rod is firmly grasped by the right hand.

If only the uninitiated were taught how to handle a multiplier in the first place, they would be far more popular reels than they are and the aristocratic aura usually connected to the user of such a 'superior' piece of equipment would be shown up for the hog-wash it really is. The multiplier *is* hard to get used to *if* you have never been taught how to wield it from the beginning.

The secret is in the setting of the bait weight adjustor! Secondly, the automatic centrifugal brake must be correctly set if the cast is to be smooth. This brake slows down and smooths out the fast revolutions of the spool during the initial power surge of the cast. The *mechanical* brake smooths the pay out of line at lower revolutions. It is manually adjustable and is for the balancing of the braking effect *considering the weight for the lure.*

The spool is released just before the cast and instead of flipping the ratchet back on as the cast ends, a thumb on the reel is far better as it can be applied with increasing pressure instead of a dead stop.

The Ambassadeur multiplier has a numbered disc on the adjustor and readings of this will facilitate easier casting once set. To set the 'bait weight adjustor', attach the bait and wind the line in until it is half way along the rod length. Now loosen the adjustor on the side until the spool frees and the bait *begins to drop* to the floor. Tighten the screw slightly so that it is necessary to actually shake the rod hard to slip the bait. It is now correctly set and the number on the side of the knurled adjustor can be read off. This number will only make sense if the dial was set at zero to begin with and when the line is free. It changes with *each* bait weight.

Casting with the multiplier is simplicity itself, provided the bait drag is set correctly. Free the ratchet and place your thumb on the line. Cast in the same manner or style as described in the previous section but use a short rod. The length of a rod fitted with a multiplying reel can be as little as 5 ft although 7–8 ft is more common in Britain. A last word of warning: if the bait weight adjustor is incorrectly set, be prepared for a few birds nests.

The fixed spool reel

Casting with this, the easiest and most common of all reels, is simplicity itself. On the standard, fixed spool reel, the line bale is opened and the loose line, which will peel off if you do not take care, is clipped onto a spare finger. The bait is adjusted to hang one third of the rod length from the tip and with the swivel on the bait side of the rings. As the line is cast, in exactly the same way already described, the left hand goes to the reel winder and the right hand releases its finger hold on the line. The moment of line release will determine the direction of bait precipitation. As the bait drops, the handle is turned by the left

Fig. 76 The author feeding line into rough sea trout water.

hand. This locks the bale arm into position, thus stopping more line from peeling off. Unlike the Nottingham or multiplier, the spool cannot overrun for it does not move, and timing is not very important except from the fishing point of view. The sooner the retrieve commences, the sooner it begins to work.

The automatic fixed spool reel is a very nice piece of tackle to use. It is simple to use and requires no fiddling or line gripping; the bale arm is simply depressed, the cast commenced and the arm released at the moment of greatest bait momentum into the required direction. Winding the crank arm sets the bait 'swimming' and retrieves the line.

On all these reels a clutch is incorporated and it is important to set the slipping point correctly. If a fish takes gently and the clutch is loosely set, there will be no force to sink the hook into his jaw. On the other end of the scale, an over-tight clutch (with no 'give') will not smooth out a heavy take and the line may snap.

Adjust the clutch to a fairly tight position so that, although you can pull line off against the clutch, it will in fact 'give' and let you do so. Once the fish is on, you may adjust the clutch at will and gradually tighten as his runs become weaker. Do not tighten the clutch while a fish is actually moving unless he is on his first run and the clutch

151

is not tight enough. When he is running, do not wind the crank arm against the clutch – there is no point and the friction plates may overheat. This instruction does not apply to some of the Abu reels which have incorporated a brake into the mechanism in such a way that lever winding is essential. If in doubt (and in any case), read the instructions concerning your particular reel.

Casting faults

Whether you are fly casting or bait casting, a number of common faults can accumulate *and stick* if they are not picked up and corrected early on.

The main difference between the two casting techniques used with fly and bait rods is that the whole length of the rod (with only a final 'hammer chop' by the tip) is used to cast a fly; whereas only the top section of a spinning rod is used to propel a bait. With a fly rod, it is the line which is the weight and the *whole length of the line* carries this weight. With the monofilament bait casting line, it is the *lure alone* which pulls out the line – the heavier the lure, the easier the cast (to a point).

An inability to get more than a few yards of fly line out in a straight line can of course be due to various reasons, but the two main reasons for this are: (1) taking the rod too far back and bringing it too far forward; or (2) letting a shooting line release before time. To cure the first fault you must watch the back cast during its execution. Absolutely refuse to take the rod tip back past twelve o'clock no matter what and never let it come down in the forward cast past nine o'clock. In other words, restrict the period of arc to three hours only and apply the 'chopping' power only during the last hour. The second fault is easily corrected; do not release the loose line until the 'chopping' blow or, if your have good timing, wait until the line tugs at the free loop before releasing it. Too much line will also cause it to fall short in coils. So will an incorrect pause between the two (fore and aft) casts. 'Pause' timing is at the very heart of casting technique and until you find a rhythm which satisfies the need of a well timed pause, you will not cast a good line. If you have trouble with the pause, count the stroke out loud. 'one, two, three', for the lift and back cast. 'One, two, three' for the pause and 'One, two, three' for the forward cast. Whatever the length of the pause, and it varies considerably, keep to it and *look behind* all the time. It is *not* a bad habit to watch the line during a back cast and it avoids bush hooking or tree tangling as well.

Another common fault, alas, one which is not restricted to beginners, is snapping flies off the cast. The usual reason for this is due to commencing the forward cast before the back cast has ceased. The solution once again, is to look behind and watch the back cast line. If the line begins to drop before the back cast is completed you are obviously not putting enough power into the lift. Try throwing the line higher into the air and do not let the rod sway back beyond twelve o'clock if there is a bank behind. Allowing the rod to come back too far leads to another fault – hitting a low bank or even striking the water with the line. Stop the rod at the vertical and throw the line *up* and backwards to cure this.

Wind knots are very easily introduced into the line. They are exactly what they appear to be – mysterious knots which appear in the line after a cast. They are more likely to occur when casting into the wind and with a long line on a short rod. When you do make a knot in the leader (it seldom happens to the line itself) do not untie it if it is severe enough to kink the nylon; it would be best left where it is. If it is near the tip, cut the line and throw it away, it is not worth the risk. To cure the fault, throw the line really high up into the air and release it late, say, nine o'clock instead of ten. This will also cure the problem of hitting the rod or line with the fly. If you are making either of these faults on a calm day and cannot blame the wind for it, you are probably not keeping the rod still at the moment of forward cast. You are taking the rod *ahead* of the line momentarily. The cure is to keep your elbow to your side and move nothing but your forearm and wrist. Do not swing the whole arm as you cast. If you *still* hit the rod, do not try casting back with the rod a little off centre to the left and casting forward with the rod a little to the right. Forward casts must be made on the same plane, never come forward to one side of the back cast plane. The resulting twist on the rod tops has caused more damage to rods in the past, particularly cane rods, than any other casting factor.

There will, of course, be many more casting faults and problems but, unfortunately, experience (and a good teacher) is the only way to learn a good casting technique. One thing is sure though; like riding a bicycle, once learned it is never forgotten.

7 *Fly Fishing*

When you reach the water you intend fishing, it must be 'read' before you can decide *how* to fish it. There is no good marching along to your beat with a fly rod unless you know everything is right for fly fishing. If the river is in high flood, your fly rod will catch more fish in a gold-fish bowl and your spinning gear should be at hand. However, assuming the water (and day) to be satisfactory for fly fishing and assuming you have spent the previous evening topping up mugs in the local hop shop when you were asking for advice, you should be in a position to tie a fairly presentable fly onto your line. Select a small fly to begin with and remember, the tone and colour of a pool can change by the hour. The passing of the sun along a pool can bring dark tree shadows to different under-water sections, or it can fling a whole cluster of rocks into brilliant illumination, so choose your fly accordingly. If there is plenty of weed around, choose a green coloured fly; if the rocks are covered in brown algae or peat deposits, use a golden brown fly. Use your common sense. After all, the laws of nature (or more accurately the balance of the environment) would be out of phase if easily seen flies hadn't become extinct long ago. Only food which can hide in a fairly successful manner would have survived a river environment at all. So this is what you must get your lure to represent – a *reasonably* hard to see (and catch) mite.

The small fly, which you should have chosen, will not 'rough up' the pool too much, frightening half the inhabitants before you get started, but an overbright, gawdy, tinselled streamer certainly will.

In the spring, you will need heavier flies as the fish lie deep when the water is cold. As the year advances the fly gets smaller until, by summer, the floating line is used almost exclusively to hold the fly just below the surface of the water. By the beginning of Autumn, say September 1st, the larger flies come back into their own – still on a

155

floating line however. In really warm weather the largest acceptable size of hook will not be more than a No. 6, with a floating line, and may even be as small as No. 12. After mid-September the sunken fly comes back into favour and the size increases. By October the fully dressed flies are in use again but remember, the heavier the dressing, the less life-like and less natural its movement will be in the water.

When the air temperature becomes less than the water temperature, fish tend to lie deeper in the water and if the difference is considerable, they will not rise for even the very choicest of food offerings. This is the time to use a sinking line. When the air temperature is greater than the water temperature, it follows that fish will come nearer to the surface and this is indeed what happens. This means the fish are disturbed more easily, for they can see moving objects above the surface much better and great care is needed.

The reason for a fish's choice of position at different seasons has a lot to do with temperature. Cold water contains more oxygen than warm water. The warmer oxygen is, the greater the velocity of its molecules and this extra energy allows the oxygen to escape into the atmosphere. The fish will therefore seek faster moving water, white water for example, which will naturally contain more trapped oxygen. (see fig. 77).

Fig. 77. Water Temperature Ratios (approx)

Water at	Temp.	contains	10 cc	of oxygen per litre
Water at	5°C	contains	9 cc	..
Water at	10°C	contains	8 cc	..
Water at	15°C	contains	7 cc	..
Water at	20°C	contains	6 cc	..
Water at	25°C	contains	5 cc	..
Water at	30°C	contains	4 cc	..

Fly fishing really needs to be broken down into more specific sections than the rather wide sweeping areas here and that is what we shall do, but just because one subject appears in one place it doesn't mean that this is the only way or reason to use it. Fishing, especially fly fishing, is so much a matter of choice and opinion, we would not wish to presume *anything* to be more than just a generalisation. Therefore, the sectioning which follows is merely in order

156

to make these pages a little neater and to make 'fact' location a simpler job. If you wish to try a sea trout lure on brownies or fish from the 'wrong' end of a pool first, by all means do so. Remember, each tiny river or lake section will be different *in some way* to any other and this is why there are very few rules in the art of fishing.

Salmon Fly Fishing

It is not usual to use a dry fly for salmon fishing although some anglers do so when the air temperature is much higher than the water and the river is crystal clear. As explained in the fly section, red fish seldom take a dry fly and if you are only interested in fresh salmon, this may well be a method of fishing to suit you. Some would say that salmon fly fishing has no scientific interest whatsoever and there is no doubt that trout fly fishing is in a league of its own. On the other hand, the salmon on a fly is not an easy thing to bring to the bank and the skill necessary to land a fly hooked salmon is not inconsiderable.

If you have a gillie (and all the best beats are usually managed by an estate which insists upon supplying one) he will be able to point out the usual lies, depending upon conditions prevailing at the time. There will always be 'best' flies on a well known river and these are the ones to start with. It is preferable to have a look at your fishing beat the day or evening before if this is possible. You may then be in a better position to select the right starting point for your flies. You may also note any particular aspects of the beat which may affect your method of fishing such as the location of trees; depth of water and wading possibilities; beaching points; rapids around the bend and so on. A mental picture of a strange beat may save a fish on the day. If you don't have a gillie to help, it is well worth looking for possible salmon lies. Submerged rocks for example or ledge overhangs. Salmon tend to lie on the bottom of smooth based rocks and with plenty of rocks around to divert the currents into channels. They like to lie close into the edge of a main current but not actually in the full blast. Where a rock protrudes above or near to the surface, a 'tail' will form behind it and sometimes a fish will lie in this gentler stream with the added protection of the shadow formed by the rock. Salmon, lying at the edge of a fast moving stretch of water, prefer the shade and will select positions under trees sooner than in the bare open.

K

Fig. 78 Jim Hardy below a weir.

Check the water level of the river, this can be detected by the countless water-line markings all along the river; bridge 'tide' marks, algae lines, dark rock marks etc. If you cannot see any marks at all, then the river is high, otherwise you should be able to see the marks just below the surface. If the water is fairly normal, the fish will probably be around the tail of the pool. If the water is low, they will move to deep, dark holes and murky pools. In warm water, salmon will seek fast running shallow stretches whereas cold water will send them to the bottom of deeper, slower water. When the air temperature is warmer than that of the water, fish will lie in the shallows – warmer water will conversely send them into deeper spots.

The best average temperature for fly fishing lies between 6°C and 10°C. Below 3°C, spinning or bait fishing is recommended – or at least very large, leaded, false flies fished almost on the bottom, and fished as slowly as possible. Above 15°C – the tiniest flies in your box are the order of the day.

There are a number of uncontrollable factors which will decide your catch, not the least of which is the weather conditions of the day. If the barometer is rising, indicating an increase in air pressure, the fishing possibilities are fairly good. When it is falling, the chances are not so good. The conditions of the river, due to the weather, will also affect the issue. The best fishing river has a normal or falling water level. When the height of the river is increasing, the fish tend to be uninterested in baits. They feel the extra pressure and visualise a move to the next pool. On the other hand, fishing is often good just before or on the first day of a spate. Once the level changes enough for the fish to sense a spate, fishing – at least with a fly – is usually over.

Spinning then comes into its own with bait fishing hard on its heels as the water rises. Once the spate is underway, much fish movement will take place. Those lying will, however, prefer to do so near the banks in favour of fighting a heavy swell – fish *do* sleep!

A cloudy day will generally offer better fishing than a completely overcast day and a bright summer day is often quite hopeless. If the sun is flinging its strong rays downstream, the fish may be unable to see your fly, being dazzled by the light. When they cannot see in this way they tend to freeze and remain rivetted to one spot sooner than risk movement in a strange environment. On the other hand, an upstream sun reflection will illuminate any bright aspect of your fly and make it appear unnatural if you have not chosen too well.

Once you reach the edge of your beat and load the line ready for action, the battle is on. Your enemies are reflection – especially from your rod if it has pretty, shiny rings to glint in the sun – and shadows; yours being the most likely to offend. Another means of transmitting your presence to the salmon is vibration. If you are wading, for goodness sake do so with some measure of care. If the sun is shining, you can at least pretend to be a bush or a tree trunk, but if you have a heavy tread, be prepared to throw an exceedingly long line – or fish from a boat! The reason heavy footed anglers catch fish in fast waters is often because that is the only place, with thundering water to shake up the earth, that his P and S waves can be concealed.

Do not look for good bank positions to cast from, these are the very spots most used by those before you, look for the unexpected and unlikely, concealed points and you may be luckier than your predecessor.

Unless you are fishing deep, use a greased line when working upstream or on a large pool or lake. The line will lift easier from the water and cause less disturbance. It will also cast a little easier. The greased line in this case incidentally, is really only a greased leader or cast; you would of course use a floating line when fishing this method. You simply grease the monofilament end of the line up to within, say, 18 in. of the fly. This keeps all the line on the surface of the water except the last few inches. Do be careful not to touch the fly with the grease (especially made for lines and sold in most tackle shops) or it will not sink.

Commence fishing at the head of the pool and work your way carefully towards the tail. Remember, every single cast may disturb the fish and cost dearly so cast carefully. A strange phenomena of fly fishing is that when one *really* thinks one will catch a fish – holding one's breath in *true* anticipation and with real expectation of hooking a fish, this very often results in a take. It is probably only that one fishes properly and with all the due care and attention at such times which is the *real* cause of success but it is nevertheless uncanny at times.

Cast across the pool and allow the line to drift with the stream to finish up in a straight line at your bank. It is when the line does straighten that a fish will very often take – he was probably lying just off the heavy current. If the line is not straight, the fly will not be working. Either reel in the line or pull the loose length through the rings until you have the right casting length free. It is important that you keep this casting length fairly even throughout the pool because you are virtually searching every square yard of the pool for a salmon and if you use varied lengths of line you may miss sections of the river bed. If the pool is not parallel – very few are – do not extend the line when you reach wider parts, come back to them after you have fished through the whole pool.

The second cast should begin one yard down from the first and if the pool is deeply coloured or very fast moving, you will need to probe its depths with much greater care and more slowly than you would with a clear pool. In other words, give the fish a chance to see the fly. The third cast is made another yard further down the pool, and so on. The technique is quite clear and very simple; a progressive zig-zag movement from the head to the tail of the pool with a return to the wider (or narrower) spots later. This is of course a very simple and basic method of fishing and would become exceedingly boring after a time if no deviation were introduced. It is therefore only meant

160

as a guide to the ideal way of ensuring a pool is thoroughly fished from end to end. Fishing the same pool in the same manner but from a different angle will probably take your fly into even more corners but the basic principle remains the same – seek your fish in every likely (and some unlikely) spots. Fish with great care; pull line gently through rings sooner than winding and causing a ratchet screech. Keep the rod fairly low and straight at all times when the line is in the water and if the current 'bows' the line, causing it to drag around by the belly, 'mend' it by lifting gently and whipping the loose line back to a non-drag position. Remember the ruse – a fly is not supposed to be attached to anything and must therefore *behave as though it were not.* No fly would be able to buck a heavy current so do not allow the line to help it do so – keep the fly natural.

If the water is fairly slow, it may be worth imparting a little 'life' into the fly. This is done by lifting and lowering the rod tip or pulling a few inches of line through the rings and releasing it. This makes the fly hop up and down and also helps it to keep swimming in a forward and upright position. If the water is fairly cold, these movements should be made very slowly. They should also be slow, regardless of temperature to some extent, if the water is darkly coloured (and thus a dark fly is in use). If the water is reasonably fast or you are fishing in a lake or large pool with a bright fly on clear water, the fly can be given more movement and at a faster rate. Do not attempt to 'bob' the fly in really fast water for you will gain nothing and possibly lose the 'line lay' to boot. It is worth keeping the rod a little higher in fast water than in slow, this keeps a little line off the water and helps to deter line 'bellying'.

When fishing deep, it is not always easy to detect a bite as you cannot see the fish. Most fly fishermen, when experiencing their first salmon bite, interpret it as being stuck on the bottom! The joy (and surprise) when the line peels off with a shriek and the salmon takes over is impossible to describe: I can only say, 'Do not fish for salmon if you have a weak heart – it will pop out of your ears on the first bite!'

The sunken fly is taken with a gentle tightening of the line and a feeling of rigidity is transferred along to the rod giving the impression of a 'hang up' and with no melo-drama or snatch (as associated with the dry fly take).

Once the bait *is* taken, the fish panics. He may stay

161

exactly where he is and try to cling to the bottom. On the other hand, and much more likely, he will take off like a torpedo. If the salmon runs towards rapids, give him plenty of line, do not attempt to pull him up or your line may break. Try to encourage your fish to turn upstream. This is done by moving ahead of the fish to show him your terrifying shadow. This will send him in the opposite direction (we hope). Never attempt to strike while the fish is first 'nibbling' at the fly. Let him turn away from you before drawing the barb into his hard, bony jaw lip with a hard jolt. The reason a wet fly is less likely to be snatched out of the mouth of a salmon before he has really taken it is obvious. The angler is less likely to strike too early if he cannot see the fly. A floating fly however, or even a sinking fly in clear water, presents an extremely frustrating situation when one can see a salmon at the lure. It takes a great deal of will power not to strike when he picks up the fly, but it would be quite fatal to do so; you *must* wait until the fish turns away with the lure. When the fish first takes, if gently, lower your rod tip gently and feed him some line – it is always worth holding a little slack in the hand when fly fishing for just this purpose. As he turns with the fly, you may allow the line to tighten slowly and, when sure he is on, give him a little stick and thump the hook in hard.

The battle is on and a firm but gentle hand is the order of things now. Keep the rod high and the clutch, if you have one, fairly tight. If he wants to run, let him do so but keep the line tight at all times. The ratchet should be turned to 'tight' if it is hand adjustable. The object of the game now is to tire out your opponent by giving him a weight to drag along after him. Only wind in when he is actually lying or moving towards you. When he runs, let him!

This game can go on for an hour or more but in general it should take two minutes per pound to land a salmon. A ten pounder should be landed in 20 minutes and it will be the most exciting 20 minutes of your life. Always keep the fish upstream of you where you can and get out of the water, if wading, as soon as possible by walking carefully backwards.

If the fish starts leaping and thrashing out of the water – a truly glorious situation – lower the rod as he leave the water and take it slightly forward of the fish. As he falls back into the water, lift the rod again and try to prevent a sudden tightness from occuring or the cast may snap.

Strange though it may seem, a fish usually fights better when in slightly warm water than when in cold and a female usually puts up a better struggle than a male. If you have been unlucky enough to hook a kelt (worn out post-breeding fish) he will usually swim in the easiest direction – downstream, whereas a normal salmon will run against the current most likely.

When the fish has given up the fight and allows itself to be pulled almost to your feet, do not assume it to be finished. It may well summon an extra surge of energy when confronted with your fearful form and gleaming gaff hook and run off again with renewed fear. Wait until he has tipped onto his side and pull him gently over the net, if this is your landing method.

If gaffing, which is far easier to do in fairly deep water but quite hard in rough running streams, slip the hook under the line and over the fish. As the point lines up with the flank, draw the shaft up and outwards with one swift, even motion. Do not assume him to be completely finished, even when gaffed, especially if you are wading, for he can still wriggle off. The tailer, which is probably the best way to land a fish, is slipped over the tail and a few inches along the body before the trip is pulled. Tailing by hand is quite simple but make sure the fish is well worn out before attempting to whip him out by the tail. Yet another method is to 'beach' your catch. This is done by drawing the fish into a shallow bank and half dragging, half letting the fish wriggle its way onto the bank. It should then be tailed by hand.

In summary, salmon prefer strong water, but stay on the edge of it. If the temperature rises to 8°C they will move to rougher water in search of oxygen. Early in the year, when the temperature is below 5°C, they will lie in deep, black pools. When walking along the bank, remember, although fish may be lying well out from the stream, they will feel the vibration of your feet – if you see the tiddlers dashing away in fear, you can be sure they will cause the same reaction as birds do when feeding near game animals. As they fly off in alarm, the game is alerted and fearful. So, small fish rushing out to the centre warn bigger fish of your presence.

Salmon often rest when entering a pool after a particularly long run and often by a rock – usually in front and not behind, where loose gravel may be churned up and taken into the gills. Also keep in mind the fact that water

163

is always deeper than it looks. Tiny trickles of water may never look deep enough for a salmon but they usually are. After taking a salmon, another may adopt his lie the next day, so always go for a spot if you have already taken a fish there before.

Salmon do not actually take a fly from where it rises. It has either moved up to that point or retreated a few yards. They prefer to take on a cloudy day, are not so good on an overcast day and are downright difficult to catch on a bright day. The best weather is cloudy but with the air temperature just a few degrees higher than the water, this will bring them up to the fly. You *can* fish with dry fly for salmon but wet fly fishing is more usual. Use a larger fly at the head of a pool and in fast water. In June and July use a very small fly – say size 10 or 12. In April use a No. 2 single or a No. 4 double.

Always keep in mind the kind of water you are fishing. If it is clear chalk stream, be very careful and *very* meticulous; if it is a wide, black 'rager', splash around to your heart's content but never forget the equipment a fish has for detecting anglers, it's pretty good!

Lastly, once you have landed your catch and decided to keep it (the decision to return a fish is taken from your hands if a gaff is used), put it out of its misery as soon as possible. A sharp crack on the skull just above the eyes with a priest – or a long piece of heavy rock or wood – will do the trick.

Sea Trout Fly Fishing
As already explained, the sea trout is an extremely shy and very timid fish – until you hook one that is! He then fights like a demon, leaping and tossing his head, terrier fashion. Pound for pound, a sea trout is the best fighter in the whole *salmonidae* family.

The sea trout, like the salmon when fresh from the sea, has a very delicate mouth. Unlike the salmon, however, the sea trout does not overcome this mouth softness, which is rather strange when you consider that the trout is feeding in fresh water whereas the salmon is not. It would seem that nature has mixed the two fishes up in this respect. The point is that you must take much more care with a hooked sea trout than you would with a salmon or trout. The answer is to use a gentle hand and have plenty of backing on the reel.

The sea trout season is a little later than for salmon and

164

doesn't really settle down until May. Night fishing is of course the best way to catch sea trout, but evening and dusk hours can give you some good sport. Coloured water will even offer up a sea trout in the day-time provided you tread warily and hide behind every possible bush, tree or rock when near the water.

Use a fine line in the daytime, up to 5 lbs. You may go up to 7 or even 9 at night.

The sea trout cast is about 9 ft long and carries only one fly, although some fishermen prefer two. Sea trout flies are shown in fig. 71 and plate 24. Always start with a No. 14 fly and work upwards to avoid unnecessary disturbance. The largest sea trout hook is around size 8 except under exceptional circumstances. If a fly is unsuccessful don't overfish a spot with it, change the fly (or the spot). Some good dry flies include Duncan's favourite;

Fig. 79 Playing a heavy fish in Scandinavia.

165

Hardy's favourite and Loch Ordie. Peter Ross, Teal and Silver, Red Palmer, Watson's fancy and Bloody Butcher are all time Sea trout 'favourites'.

The best fishing conditions are to be found when the river is normal. Fishing commences at the head of the pool although the fish tend to drop back around dusk so start in the middle or even lower at this time. This prevents unnecessary pool disturbance when there is little likelyhood of catching a fish at the head and much less chance of frightening fish at the tail before you get there. Sea trout fishing is usually better when the surface is disturbed by a wind or even by rain, although estuary fishing prevails on a dry day.

Night Fishing

Although night fishing is certainly not restricted to sea trout, we have included it in this section because it is far more applicable to sea trout than to other fishes. Indeed, many experienced sea trout fishermen will tell you a sea trout caught in the daytime is little more than a fluke and in some waters this is certainly true. However, the following points on night fishing are general points and are applicable to any fish except where otherwise indicated. After all, when the cows have stopped tramping around the fields and pedestrians have gone· away from the river-side, peace and quiet will prevail and this, at last, leaves the fish in peace and allows them to feed. This hunger period is free for all.

The best equipment to have for night fishing is a good memory. Visit the scene of your intended beat and make a mental note of bankside trees or bushes. Check on snagging points and dangerous hook-up possibilities. Also try to keep in mind ·any possible landing or beaching spots, extra shallow and extra deep pool sections. Find a marker spot, which can be easily located in the dark, to stow your tackle – and any fish you may catch – and *mark the beat,* either with a rock on the footpath or bank edge where the pool finishes or by locating a whitish object nearby to recognise in the dark. You may also wish to mark restrictive casting points, or, alternatively, long casting points.

Apart from your excellent memory, (indicated by the number of marker rocks and white painted trees strewn all around the pool), you will need one or two items. A good torch is absolutely vital and if you can find (or make) one with a good mask on it of the type used in the last world war, so much the better. Incidentally, a pair of infra-red night glasses, if they ever come your way, would be really something. If you come across an unwanted set, contact the author immediately! It is worth binding the front edge of your landing net (tailing and gaffing is tricky at night) with white tape to make it stand out in the dark; pieces of this tape can be stuck to other items which may be mislaid in the dark too, although it is well worth a trip back to the river the next day in search of possibly mislaid gear.

A long rod is best for night fishing; this helps you to keep in touch with the fly. The fly should be of the double hook variety, tied to a 9 ft, 7 lb. cast. One fly is sufficient and certainly less dangerous snag-wise, and you should carry a few spare casts.

Carry as little gear as possible at night and keep what you must have with you all the time. This reduces the chances of losing it and removes the temptation of constant gear changing. If you only have six flies with you, you will not be re-flying every few minutes. A very definite must, if you object to being bitten from head to toe, is anti-midge cream. This is invaluable when night or evening fishing. Most of the well known makes are effective but make sure you do not get any on the line or fly; fishes have a pretty keen sense of smell and they most definitely dislike anti-midge cream.

Night flies and what to use after dark in general is a very controversial subject. One can only lay out ideas based on personal experience and this is precisely what the author has done. There are, however, certain scientific facts which cannot be denied and which will have a great deal of bearing on your fishing. The obvious way to select from the wide variety of information is to consider these facts when making estimation *at the fishing beat in question,* for only there will an interpretation be possible. Much can depend on local information, so get as much of this as you can. Then apply your technical *facts* to this, and a few dabs of information collected from books (like this one), and you should catch a fish or two! It boils down to common sense, experience and carefulness, there is nothing mysterious or difficult in fishing, day or night.

Fish most definitely *can* see at night. There are *always* some light rays reaching the water even on the very blackest of nights, there are also light rays which are not of the normal (visible to human) lengths, such as infra-red rays. Fish can collect certain light rays on a 'reflector' behind the eye, which cats, owls etc., share the ability to do, and light is reflected back. Unfortunately for man, his sight covers a small range of the spectrum – between red and violet – but fish can exceed this range. A certain fluoresence is radiated by some animal tissue. Hen's hackles, mole's fur and heron feathers for example, absorb extremely short wavelength light called ultra-violet rays. These furs and feathers may then give off rays of a longer wave length and be spotted by fish if used on a fly. Some animal fur does not reflect rays in this manner. Experiments will soon show you the most interesting flies on *any one specific night!*

Apart from vision, which would seem of secondary importance in darkly coloured, peaty or muddy waters, fish have a very efficient sense incorporated into a 'vibration area' known, from an anatomical aspect, as the lateral line. As previously explained, this delicate radar-like 'instrument' carries nerves which collect aquatic vibrations and waves. It can feel and locate direction and current strength within minute degrees. It measures current strength and wave amplitude by pressure 'sensors'. To back up this highly sophisticated 'organ', a fish can also 'hear' vibrations in much the same way as the human ear is stimulated. There are two cavities, or hollow bones, behind the brain, which deal with balance (just like the semi-circular canals of the human ear). They can also detect vibrations and transmit an interpretation to the brain for comment and action. Fish have a jolly good sense of smell too!

Lastly, fish have yet another advantage over the angler. He is alone – they are not! Nature (or should we say environmental evolution) has developed a 'sense' among shoaling creatures called 'mass control sense'. This 'sense' is more of an instinctive alertness, precipitated by unnatural movements of other creatures. A good example is sheep. *One* sheep wandering in *one* direction usually takes all the others with it. If a dog barks, they move by 'mass control' and even those sheep not hearing the dog, move with the others by 'mass control sense'. Shoaling of fish is almost the same thing, so take care not to disturb *any* creatures in or near the water, it may mushroom into 'mass hysteria'!

As the sun drops out of sight, two basic changes occur;

168

the light fades, and the temperature drops. This, incidentally, is probably why a cloudy day is a good fishing day – the *changes*. For half an hour or so after sunset a trout or sea trout rise usually occurs. The sea trout usually migrate to shallower waters and pool tails at this time. *Really* rapid water is avoided now as fear of discovery lessens with every darkening minute. A cold night is seldom very good and a misty or foggy night is well nigh hopeless.

After the first half hour of 'evening rise' there is usually a lull, but in an hour or so it will probably start again and stay good for the rest of the night (provided it began well in the first place), with a pause between one and four a.m. During the first rise, the sun is very often still visible and casting should be in the direction of the sun-set if possible.

As darkness approaches, the size of the fly should increase from, say, size 12 to size 10, or even 8, depending upon whether you use a double hook (advisable) or not. A calm night is a difficult night and extra care is needed if fish are not to be frightened. Wading is not very safe at night unless you know the water exceptionally well and wading on a calm night is most definitely out. If a breeze is blowing, your chances of catching fish increase and 'familiar water' wading is possible.

If you are fishing a stream, the dry fly comes into its own at night although a lake is usually fished better with a wet fly. Dry flies are of no use whatsoever if the night is misty or foggy as the fish tend to lie low and feed on nymphs. They will also prefer to nymph if the night is bright with moonlight.

When casting, listen for cracking on the back cast. If this occurs you have probably lost the fly. Do not take the rod past twelve o'clock on the back cast as this takes the line too low down and may result in lost or damaged flies. Check your fly every now and then and, if the cast entangles, let it go and tie on another – it is less frustrating!

Finally, make sure you *can* fish at night before setting off. In many places, Scotland in particular, night fishing is illegal!

Trout Fly Fishing
Fly fishing for trout not only deserves a chapter all to itself, it really needs a book to itself (perhaps I may write one sometime). However, not to be biased in favour of any one member of the *Salmonidae* family, I have allotted

this part to brown trout fly fishing and that's that! Rainbow trout are not included in this section as such and are dealt with in chapter nine – with lake fishing – as we discuss rivers, streams and burns here. Much of this section is, however, most applicable to rainbow fly fishing too. If you can remember that rainbows do not live in rivers normally in Gt. Britain, you may share most of the following techniques and facts – plus a few of the theories.

Trout fishing *can* be classified into water type groups but it all becomes very bewildering. For example, there is chalk-stream fishing, pond fishing, river fishing with sunken fly, dry fly fishing, nymphing, rain fed river fishing, still water wet fly fishing, lake and boat fishing, stream and burn fishing and so on. Where does one begin? Unfortunately the answer is – with experience! Most basic methods of fishing are the same, regardless of where it is performed, the differences are somewhat subtle and will only be adapted to wide use within the capabilities and intelligence of the angler. Nothing which follows can be strictly accorded to one specific method, so gather all the data you can and apply that which is applicable to the situations you will meet *when you meet them*. There is no such thing as 'do *this* when water is like *that*', one can only generalise, it's up to you to interpret or read the water hour by hour. The following 'sketches' are meant only as such – sketches.

We have already described, in chapter one, how trout are territorial creatures with a boundary or feeding area limit around their lie. This is, however, not the complete story and there are times, as any trout angler will tell you, when they shoal. To be more precise, the trout season begins in November when they repair to the upper reaches for spawning purposes. This lasts until early January, depending upon the severity of the winter. During January and part of February, after spawning, the exhausted trout drop back downstream with the ever increasing current until they find large, sluggish resting pools and wide, shallow patches. Then follows a period of recuperation, during which the spent fish rebuild their tissue. By April, they have ended their convalescence and begin to adopt the territorial areas we have mentioned. This will all depend on the size and aggressiveness of the individual and tough boys will take the choicest spots. Unlike the salmon, trout seek true hiding places *under* rocks or even under hollowed out banks instead of more temporary *current* deciding spots. This territory will be guarded tooth and fin until Autumn turns their heads once more and the lure of better things overcomes the desire to feed. Trout will feed a little on their way upstream but will positively refuse food when waiting a chance to scale a rough section or water-fall. The rougher the stretch ahead, the less likely they are to feed on flies and only a spinner, imitating a small annoying fish, will possibly induce them to take. At this time the fish shoal and hang around tributaries and forks seeking a mate to court.

Depending upon water conditions, fish may be found almost anywhere and although there are some places more likely to produce a fish than others, you should not be deterred from trying all the usual places – and then some of the less likely spots; it is often the unexpected which occurs in trout fishing, indeed, that is the art of the game.

Normally, trout are to be found just off the main current; in slow, deep pools or, if in faster pools, either just in front of a rock or a few feet behind it. If there is enough room, he will prefer to slip under it. Trout may also be found in the slackish water just up from rapids; in the gentler sections of a pool tail, or where currents swirl, due possibly to an island or a burn entry into the river. They love to lie in the lee of a small island and much prefer dark, shady spots to open, sunlit stretches. The bank usually overhangs a river water edge and tree roots afford lovely refuges but remember, light rays bend when they pass through water and although you may not be able to see a fish just over the edge off a bank, he may well be able to see you as your image *can be bent with the light rays* and be sent into his field of view! An astonishing example of this phenomena was illustrated in 1905 when the Canigou mountains near Perpignan were photographed from Marseilles – over 250 kilometers away. The radius of the earth over this distance places the mountains below the horizon! In fact the light rays were following a curved path around the surface of the earth and, of course, the image was carried by the rays. The complexities of this strange effect are summed up by 'Fermat's Principle of Least Time' but we are digressing somewhat – the lesson is clear – don't stand too close to the bank because fish *can see around corners!*

In a river which is rising, trout tend to move towards the centre of the stream, but once the water height reaches flood proportions, they move very close into the bank and seek less ferocious currents. They will also move into the banks when the reverse occurs – low water.

If the temperature is very low, most fishes, including trout, lie on the bottom and become sluggish. This is because they are unable to maintain their own body temperature and must rely on the surrounding heat to determine their rate of metabolism. If this drops to any appreciable low, their rate of energy production drops too and a state of semi-consciousness, rather like hibernation, sets in. They are not sluggish though and will react to normal dangers – they just won't go out of their way for food and it must be taken down to them.

We have discussed 'pools' many times throughout this book and no doubt you are well aware of what a pool actually is. For trout fishing with the fly, it is important to know the precise parts of the normal pool and so, for those in doubt, a pool is hereby described in detail. A pool is a deeper, slower part of the river or stream where the water widens and the fish lie in search of food or rest. A pool begins fast, usually as the result of a level change in the river bed. A waterfall may begin the pool and this part of the water is called the head. It is the part where the water *enters* and not, as some people think, where it leaves. There is usually a slim, deep depression just past this point called the 'neck' of the pool. In the centre of a pool there is often a deep, black, calm area. This is called the hole, or well. The pool then becomes wider and shallower; this is the apron. Then the pool speeds up and finally rushes off as white water to boil into the next section of the stream; this final part of the pool – so often called the head by the uninitiated – is the tail. This rather diagrammatic explanation will of course differ pool by pool, but the essence seldom changes.

There are many ways to fish for trout with the fly and it is only possible to describe the more popular methods here.

Wet Fly Fishing

Most forms of trout fishing are best after April and there are many rivers which do not permit fishing at all until March but, if fishing earlier, you may be sure that wet fly fishing or nymphing is the only possible way. It is sometimes argued that the May fly introduces dry fly fishing and there may well be some truth in this.

Having decided to fish the wet fly, to begin with at least,

caption on page 191)

you must then decide whether to do so *up* or *down* stream. If you haven't had very much experience or are a complete beginner, then learn to use the wet fly downstream first and keep off the super light tackle. If you are more adept at fly fishing and can afford a decision then consider the conditions of the day and the water. Down stream fishing is usually better when the wind is blowing downstream. It is also more favourable on a dull day, when the current is reasonably swift, or when the water is coloured. The reason for these considerations boil down to one element – the fish are facing *you* when fishing downstream and all the above phenomena counteract the chances of them seeing you! It seems logical that a trout would see you creeping towards it when the stream was crystal clear but it may not do so when the water is cloudy. Whatever the conditions are, you must fish for trout like a commando in enemy territory; with extreme care, silence and animal caution. The glint of a rod ring, the scrape of gravel or a fleeting shadow and your quarry will vanish.

Having decided to work downstream do not worry too much about the rightness of your decision for, after lunch and after fishing through all the pools, you may then fish your way back – upstream!

You will need a fairly long line for downstream fishing and the cast should be almost the length of the rod. Three flies are tied to the line at intervals of 3 ft. The first fly is called the 'bob' fly; the middle one is called a 'dropper' and the last is the 'tail' fly.

It is advisable to use rather small hooks for downstream work, say size 12 or even 14 to begin with on a reasonably heavy line, say 6–8 lbs. It is not clever to fish over-light and the agonies suffered by a fish with a broken cast trailing in its mouth for days or weeks need no further description.

When fishing the wet fly, bear in mind how natural your bait must appear to the fish. After all, he is an aquatic creature and eats far more sub-aquatic food than surface food. The fly is cast across and downstream, usually from a vantage point in the water, (thus a need to wade) and allowed to drift downstream with the current. The fly should be sent in all directions, searching every rock or other likely trout hiding place waiting for insect life to drift near enough to allow a quick dash and a snap. If the distance from their 'home' is too far for safety they will ignore the food. And so it is necessary to take the fly

L

almost to his door. Much will depend on how well fed (chalk stream) or how desperate (mountain burn) the fish is.

If you are fishing a small stream, keep well away from the water and use very small hooks – 14 to 16 even. If the current is strong in a burn, fish upstream. Always check the action of your flies in the water. If the wet fly will not sink, suck it in your mouth for a few moments, rinse it in the water and it should then sink.

A greased line is sometimes advisable when fishing downstream although it may cause bad 'bellying' of the line in fast water. I have already described the method of curing or mending this problem from the bank and there isn't much difference when wading except that you are now at water level and must lift your rod top to compensate. The objectionable aspect of a curved line is that, as a curve, the current force will pull the radius of this curve at different speeds! It is rather like the line of chorus girls walking round the stage arm in arm; the centre girls simply mark time, whereas the outer girls have to step very fast indeed. Well, the fly is analogous to the outer girls when the line curves and the greater the curve, the faster it will travel. No insect could possibly move *across* a fast current under its own steam. It is

Fig. 80 Stream trout fishing.

176

this unnatural speed which deters a trout from taking.

If in mid-stream, fishing across, take care not to 'mend' your line too sharply; the lift must be gentle and the rod motion restricted to a small arc. In fact, the rod tip should move in a neat circle from the direction of the drift – a 'whip' round to the opposite side, rather like a short hammer blow again, usually in an anti-circle.

If you elect to fish a greased line, decide on the depth of your fly and grease the monofilament to within that distance from the fly. If the water is fast, cast upstream a little or the fly will not sink appreciably. Fish into ripples of wind blown water sooner than smooth surfaces. Don't bother with white water, this is the domain of the sea trout and your tiny fly probably won't sink there anyway.

If you see the fish take your fly, wait until he pulls on the line before striking and even then you should *pull* sooner than snatch.

In deeper or calmer waters, the sink and draw method of fly presentation sometimes coaxes a trout out into the open. The idea is to impart motion into the fly by nodding the rod top slowly, but don't make the mistake of letting the fly buck the current; keep to natural movements. A good time to 'nod the rod' is when retrieving from the slack side-water for a new cast – a time when a trout may well nip out from the bank to snatch a fly.

Although the principle of downstream wet fly casting is to toss the line at a 45° angle downstream and allow it to drift to your bank, with an occasional mend in the middle, this is not the be all and end all of the method. On the contrary, this is simply the foundation of a principle. It is rather like teaching a person to drive a car: once he can handle the controls, he may then go on to drive in a Grand Prix. But although he knows how to use the controls, it takes considerable skill, practice and personal qualities to win a race in the end. The principles of down stream fly fishing are basic but they are extremely elastic and variant. Just as each circuit needs special gearing, so a fishing beat will have its own demands. It is up to you to study the ground beforehand and fish accordingly. It is a very strange river which does not require a little upstream fishing even as you fish down it.

Fishing the trout fly upstream is perhaps the most artful method of catching fish there is. It is certainly one of the most skilful and rewarding ways to spend a day. With upstream fly work, you cast to a specific fish and to do this, you must be able to read the water and judge the position of a single specimen. The joy, when a trout snaps your fly up just where you figured one should be, is incomprehensible to one who has never experienced the feeling and there comes a flood of self satisfaction comparable to that a scientist must feel when a planet he predicted by mathematics suddenly appears in the screen of a telescope.

You *must* know the water to work an upstream trout fly. You should be able to wade without letting him know you are there – rather like creeping up on a gazelle; it is pretty tricky! You will have some advantage over the trout if the water is fairly rapid because he will have to face the current. A strong current from behind would force the gills apart (or closed) and drown the fish. If the pool is large and deep the fish will wander around in search of food in all directions, they are then called 'cruisers' and you will not creep up on a cruiser! Another advantage of upstream fishing in fairly fast water is that the current will not carry smell or vibrations to the fish. The force of the current completely removes the possibility of scent travelling upstream and restricts (or even overcomes) the effect of sound wave radiation and other vibrations liable to warn the downstream fish. Stealth still remains of paramount importance and always bear in mind the 'sentinels' of the river! Imagine you are in a jungle stalking deer. You are already downwind and have overcome the senses of smell and sight by getting – in this case the water flow – ahead of you (the fish are all facing ahead!) The other senses, sound and vibration, are masked by the force of the current. But, wait a minute, you have only overcome the senses of the fish you are sneaking up on, you are ignoring all others. What about the eels curled up in horrid dark corners? What about the ever present tiddlers? Every step you take may disturb some form of under-water life and many of these will flee *upstream* – right past the nose of your trout! What would you think if you were a nice fat juicy trout, basking under the shade of a willow tree, waiting for choice caterpillars to drop into the water for supper and suddenly dozens of tiddlers go rushing past your doorway in panic? After all, they wouldn't dare go near you at all for fear of joining the caterpillar queue under normal circumstances. Just like the deer, the trout is warned of imminent danger by lesser life around. The only difference, in the case of deer, is that the sentinels are birds.

178

The lesson is plain, you will not only need to overcome the senses of the trout, but those of its sentinels, and stealth is your only weapon. It cannot be stressed too greatly – stealth and caution, cunning and craft, patience and silence are the absolute essentials if you are to catch a fish – any fish. If you bear these thoughts in mind, your day will almost certainly be a good one; fishing ability comes next.

To return to the method; it is not wise to have more than one fly when fishing upstream. Don't forget, the fly comes back to you, and to keep touch with two or three flies is not easy. The chances of being snagged on the hook yourself increases and there is nothing more annoying than a pin hole in waders – especially if you are wearing them at the time!

Although you are casting to a specific fish, a certain amount of searching is inevitable. Casting should be either forward and across the stream or directly upstream, depending upon the geography of the water. When I say geography I mean underwater topography as well as visual scenery. You will, of course, cast to where you think a fish may be. The line is kept fairly short, not more than twenty-five feet, and must be retrieved in such a way that the angler is always in touch with the fly. This is an exceedingly difficult accomplishment when the water is fast. A good way to retrieve is to pull the line back through the rings and let it drift to the rear with the current. In this way you are also fishing behind and there is always the odd suicide fish hungry enough to ignore the usual danger signals. He is probably tempted to follow your wading course by the countless insect life kicked up from the mud or dislodged from stones as you pick your way through the river bed. This is one good reason for returning along the beat, nymphing downstream, once you reach the end of your section.

Another method of line retrieve is to raise the rod as the current returns the fly. An important point to remember when casting to an upstream trout is that although the fly is (or should be) deposited a few feet in front of him, just in his field of view, the line will land right across the length of his body – fore and aft! The care with which the line hits the water is absolutely vital and this is why it may be better to present your cast from a slightly diagonal vantage point.

The fly must, of course, be retrieved reasonably fast,

depending upon current speed, and the strike must be equally fast too. The usual drag and slow tightening is forgotten when upstream striking, because the fish is facing the right direction anyway and an upward strike should bury the hook in fast and deep.

The last foot or so may be left dry if you use a greased line but try different fishing depths if unsuccessful.

Upstream fly fishing is best when the wind blows upstream and when the water is low or clear. It is also advisable on a very bright day; it is not a method of fishing fast water as you would not be able to keep up with the retrieve.

Nymphing
Nymphing is a sunken line, insect bait method of catching trout. Nymphs were very briefly described earlier, but when fishing on a 'nymph' basis, it is worth remembering that the diet of a specific fish will depend on its environment and *nothing else*. If a specific insect nests in your fish's area he will probably feed on it, given the chance to do so, as he has probably tasted one before. An extraordinary example of insect-fish evolution can be seen in certain yellow and black striped flies. A yellow and black striped body usually denotes a poisonous or stinging fly, such as the wasp or hornet, and flies with these markings are usually ignored by birds, (the insects' greatest enemy) predatorial insects and fishes. Some insects, which are completely non-poisonous, have survived the relentless selection of evolution by developing yellow and black colours! They become almost immune to predatorial dangers in this way – and would subsequently be useless as bait in an area where *real* poisonous yellow and black striped insects live. In a river which does not usually see such insects, the fish will *not* have developed a fear of them.

The above example is quoted merely to give the prospective nymph fisherman an insight into the complexities and fascination of the sport. If you are interested in more serious nymphing, you could do worse than read a little entomology first. An understanding of insects will enable the angler to read conditions at a glance. One thing is certain, for every 'fly' a trout takes from the surface, he takes many dozens more below the surface.

Finding the right depth to nymph is the first problem. This is accomplished by greasing the line up to, say, 4 ft from the end, depending upon the depth of the water, and then greasing more and more until the sub-surface length is only a few inches. The only reason for starting at the bottom and working up is that it is easier to grease a line than to de-grease it! On the other hand it could be argued that a line fished from the top downwards would disturb the pool inhabitants less than would one vice versa. A possible answer, then, is to fish three nymphs to the cast: if you do this, try a dry fly on the top. Do not hesitate to change depth – up or down – if unsuccessful and never thrash a pool to death without reaction – the first three casts in *any* pool under *any* circumstances are always the best chances you will have to catch a fish. From then on your chances get slimmer.

Most nymphing fish take the unfortunate insect just as it reaches a few inches from the surface when it has emerged from its 'shell'. This suggests that the trout has either followed the nymph up from the bottom or that it cannot see the nymph until it reaches a point above and becomes a visible silhouette. Whichever the reason, it is often more successful to 'bob' a nymph, especially in calm water, to impart a certain natural motion into its character. As the insect hits the water it sinks, whereas most insects, which fall from trees – natural foods – float very decisively; their weight simply doesn't overcome the surface tension of water. It is therefore unrealistic at this point. But then the current takes hold and at least *some* natural movement occurs. If the rod tip is gently bobbed up and down, allowing the insect to 'sink and draw', part of the motion should look like the last few inches of a normal nymph lift.

There are of course countless creepy crawlies, which fill the trout diet, creeping and crawling around the bottom of the river bed although these are very difficult to imitate. Always try to make your nymph look like some unfortunate insect, struggling for its life – that's a trout's delight. Never make a nymph 'swim' against the current, that is almost impossible.

Like any downstream wet fly fishing, nymphing is essentially a random search system and every possible corner of the pool should be investigated. Casting is down and across, as already described, and if you really want an absorbing and worth-while hobby – try adopting the science of chalk stream trout nymphing and everything that goes with it!

181

8   *Bait Fishing*

A bait, technically speaking, is the lure on the end of the line. But we refer here to heavy solids delivered on a nylon line and not to flies, which are delivered with a fly rod on a fly line. As already pointed out, there is no limit to the kind of bait you may wish to use, but there must be some point to start from. If you keep a fishing diary you will soon learn which baits are the most effective and on which rivers. The decision to use a bait and not a fly may not be yours. Many river authorities insist on fly only at all times. This may seem a little short sighted but is often more objective than it appears. There would be no point taking a fly rod to a heavily flooded, black torrent and although fishermen may long to toss a big fat minnow into the water, officials may not allow this because they wish to rest the water. The law of 'No Sunday Fishing' may be very annoying at times but it does rest the more popular beats and Monday mornings are usually good fishing times simply because of this rest. There is also a difficulty in deciding which is fly water and which is not. Many associations decide by the water level, although this is not always a complete answer.

The first thing to do when contemplating a beat is to read the regulations and ascertain if baits (and *which* baits) are allowed. If you think the water is not worth fishing with the fly and they do not allow spinning, either use large, false flies or don't buy the beat!

By now, if you have conscientiously read all the fishing data presented in this book, you should be able to 'read' a river well enough to decide whether to use a fly, spinner or bait. If in doubt, ask the locals, you will probably then be able to narrow down the possibles just by listening to their arguments (they will differ at all times) and, deciding which would be the more enjoyable method, even if you do not catch any fish, off you go the water. Always take a fly rod *and* a spinning rod; even if the weather doesn't change, you could have an accident and break a rod or reel.

183

NATURAL BAIT FISHING

Although a little messier and somewhat distasteful, natural baits often succeed where nothing else will. The absolute need for natural baits when fishing for large ferox and other carnivorous fish is discussed in the section dealing with lakes and ponds, where these creatures are usually found. We are concerned here more with the small, smelly, grubby little tins of 'live stock' which many of the old timers are so fond of and which most schoolboys have dangled in a water at some time or other. Natural baits are precisely what they say, they are natural. The one advantage such a bait has over any other is that it smells. Small fish, shrimp and prawn, worms etc., all are part of a fish's diet and will, on the right day, kill fish.

Worming

The man who tells you that worming is not for gentlemen is no fisherman. He has never wormed upstream in a crystal clear chalk stream, nor has he picked a half pound trout from a tiny Scottish burn in a hill of heather. Worming *can* be a sadly mis-performed business and is undoubtedly the reason for so much controversy among anglers. The chap who tosses a bundle of lobs into a deep pool and sits back waiting for a salmon to gorge them deep inside its throat, giving yards of line for just that purpose, is undoubtedly worthy of a fly man's contempt. For some strange reason the salmon will gorge a worm although the author has never come across a salmon with worms (or anything else for that matter) actually in the stomach. It is, however, necessary to give a salmon plenty of time to decide whether he wants the worm after the first initial probe.

Worming for salmon is usual in a spate, when the river is unfishable with the fly, or in low, clear water conditions. Worming for sea trout is a fast or coloured water method and worming for trout is just a matter of choice. Do not be put off by 'snobs' who insist that no gentleman would soil his hands with worms – let the wife hook them on for you!

Catching worms and their types has already been described in chapter 4. The decision to use them now depends upon weather conditions (and the rules of each river). Spate worm fishing is self explanatory; flies are out of the question on a big heavy river as the fish are unable to see them and, unlike normal conditions, are not moving around very much. They are hanging in side currents or skulking at the bottom of deep pools, waiting for the pressure to decrease.

The choice of tackle for worming varies. Some anglers prefer to use a spinning rod with a multiplier or a fixed spool reel, others prefer a fly rod with a Nottingham type reel. A fly rod is perfectly alright for light worming but no fly rod is made to cast anything but a line and a huge bundle of heavy lob worms is a very tricky weight to present on a long slender rod. The heavier the bait, the less likely is a fly rod practical and a spinning rod or even a bait caster should be contemplated. And, somehow, it seems rather a shame to hang a smelly worm on the end of a beautiful hand-made, cane fly rod – rather like towing a caravan with an Aston Martin. Using a fixed spool reel means a completely monofilament line and this may be perfectly all right in deep holes, but it is not always possible to keep even a well greased line on the surface in heavy water. A fly line is quite useful for worming and a sinking fly line, which can be greased to float at any height, is even better. Lead can be used, usually as two or three split shots a few feet from the worm. It is important to have cast just a pound or two less than the breaking strain of the line and connected by a swivel to prevent long line loss if a particularly hairy fish breaks you. The hook decision – single, double or triple – will depend on the worm size. For stream trout, a small worm on a single 12 or 14 hook; for large salmon, a bundle of huge lob worms on a single size No. 2 hook or the lob on a stuart (triple hook) tackle. It really is a matter of taste. Upstream fishing requires one worm, whatever you are fishing for.

A very useful worm accessory is a stout cloth bag, which is hung round the neck, at a suitable distance from the nose, and used to carry the supply of worms. Keep a handful of damp moss in the bag for the worms to wriggle into and change it frequently. Don't use mangled or damaged worms – except as ground bait – and throw out any sick or feeble looking specimens or they may pollute the rest. There is no need to close the bag for the worms will not come out into daylight.

The very best worm fishing is usually in the spring when the rivers are just growing strong enough to wash worms off the banksides as the water rises and loosens the dry earth. Worming then pauses, unless a spate occurs, until around August, when clear low water conditions

185

occur. It is not considered 'quite the thing' to worm when conditions are right for the fly. It is seldom worth worming on a very cold day and, if you intend upstream fishing in clear water, you really need at least a light breeze upstream to help conceal your presence. Heavy water worming returns in the Autumn.

Although techniques for worming vary slightly for the fish you are aiming at, the art of worming differs little in the long run. If you are working upstream you will need very light tackle, whereas spate worming permits a pretty heavy line. For heavy salmon fishing or even sea trout worming, you may need a spinning rod and if you are worming a really wide river a fixed spool reel is essential unless you are proficient with the multiplier.

Spate, or coloured water worming, is a downstream method and the style you use can be chosen from one of three basic ways, with many variations to choose from. The most popular method is trundling, which means casting across to the opposite bank and allowing the bait to bounce along the bottom like any real worm washed from the bank would be. The worm is left on the fisherman's bankside when the current brings it back for a few moments before reeling in and the process is then repeated a yard or so downstream. The pause at the end of each cast is very important for a fish will usually follow the current held worm until it stops against a rock or other obstacle. As the worm is attached to a line the current will cause a force which will lift it when taut and the worm will rise to the surface and be no longer 'fishing'. If the worm comes to a halt under water, leave it awhile before re-casting. Keep the worm bouncing and 'trundling' along the bottom of the river bed by adding just enough lead to keep it moving yet deep. The more lead used, the more likely are 'hang ups' on the bottom. It is invariably the lead which catches in a rock, hooks being particularly partial to under-water branches or tree roots, so only use lead if absolutely necessary. If you value your line and trace more than the lead, a piece of economical common sense, do not attach it too firmly to the line. In fact, some anglers prefer to tie the lead on by fine cotton although this is somewhat unnecessary. Spherical lead shot seldom catches up on a rock and can be pinched onto the line fairly tightly. If it isn't on tight it will tend to slide down to the hook but beware of tightening too much as the nylon becomes flattened under pressure and *always* throw away

186

the piece of nylon which has been used for lead-shot purposes – lead and all.

Keep in touch with the trundling worm and always leave a little line slack in the hand ready to give to an interested fish. Wait until the worm is actually picked up and the fish has turned with it in his mouth before slowly tightening the line. Once real resistance is felt, it is a matter of all or nothing and a sharp 'yank' should sink the barb past the horny mouth part so essential to find if a fish is to be landed. A 'strike' is best made by pulling the line through the rings when you feel the hard bite of a real pull. An upward, or sideways strike may take the hook away if your fish has the worm only in his mouth but never allow too much time for the bait to be taken and swallowed. There can be no feeling of satisfaction to pull out a fish with the hook embedded deep in its entrails, the agony it suffers must be severe indeed. And for those who insist a fish cannot feel pain we have only the deepest sympathy for their academic upbringing. A fish *does* feel pain. It has a perfectly good and very sensitive nervous system. Haven't you ever seen a fish jump when touched? Not having any vocal cords makes it pretty difficult for a fish to scream but they probably would at times when dragged through a pool by their insides. *Don't* let a fish gorge a worm this far and if you do happen to land a gravid hen or a kelt hooked, albeit accidentally, in this way, do not attempt to return it to the river, it must be rapped smartly on the head and disposed of there and then; it wouldn't have a chance in the water.

There is absolutely no need to fish fine in spate water unless you feel competent to do so and will not leave fish running around with lines dangling from their jaws. Remember, a thicker line needs less mending than a fine one and a worm is not 'fishing' if the line is dragging it across the current.

There is of course no reason why spate worming should not be performed upstream as well as downstream, although it is far more difficult. The current is usually too fast to allow the worm time to sink and if a large piece of lead is used it will be the very devil of a job to continually dislodge from 'hang ups'. A good method for the would be upstream fisherman is to use a large bundle of worms, hooked by their tails on a large single hook. Their weight will carry them down and yet allow a certain amount of give when obstacles present themselves.

Fig. 81 The mighty River Spey.
(courtesy of the Scottish Tourist Board)

Although upstream fishing is usually a wading method, it is seldom possible to wade safely under spate conditions and both up or downstream worming should be carried out from the bank unless a complete knowledge of the river geography *under spate conditions* is to hand. If you must wade in heavy water, for goodness sake use a stout wading pole and, even better, tie a lanyard to the bank; and never wade heavy waters, especially strange ones, alone.

Another spate worming method is 'trotting'. This is precisely what it says and involves one cast followed by walking along the bank with a slack line until the bait is arrested by some obstacle – or a fish. The bait is then cast across the river again and the process is repeated. This form of fishing requires a tree-less bank and a long pool. Pools do of course enlarge considerably during a spate and many false pools occur. When trotting fast waters be prepared for a sharp take, especially if salmon fishing, as fish in fast water must grab the worm as it passes or lose the chance. On the other hand, a fish in slow water can follow the worm, examine it, poke and push it around for a while and then pick it up to take home for an even closer inspection in its lie. When fishing the calmer waters, do not be surprised to pull out all manner of unexpected creatures, especially eels, (which should be promptly killed as they destroy the breeding redds and compete with the game fish for food). If the water is really slow there is no reason why the sink and draw method, used by flymen, should not be used for worms too. The worm is cast across the stream and allowed to turn into the current. If this is very slow, motion may be induced by nodding the rod tip up and down as the worm comes round. Always allow a fairly long pause before lifting the line out to allow for final inspection if in progress.

For faster, shallow waters a float is sometimes useful. A float will allow a bait to take the full extension of a dragged line without floating itself. In other words, instead of the worms rising to the surface as the line reaches maximum length and the current pulls them up, the float stops at the end and the worms can stay submerged for quite a long while after the line has risen. The float not only allows the fisherman to see where the bait is in turbulent stretches and when a really long line is out if 'long line trundling', it tends to act like an artificial 'otter'. We mean of course, the line de-snagging otter and not the fish-eating variety. Snagging is considerably reduced when float fishing in rapid shallows although most salmon and trout men will throw up their hands in horror at the idea of using a float under any circumstances and no Scottish tackle dealer would even consider stocking floats. The choice is yours.

The art of upstream worming in low, clear water is something only the most patient of all anglers will ever learn. It needs the delicacy of a Chinese water artist, the skill of an engraver, the cunning of a jackal, the tread of a fairy and the patience of Job. And that's just to start with! Added to these attributes should be a lifetime of fishing, a detailed knowledge of under-water topography, an eye like an eagle and an experience of casting good enough for you to pick the eye from a frog at twenty paces. If we haven't deterred you from upstream worming by now, you *may* have the makings of such a craftsman yet.

Not having these qualities himself, the author will not attempt to pass on any great words of wisdom. He can only offer one or two morsels gained from little river-side frolics (George Mortimer has only been fishing for sixty years and Tom Ravensdale is still wet behind the ears with a mere fifteen years fish research).

Upstream, low water worming is conducted with an upstream breeze helping to cover the glint of your rod top or the flash of your teeth as you crouch down like a midget whilst dresssed as a commando, peering through polaroids (the less experienced) from under a wide brimmed, floppy hat more precious than the missus – Whew! Each and every step is carefully planned and the tiny, leadless worm is propelled with astonishing accuracy a few feet beyond a 'stalked' fish to roll and bump along on invisibly thin nylon into the scent area of his nostrils. The first refusal is followed by a long pause and another upstream cast, 6 ins to the right, and perhaps another, 6 ins to the left. If he *still* doesn't take, either pack up and move on – he's seen you – or try a smaller worm.

As you slink along with scarcely a ripple from your dull matt waders, using every piece of water craft you have ever learned and hiding your shadow behind rocks, or coughing only when a bird screeches, you will have the tautness and expectancy so vital to a fisherman's success. You are aware and ready at any moment for a take and this is how fish are caught.

As already explained, the tackle is fine – it has to be. The hooks, unlike spate worm fishing, should not be eyed. They should be plain, round bend hooks lashed to a thin nylon leader. This allows the small worm to be threaded over the bar and passed along the shank onto the nylon. All of the hook must be concealed and no lead should appear. A swivel, if really wanted, can be introduced about 2 ft up the line to act as a weight if the water is moving fast. The best of upstream worming is that the worm can be tossed into corners and cracks no fly or spinner could ever reach in a *fishable way*. The toby may well reach a hidden spot but it will not start actually fishing until the current picks it up and commences to spin it. The upstream worm fishes from the start.

See illustration on
page 174

27 Fred Farringdon spins
a deep pool in Banff-
shire, Scotland; a par-
ticularly beautiful spot
near Tomintoul.

28 A lively rainbow trout:
when boating, keep your
play at the 'blunt' end.

29 Dr. Seymour Chissick of King's College, London, using a Hardy Wye on a tricky sea trout stretch of the River Avon, Scotland.

A long rod is needed for these conditions. The line is cast directly upstream where possible and the worm is permitted to rattle and roll along the bottom towards, but slightly to one side of (to prevent the line from touching the fish), the suspected lie. The worm *must* touch the bottom as it rolls and if the line catches on the bottom, do not lash about with the rod, wade to the spot and dislodge the hook, making sure the point is still needle sharp before re-casting. Change worms frequently and only use very small 'plop-proof' ones. Keep the loose line under control with one hand and *keep in touch with the worm*. A little slack always in hand as the current returns your line is very useful when a fish takes. As the fish will be facing the opposite direction (theoretically) when he takes, an immediate strike is in order if you are sure he really *has* taken. The strike is best executed by a sharp hand tug on the line, which is already held in one hand ready to 'give' or 'take'.

Upstream, clear water worming can be a jolly fine pastime, but it can give you a pretty stiff back the next day too. If a fly man ever sneers at your worming intentions again – pull out this book and show him the last few pages, it may change his tune.

Prawning

Although there is no such word in the English dictionary, there is no other to describe what a fisherman means by 'prawning' so let's proclaim it a word and be done with it! After all, we refer to a ghillie when we mean gillie, so why not? Prawning is rather like worming in that many of the fishing 'aristocrats' refuse to accept it as a method of catching fish. This is just nonsense for, like worming, prawning can be a very precise business when conditions are difficult.

Prawns are really a salmon bait although many a fine sea trout has been banked by a small one and very few brown trout will refuse a firm piece of white prawn meat on a size 12 hook in the summer. Unfortunately there are two drawbacks to prawning; it may prove fatal to toss a prawn into a salmon pool and it is very difficult to hook a fish on a prawn tackle. More fish have been lost to the prawn than any other form of bait, except perhaps the worm. The fish *always* 'kills' his sharp edged prawn first, he then takes it back to his lie and *only then* is the bait firmly in his mouth.

But, to return to the method; as already explained, prawn fishing should only be considered when all else has failed. When you are quite sure that you have no chance of catching a fish on any other lure and that you will lose nothing by scaring the fish out of the pool, by all means try the prawn. But, a word of warning, make sure your permit allows prawning and do not consider it as a last resort if other anglers are fishing the same beat that day – give *them* a chance.

Prawns come in all shapes, sizes and colors. They range from little, $1\frac{1}{2}$ in. pale pink jobs, to a fine, ruddy, 6 ins. A happy medium would be a nice, red 2 in. female, preferably carrying berry, (a bundle of roe between the rear legs). If you have no success with one particular prawn, do not hesitate to try a different size – smaller if possible.

The prawn should be mounted, as described earlier, on a special prawn tackle, but a good darning needle with a treble at one end and a swivel bound to the other will do the job quite well. The prawn must be firmly bound to the tackle with wire and should be pulled through the water by the *tail*! With the needle mount, lead may be bound around the centre and rolled along the length. This ensures a fairly level swimming bait and not a nose down or unnaturally 'posed' prawn. If a swivel is introduced to the trace – and it must be if a vaned (winged) tackle is used – place it 2 ft from the prawn. The prawn may be fished with the sink and draw or plug basis when water conditions suggest a slow moving bait – such as cold or coloured water. It may be spun when the opposite is the case.

Prawning is really a warm weather, low water method (when all else has failed) and is seldom very successful much before June. It may be fished when water is normal but never when it is very cold.

The prawn must be very fresh and preferably tough and stringy. A soft prawn will not last five minutes in fast water with plenty of rocks for it to bash into as it bounces downstream. If it hasn't been wired very tightly, it will get easily damaged and will soon look a very raggy mess once the current has pulled it for a while.

The prawn is really too heavy for the fly rod but there is no real bar against using one as long as the cast is not too vigorously executed. Better still, use a stout spinning rod with a fixed spool reel – it's made for the job.

Whether you put a 'bent' prawn on and pull it through the water in a bobbing fashion – sink and draw-wise, or

194

Fig. 82 Float fishing for trout.

use a straight, slim, spinning job fitted to an archer tackle, you must never rush a prawn. The prawn should be slowly fished. It may be trundled in the same way as a worm (called roving when applied to a prawn) or even trotted downstream. Like the worm, a prawn is taken very slowly and must be 'fed' to the fish slowly. Try to overcome an irresistable desire to strike when the salmon or trout takes, and wait for the fish to turn before pulling the line through the rings in the same manner as a worm strike. Keep your rod high at all times or the prawn will 'swim' unnaturally and always keep a little line loose in the hand ready to give or snatch as conditions warrant. Lastly, if the spinning prawn is not accepted, cut off the vanes and use the sink and draw method, or puncture holes in the shell of the bait, it will make the scent stronger.

Shrimps are often acceptable when prawns are not and, although some experts believe a fish can differentiate between prawn and a shrimp, the author feels this to be unlikely. The main evident difference is one of size and we all know how vital bait size is. After all, a prawn is a pretty big bait isn't it? Another variation is that brown shrimps may be obtained instead of pink ones and the comparatively successful employment of brown shrimp over the pink variety suggests that they blend in with natural surroundings a little better than the rather un-

195

natural pink ones do. British coastal shrimps are of course transparent when alive but who knows what colours radiate from Atlantic shrimp, which are feeding on some-times irrisdescent plankton, under the polar pack ice? One fact is certain – brown shrimp fish better!

The shrimp is a more 'believable' bait than a prawn when low water conditions arise. The shrimp is more of an upstream bait at this time and should be cast to a fish and not used as a searching bait like the prawn. When the air temperature exceeds that of the water by several degrees the shrimp comes into its own.

Set the shrimp on a single hook; if upstream fishing use size 4 or 5. A double fly hook hides well in among the legs and even gives a more natural look to the bait if cunningly placed. The extra weight of a double hook also helps the shrimp to sink. It should be fished worm like, in a free swimming, current speed manner and must touch the bottom as it free-wheels back to the angler's bank.

Needless to say, the shrimp needs a little more experi-ence to fish in this manner and the easier methods, identical to worm fishing practice, are best adopted by the beginner until he has more experience.

Minnows

Minnows (and sprats) are essentially early spring baits for use in heavy water and cold weather. Although they were once very popular, only the older, more experienced fishermen bother with them any more and if a newcomer to the sport does use a minnow it will probably be a preserved one at that. Manufactured spinners are so much cleaner and easier to use, it is not really so surprising, but a natural bait will often score when an artificial one will not – the real thing *smells*!

Preserved minnows and sprats come in a variety of colours, the most popular of which are silver or gold. If you wish to catch your own (see chapter 4) you will be assured of the freshness and a fresh bait is ten times better than a preserved one. If it is the colours you want, why not dye your own? The silver is obtained by keeping the bait in sand or earth whereas the gold can be gotten by an overnight soaking in two parts per thousand acriflavine solution.

Strangely, natural baits may be up to twice as big as imitation baits for the same conditions. A rough starting point for natural baits can be seen in fig. 83.

196

Fig. 83. Natural bait sizes

Temp. °C	River height	Current speed	Water colour	Bait length ex. hook
2	normal	normal	normal	6 ins
2	low	normal	normal	5 ins
2	high	normal	normal	5 ins
2	normal	slow	normal	4 ins
2	normal	fast	normal	5 ins
2	normal	normal	clear	$4\frac{1}{2}$ ins
2	normal	normal	cloudy	5 ins
2	normal	normal	normal	$4\frac{1}{2}$ ins
5	normal	normal	normal	4 ins
10	normal	normal	normal	3 ins
15	normal	normal	normal	$2\frac{1}{2}$ ins
20	normal	normal	normal	2 ins

Sea trout are partial to the odd minnow and a take is usually quite a ferocious business offering plenty of sport. They take this sort of bait very fast, quite unlike the usual 'sniff and probe' dawdle of the salmon. Brown trout and rainbows will also take a minnow, but usually only the bigger fish, which are found in lakes.

As already explained, the head should be snipped off a bait minnow, the bait is mounted on a treble hooked tackle by a leaded needle and the skin should be punctured to let out the smell. If the bait is unsuccessful, try snipping a chunk off and shortening the body. Fish it at all depths and quite slowly. A sink and draw method is quite acceptable and the trick of fixing the fish onto a vaned tackle at an angle to make it wobble through the water, helps to send out very strong vibrations and attract predators that way, but draw a wobbler bait even more slowly.

Sand Eels

These tough, wiry little baits are described in chapter 4. Their method of fishing is explained in chapter 9. Sand eels are seldom used outside estuary waters. They are mainly for sea trout although an occasional salmon may tackle one and, once taken, the sand eel usually hangs onto its fish. The single hook, attached to the mouth of the sand eel, isn't noticed by the taking fish until it is well inside the mouth – provided the fisherman has given a little line on the first knocking.

Elvers fall into the same category as sand eels and should be fished the same way.

197

Grubs and Maggots

These small baits are used almost exclusively for trout and especially on lakes or small streams. They will occasionally attract a sea trout but very rarely will a salmon look at such a tiny lure. A single hook as small as No. 14, or even 16, is best and a few lead shots will be needed to take the bait down. A float is sometimes used and, on the deeper pools, a very careful assessment of the water depth is necessary. Fish the maggot a few inches from the bottom and use plenty of ground bait. A handful of maggots thrown over the spot you are interested in ten minutes before fishing will enhance the chances of catching a fish or two. Ensure ground baiting is legal though.

There are many kinds of maggot or grub. There are the offspring of blue bottles, blow flies and so forth. The caddies fly larvae is sometimes successful and even a caterpillar will be taken. Creeper fishing (Stone fly larvae) is a very exacting sport and much fun can be had with a bottle full of daddy-long-legs and a fine trout lake. The creeper is fixed to a special double hook creeper tackle and fished downstream in a river. It can be a very successful method of trout banking in a low water if you have the patience.

Moths, dragon flies, daddy-long-legs and black beetles – all will interest the ever hungry brown or rainbow trout and several can be used at once on various droppers if a fly line is used. Do not be afraid to experiment. If you see a small frog in the grass, whip him onto a hook (after rapping him on the head first) and chuck him in – you never know with fish!

ARTIFICIAL BAITS

The array of artificial lures available to the fisherman would surely dazzle even the most advanced case of gimmick collector. It is not so much the sheer quantity of choice, more a case of which ones *actually* work and which do not. In actual fact, almost any lure will work provided it is the correct size so don't collect a huge array of plastic and cork around you, make a fair selection of sizes and colours and leave the rest to an ability to fish. Being able to use a lure is far more important than the reality of the lure itself.

Although we are constantly referring to 'artificial' bait fishing and although plug fishing is an art in its own right, we really mean *spinning*. Most artificial baits are either spun or at least offered on a spinning rod.

One thing to keep in mind before commencing to spin is that a few heavy casts into a pool will probably ruin the water for fly fishing, so don't use the spinning method unless you are sure the fly is not a plausible bait. You should also be prepared to stop fishing if a fly man arrives on the scene. He has right of way over a bait or spinning fisherman – provided he has a permit.

Spinning is really a big or coloured water method of catching salmon or trout. The *big* trout are a different story however for they are usually to be found only at the bottom of deep lakes and will seldom come up for a fly. These big boys are almost certainly purely piscivorous (live on fish) and are found either as cannibals, with a nice brownish sheen to their coats, or as kelt type monsters with huge heads filled with teeth and jet black flanks. Needless to say, these boys are quite inedible and serve only to deplete the stocks of normal fish in the same area. Perhaps the best of the big trout are the huge, healthy looking, silver sided ferox. Whether you seek trout for culinary or sporting purposes, the really big ones will only respond to really big baits.

Although spinning is considered a spate or coloured water method, we shall deal with all conditions as there is always a time when the fly just won't work; there isn't always a reason – they just will not take and that is that!

Spinning lures have already been described in some detail so we will concentrate here on their use only. If you separate heavy and low water spinning into their individual classes you should really separate the equipment too. For big waters, in search of salmon or large sea trout, a heavyish cane rod, such as the L.R.H.2 (now, sadly, no longer manufactured) with an Ambassadeur 6000 multiplying reel, is an excellent outfit. A twelve or fifteen pound breaking strain line, preferably braided nylon to lessen the overrun risk, is advisable. Attach to this a stout swivel and join on a very slightly weaker nylon monofilament trace to finish the job. Always select a swivel of suitable strength and yet of sensible proportions. For summer spinning, or even heavy water trouting, you would be better off with a lighter, one handed, glass rod and a fixed spool reel. Ten pound monofilament is a fair line weight for salmon and six pounds would be an ample sea or brown trout spinning line. If you intend upstream spinning

you should reduce your line to 5 or even 4 pound breaking strain for trout and 8 to 9 pound for salmon. With all reels it is important to keep the spool correctly filled, but with a fixed spool reel it is much more critical. If you do not fill it enough, the line will not slip off easily as it must overcome the deep lip of the spool. If it is over-filled, the loops of line will slip off when they are not meant to and a tangle will result, especially if thick nylon is used. The best argument for a fixed spool reel is that you may carry spare spools filled with different line thicknesses. Changing from one line to another is, thus, a two minute job.

Whatever your choice of spinner, spoon, devon or toby,

an anti-kink vane is needed. If you use a multiplying reel it is not quite so important, but with a fixed spool reel it is essential, unless you prefer to alternate between the left and right handed spinning lures. Although we have already described the lures, it is worth re-capping on bait weights. Of course, each water will demand different circumstances but it is pretty obvious that metal lures will swim lower and cast easier than wooden ones. If you wish to use a special model and only have it in wood or quill, which is not heavy enough, use a piece of lead. In preference to adding it to the line directly, try to twist it around the wire which passes through the centre of the devon; if it must go on the line, place it *above* the swivel, this will assist the spinning motion and deter line twist. If you are fishing particularly coloured or heavy water, try using a reflex devon. This is simply a flat sided model fish, which disturbs the water waves much more than a normal one will. The shape of a lure will, of course, determine the waves it transmits, but fast water tends to swamp this effect. The colour of your spinner will depend on weather as well as river conditions as already explained, but for some strange reason the 'cold' colours, such as silver, black and blue, seem to work better in the spring, whereas the warmer colours, such as gold, yellow and brown, are quite good in the autumn. Grilse are particularly partial to the intermittent striped lures which flash alternate colours. Blue and silver seem a good combination under most circumstances. Red seems to frighten some fish but perhaps this is because it suggests blood – and subsequently a dangerous enemy in the neighbourhood. On the other hand, pike are notorious for liking red tipped baits! Red flies do not seem to have the same adverse effect as red spinners.

In general, and at the risk of disagreement, it is usually easier to spin for fish than by any other method so far mentioned. This does not mean that all spinning is easy; on the contrary, there are forms of spinning which require great experience and river sense, but the basic principle of spinning is simplicity itself. The normal cast is made across and slightly downstream. If the water is fast there is no need to reel in to make the bait spin. If you cast slightly upstream though, keep an otter nearby for you will almost certainly become snagged on a rock if you do. It is perfectly alright to cast upstream *if you mean to* and can wind in quick enough; indeed, the art of upstream spinning is to retrieve at a speed just slow enough to interest fish but fast enough to prevent hang ups. When spinning slower pools you can, of course, cast in any direction; you may even be able to impart a little life into the line by sinking and drawing, or even changing the direction of your lure. This is done by casting well to one side and retrieving very slowly. Then the rod is taken over to the other side, which changes the direction of pull on the line. Another switch of direction before reeling in gives yet more evidence to a suspicious follower that the lure is not attached to a sloppy hatted rotter on the bank.

When fishing quiet, deep waters with plenty of space for such manoeuvres, do not make the mistake of allowing too long a line to run out, especially if seeking the fast taking sea trout. Some monofilament nylon stretches a great deal and the more line you have out, the less effective will a strike be. The elasticity of your line could well give the fish that split second it needs to prevent the barb from sinking home.

Sea trout are not really likely to 'take' in quiet waters during the day but there is always the possibility. In fast water he usually comes in with a bit of a wallop and whatever water you fish, if you are seeking sea trout, draw the spinner in at a fairly rapid rate. Do not give a sea trout time to study the bait. Salmon on the other hand, do not always care to leave their lie and it is necessary to draw the lure right past their noses to encourage movement.

If you are downstream spinning in heavy or coloured water it is always better to cast into shallow water at the commencement and 'fish' the lure into the deeper section. As the current picks up the bait and puts a spin on it, you will not need to wind in. As the bait comes to your bank and slows down, commence the retrieve, but do so slowly for this is often when the fish will take. If you get stuck on the bottom, walk past your lure with a loose line and try to release it from the opposite direction. If it still clings on, make use of the elasticity we mentioned by pulling hard on the line and then suddenly releasing it with lots of loose line. This often acts like a bowstring and the backward jerk should lift the hook away. As a final attempt to release your favourite lure you may try out an otter, as described in chapter 3 (and usually more valuable than the lure). Of course, as a really last resort, one would just have to send the wife in after it.

In heavy spring or autumn water, always fish the

202

spinner deep and slow; as long as the bait moves, however slowly, it will be fishing. If the water is very cold, the fish will hug the bottom and only move when really stirred. The take may be sluggish too – almost like being hung up on the bottom and in really deep water it is not always easy to bring a sulking fish to the surface. If a hooked fish, a heavy salmon for example, decides to bed down at the bottom of a hole, come out of the water at once and go to the spot where he is lying. A few stones tossed onto his nose may move him, but if he is really stubborn, slip a ring of lead round the line and let it slide down to give him a sharp rap on the snout – that should do it.

As for the actual choice of a spinning bait, this depends very much on the water, but as a general guide, go for a multi coloured bait in coloured water and, if it is really black, use a toby. The stronger the water, the *heavier* the bait but not necessarily the *bigger* though. If the spinner does not touch the bottom every few moments it is not heavy enough. This does not refer to upstream casting in which it is fatal to allow the spinner to touch the bottom. Incidentally the upstream method, with a fast retrieve and a deep swim, is best suited to sea trout.

For low water work the fixed spool reel on a light, hollow fibre-glass rod, with a very light line, is the order of the day. The lure must be very tiny and the swivel a good two thirds of the rod length from the hook. On the subject of hooks, it is often better to use a single hook with these tiny baits; say up to 1 in., as a treble makes a bit of a splash in gin clear water. If you go much smaller you may as well use a fly rod and spin with that – it has been done before.

One of the points which makes upstream, low water spinning so tricky is that an interested fish usually turns to follow the lure as it sweeps past in order to nip it by the tail. When this happens the fish is facing you and has a splendid view of the line, the rod and of course their owner. The answer is to fish like a redskin, as explained in the upstream worm fishing section – it's great fun.

I end this chapter as I began, with the advice all anglers love to give. If you fancy a bait – chuck it in. Fish have the very devil of a job feeding themselves so try it – you will not catch a fish unless your line is in the water.

"A wise old owl lived in an oak. The more he saw the less he spoke. The less he spoke the more he heard. Anglers should copy that old bird."

9 *Lake and Boat Fishing*

Fishing a river or stream requires a knowledge of the water surface, an understanding of the bankside and a reasonable ability to make a shrewd guess at the sub-surface situation. It requires an ability to read weather conditions and a great deal of water craft. All these qualities need not necessarily belong to the actual person who tosses the bait in though. The answer is of course that it boils down to a good gillie to set you off on the right track. Well, the same applies to boat fishing, lakeside fishing and estuary fishing. The only difference is that the gillie is now called a boatman – first catch your boatman! Without a good boatman your fishing days may well be fruitless, but there is no reason why you should not try your hand at lake or estuary fishing from the bank – most fish lie well in by the bank and only the very big boys (so we are told) are silly enough to venture out into the middle of a big lake. If you have manged to lay hands on a good boatman, you may lay down this book and do what he says because, like the gillie, the boatman usually knows his water like a racing driver knows his circuit and once a water is known that well, no stranger can improve on it.

ESTUARY FISHING

Estuary fishing is usually a sea-trouting business but many a fine salmon, glistening silver and fresh from the sea, has fallen to the streamer of a surprised trouting man. Of course many other, even stranger, things happen near the sea. Eels and dabs, gobies and crabs, almost anything which is hungry (in the sea?) may fasten its beady eyes onto a seductive lure pulled past its proboscis by an invisible line, so take a hefty priest with you when tasting the salt air, you may need it.

Never, ever, go out in a boat alone on a strange tidal water. If you cannot find a boatman, fish from the bank, it's really not worth the risk and you will never find the fish channels alone.

Boating

Before going any further it is perhaps worth a few moments to consider some of the aspects of boating which may effect your fishing. Boatmanship is one thing, but fishing from a boat does require a little of the boatman's knowledge and the technique of fishing from a boat requires an understanding of what the boatman is doing, apart from rowing or handling the motor. As a boatman will be needed when lake fishing as well as tidal fishing, the following is a very general list of issues appropriate to both cases.

First and foremost is safety – wear a life jacket in deep water and never go into sea water without one whatever the circumstances. Tie the outboard on with a lanyard and stow all other gear safely under the gunwales. And remember, not many boats have a dry bottom so keep your gear high up and over the footboards. On the subject of outboard motors, carry a few spare sparking plugs and a couple of spanners and, needless to say, a can of petrol, correctly oiled and mixed of course; the mixture details are usually on the filler cap. When conducting minor repairs, do so *in* the boat and avoid losing gear in the water. Always wash your hands very thoroughly after working or you may muck up your fishing tackle.

Clothing should be extra sombre as there are no trees and bushes to hide behind in broad waters, in fact it is quite the contrary, the fisherman stands out like a sore thumb when his silhouette breaks the skyline. Wellingtons or other soft bottomed shoes are best and the same care should be taken on a boat as when upstream, low water fishing. Oars should be handled with the greatest of care. One piece of equipment worth taking aboard is an anchor or, better still, a sea anchor, to slow down the boat drift.

Keep well clear of bank fishermen and allow plenty of room for other boat anglers who may have a very long line out.

Lastly, in England and Wales at least, there is a public right of fishing up to the high water mark in estuaries but this is provided you have the land-owner's permission to use his bank. Boat fishing is the answer when you do not have this.

The Sea Trout

To return to the art of estuary fishing, we can expect to attract mainly sea trout as already explained. These fish are best sought in June and July although a few will be around from as early as April. August and September are rarely good sea trout months and October to April are hopeless for estuary fishing. An exception is that September estuary sea-trout fishing in the Shetlands is reputed to be the best in Scotland although no first hand experience of this can be admitted. The fish tend to enter the river on a rising tide, usually high, but will not do so if the sea is rough.

An extraordinary coincidence (or is it a wise old mother nature again) occurs in the spring and this certainly accounts for the lower post-breeding death rate figures for trout compared to salmon. The story really begins thousands of miles away in the Sargasso sea, where the common eel is born. Some strange force, similar to that which grips the migrating salmon and sea trout, send the tiny eels, or elvers as they are now called, across the high seas and up into the fresh water breeding grounds of our quarry. By some strange coincidence, the elvers enter the rivers just as the spent sea trout kelts arrive at the estuary. Needless to say, they provide an excellent opportunity for the kelts to feed and regain their strength. As the spring run of sea trout on its way upstream occurs at this time too, the unfortunate eel fry suffer great losses. It also offers the angler a slight problem in recognising kelts for they are almost as fat and juicy looking as the inbound fish. One method is to press a thumb into the soft belly and bring it up to the throat slowly. If a mass of elvers appear in the mouth of the fish it is probably a kelt – loaded to capacity.

The best time to fish is between half ebb and half flow with a pause at full tide. Most locals know the tide times and flood tides are often better fish movement periods as the usual obstacles become submerged at these times. All coastal newspapers give tide tables each week and remember, there are always two tides a day – one every twelve hours. Two hours either side of high tide is, as explained, the best running times but if the water is low the fish will not be able to get past the first sea pool or so and they will be forced to go in and out with the tide until high water arrives. This is a good time to catch sea trout for they gather in large shoals. You may even follow them out to sea as the tide recedes for they will not go far from the coast and, having been thwarted in their attempt to run up river their thoughts turn to food – especially if elvers are around.

When the river is high, the fish usually run straight up without a pause. It seems that the transition period from salt to fresh water is rather like the coy swimmer who wades into cold water with such a lot of finicky fuss after wetting the tip of his toe a dozen times. He would have no trouble if he closed his eyes and jumped in. Sea trout tend to get to the edge (a brackish transition point where the incoming tidal water meets fresh, usually marked by the two different coloured waters) and hang around before making a dash into the enticing yet breath-taking fresh water. For this reason (another theory) they tend to congregate near this water die-line and the best catches come from the first three pools from the sea. They follow pretty regular channels once in the river and only deviate when in really wide waters.

Occasionally one may come across brackish water brown trout, they tend to move in and out with the tide and are often taken for Finnock (sea trout grilse). Although they are difficult to tell apart from sea trout, there *are* differences (see chapter 1). They are probably living on elvers.

Fishing tackle for estuary work need not differ from normal tackle although lures are a little different. You need to take much more care of tackle used in salt water. Rods should be washed and oiled or waxed: hooks, lines and lures must be soaked, rinsed and dried: flies should be thoroughly washed by hand and the hooks oiled (very lightly – or the fly won't sink again). The reel should be totally immersed in water and put under a running tap. All other items which have been exposed, even to salt air, should be tended as suits their make-up.

Flies are seldom any use when mist or sea fog is around but sea trout are far less timid when first entering the river – they haven't yet passed through the gauntlet of rods and nets! Three flies may be used in open water with little fear of snagging but beware of the hooked fish running under the boat because a hook will stay put if it touches wood. Always fish from the blunt end of a boat to avoid this if you can. If a hooked fish does run at the boat, which is most unlikely unless you are between him and the open sea, stamp on the floor boards or ask the boatman (he

208

should do it automatically) to splash an oar. The oars, incidentally, should be pulled in the moment a fish takes.

In daylight, use size 10 or 12, double hooks but when dusk arrives, the larger 'flies' such as terrors or demons may be used. Terrors and demons are very long pennell (double hook) tackles with bright feathers or floss, simulating worms or eels, they are not true flies. Daylight line should be around the 5 to 6 pound mark increasing to 7 or even 8 pounds at night. If heavy spinning is envisaged, a multiplier is recommended. Terrors may be as long as 3 ins, depending upon temperature and water size but if really small lures are used, a sink and draw method is best. Prawn and sand eels will attract sea trout as will worm – fished from the bank on a pennell tackle – but the elver must surely beat all other forms of natural bait. Elvers can be found under rocks and in clumps of seaweed left in beach pools as the tide recedes. They are the very devil to catch and you will need a very fine mesh net and quick arm to fill a jar. Although most sea trout men use the elver alive, it seems rather cruel to do so and no really big advantage is gained by making the poor thing suffer so badly just for pleasure. Of course, the same may be said for worms and the same is probably true – the choice is yours.

Blue-silver demons are excellent attractions on the right day and spoons or tobies have an impressive record too, but do not use large baits unless the smaller ones fail. A one inch gold or silver mepps spoon or a $1\frac{1}{2}$ inch toby is usually quite big enough. If there is fog or mist about, fishing is usually bad but you may at least try a bait – flies are hopeless under these conditions and boating is downright dangerous.

Strangely, a downstream wind is better for fishing during the daytime but a dead still night often results in filled baskets (a salmon basket is called a bass). Cast upstream and allow the line to return to the side when bank fishing, then move a yard upstream and repeat. This is the old principle of pool searching and although it applies here, a certain amount of imagination is helpful. Fish every inch of a strange pool and fish the rough part even more thoroughly at all levels. In brackish water, keep the lure moving fairly rapidly as sea trout like a lively lure and a fast moving bait prevents a really close inspection. There is plenty of competition for food in a shoal of fish and the real caution so typical of a river sought sea trout does not show at this stage. This light-headedness soon wears off, so you will do well to take the chance while you may.

One danger which so often causes the downfall of a river angler under estuary conditions is the realisation – or non-realisation – of the delicate nature of the sea trout mouth as it leaves the sea. It is all very well being aware of it as you first begin to fish, but the excitement of a take and the battle (the sea trout is a really savage fighter when this fresh) may produce an under-estimated rod arm strength as the adrenalin flows. The solution is to fish a pound or two less than you do in a normal river. The knowledge of a light line is the first thing to sting the mind of an angler when he has a take and it is a constant worry throughout the play, so make use of this psychological effect and avoid tearing hooks from too tender mouths when near the sea.

If there is a scarcity of fish and you are boating, you will need to locate the actual fish runs. There are usually several in a wide estuary and you must pick the best. although this is largely a matter of luck or skill on the part of the boatman, you may like to improve your chances of finding the stream by purchasing an estuary map from the local post office. Most ports and fishing towns sell maps (called charts for some reason when dealing with water) and deep, submarine channels are well marked and will show a very definite course most likely to be adopted by the moving fish. Sadly, the estuary netsmen will know every single fish lane in the area and if you don't mind a word or two with these people, you will probably learn a great deal; after all, they are only doing their jobs. If fish are plentiful, it is hardly necessary to seek channels for they will be all over the place and in no particular direction, seeking food (we hope) and the boat may be allowed to drift where it will. The best spots are patches of dark water, which suggest seaweed, rocks or water depth. In a full tide you may even wish to use a float and let the line drift over long distances. A full tide is, however, rarely a good fishing time and a spate will prevent the fish from settling or even deviating from the path upstream.

After high tide, fishing usually gets better and spinning comes into its own, especially if you spin from the bank. Nod the bait in a sink and draw method as you would in a deep pool when confronted with fog or mist. If you can see fish rising, discard the spinning rod and use a fly. If the

210

rise is only the backs of fishes and not their mouths, pop a lead shot or two on the line and, if it is springtime, put plenty on as the fish usually lie deep as they seek underwater crevices to pass through.

Harling

Harling is so often confused with trolling, it needs a little clarification. Trolling will be dealt with in the lake fishing section. Harling is described forthwith. Some fishermen 'harl' with two rods at once, others fish a normal rod and leave another set up on the rear of the boat 'harling'. Yet others simply 'harl' with the one rod and consider this a good day's sport. It may well be, but most people would get a little bored with this after a while. To 'harl' properly, a good boatman is essential. Whatever lure you use, and a terror is probably best, cast a line of 20 or 30 yds over the stern of the boat. If you use two rods, fish them at different distances from the boat and at different depths. Once the lure has drifted over a likely spot, the sea anchor or even bottom anchor is used to keep the boat steady. Even better, the boatman should keep the boat still. If no success is forthcoming, move downstream to another possible spot, letting the lines fish as you go. The object is to sink a deep line and search the bottom with a trailing (or trolling) exercise in between. If a fish is hooked, the boatman should pull in any extra line at full speed and boat his oars.

A final method (for this book at least – there are countless other methods) of fishing an estuary is ledgering. This is done from the bank and involves fresh baits. A large piece of lead is attached to the line and the bait is thrown well out. The line is then left until a fish takes the bait lying on the river or sea bed. It is a rather uninteresting form of fishing but may serve as a second line provided you can fish another rod at a suitable distance from it and have a pal to pull it in if you get a take on the 'real' rod.

There is probably less known about estuary fishing than any other form of angling but this should not deter you from having a go. On the contrary, it offers the chance of much experimenting and may produce many a surprise.

Lakes, Lochs and Loughs

Perhaps we should include reservoirs here, but as this is simply a man-made lake, we will consider it as such. The three titles above refer to the English, Scottish and Irish spellings of the same water bowls respectively. All are

sheets of water within land to the angler although strictly
speaking, a loch is 'an arm of the sea' and so is a 'lough'.
To avoid confusion, we will refer to all three as lakes or
inland water pools and leave it at that, with no offence
meant to anyone. However, it will be realised that rainbow
trout are not usually found in lakes which *do* connect with
the sea; neither are salmon or sea trout found in lakes
which *do not* connect with the sea.

Fairly large lakes have usually been well mapped and it
is not difficult to get hold of lake charts. The local angling
association will be able to help here, if not, try the
local inland water board. If all else fails you must rely on
local knowledge and this is usually the best thing you can
do anyway.

Reservoirs, or man-made lakes, are usually quite good
trouting grounds as the bottom foods have not been
trapped deep in the mud yet, but any water deeper than
fifty feet is hopeless in the middle. Fish are usually found
between 5 and 25 ft down, dependant upon the sun and
temperature. This may be best understood if the 'food
chain' of fishes is described. Sunlight is essential for the
growth of algae (a simple green or red plant) and ray
penetration to any depth under the water surface will
depend on light intensity. Feeding on algae are millions of
minute fresh water plankton (tiny aquatic animals). Feeding on these in turn are the tiddlers or fish fry plus of

212

course numerous under-water insects. The fish we seek feed on both the insects and the tiddlers and so they will generally be found in the same place as one or the other. In fact, in ideal circumstances, all should be in the same area together and this is very often true. In this case one could say that as the sun is unable to penetrate the depths at the centre of a big deep lake there will be no fish there and this would be very often true – most of the aquatic life is to be found around the banks or in island shallows.

The movement of smaller food in the chain link usually means the movement of all others higher up on the scale and if the sunshine is exceedingly bright, photo-sensitive creatures will seek shade – or depth – and their pursuers will have to go down with them. On the other hand, the sun may heat the water up so much the oxygen content of the water is drastically reduced and the fish are forced to move to the shallows or stream entries into the lake. When the temperature is much below 10°C, the fish are subjected to a condition of semi-hibernation as their metabolism rate slows and they will lie listlessly on the bottom. They may also go down below the heat band at a certain level when the top water temperature exceeds 15°C. Come summer, the weed beds will have established themselves quite well and the food chain will occur around weedy areas. Weed gives off oxygen during daylight and provides yet another reason for fish to seek it apart from the obvious hiding places to be found there. Conversely, an over-bright sun on a very weedy area may cause an excessive stimulation of oxygen by the plants resulting in the same effect. Fish can no more stand an excess of oxygen than they can a shortage. And so we see how apparently mundane matters affect the movement of fish. The influence of tiny microscopic life and the condition of the sun, the speed of the wind and the shelter afforded by the surrounding landscape – all go to make the lake anglers job very difficult and a very interesting one indeed.

The best time to fish a lake is very often in the spring (one never says anything more definite than 'probably' or 'usually' or 'very often' where fishing is concerned for there is a 'no' to every 'yes' and a 'right' for every 'wrong' at all times). If the weather is still chilly they will lie very deep and will not stir from their beds much before noon. In April and May it is usually best to nymph from the bank as long as you can manage a fairly long cast. Once the air temperature rises you may bring out the May fly

Fig. 86 Norwegian waters demand heavy tackle and a strong arm.

Fig. 87 A nice brown trout taken on Abu gear in a quiet lake.

and in summer the wet fly is unbeatable. By September the cold chills begin to set in at night and you must revert to the big, deep swimming flies again and it is at this time that the really big fish begin to come in-shore.

It is not easy to find fish lies in a strange lake. One can always make a few educated guesses though; streams trickling into a lake will obviously bring plenty of food and there will always be a few fish hanging around the mouths of such waterways, especially if the water there is fairly fast. This offers a small current and is preferable to sluggish lake waters.

Sea trout arrive in most lakes during June and July, although it is best to consult locals before planning a trip for a specific lake fishing holiday. The finnock, or sea trout grilse, will stay in shoals during this stop in a lake but salmon seldom gather in numbers exceeding a few dozen. Brown trout begin gathering in shoals when autumn nears. They build up around the entrances to heavier streams ready to run up for spawning. The bays around a single inlet stream of a long, flat lake usually team with brownies in October and November.

Salmon will also lie near the infalls of rivers when they first arrive. They may lie there for several days getting over the exertion of the long run up-river before moving off and, once they have nosed around for a look at the lake, they will pick up lies near the outfalls of rivers. The stronger the current at these points, the more likely salmon are to lie there. They will tend to lie under or near rocks and they like the shade of an island, no matter how small, as currents tend to build up near submerged bodies. The salmon are, of course, only pausing for a rest in a lake. They probably regard the lake as a huge river pool for they have arrived by a river and they will leave by one as soon as water conditions are right and once they have regained their strength.

Bank Fishing

If you know the lake well, you will probably fish from the bank, but if not, a boat is quite a useful way of reaching the shore points you wish. A cast of at least twenty yards is best and the lee shore or island lee is a good starting point. With a clear beach and plenty of space behind, lake bank fishing is an ideal casting practice situation. Wading is not likely to be hazardous as most lakes have a gentle incline to the water, (check this though) and a fairly long

214

back cast is possible. A long cast *is* necessary for lake bank fishing and here is an excellent opportunity to practise and lengthen your cast. You will need a really well balanced outfit and a good double tapered or even a shooting taper line should be used. If a stiff head breeze picks up it would be advisable to either fish from the other end of the lake or change your cast for a good heavy tapered job.

When fishing still waters from low level, as you would be when thigh deep in lake water, great care must be taken not to hit the water behind on the back cast. The line must be lifted off the water gently and thrown high at the forward cast in a smooth arc to ensure the *fly* hits the water first and not the line. An overhead cast is best or even a double handed side cast with plenty of punch in it will do. If you can reach a stream inlet, cast into its current from the furthest distance you can and allow the fly to cross the main water path.

Use two flies when bank fishing for sea-trout; three for

Fig. 88 Lakeside fishing is most restful.

215

brown trout if using wet flies and one single fly for salmon. A 9 ft cast is quite long enough although a 12 ft cast may be used if the rod is at least this long. Dapping flies is quite feasible from the bank but this is explained and described a little further on. It is usually better to fish from the bank when the weather is cold and although the fish will be lying deep, they may be tempted to move with a natural bait. Natural baits always do better in the cold.

Lake Boat Fishing

The art of boatmanship has already been described very briefly; fishing from a boat requires only an adaptation of river techniques plus a little common sense. Simply drifting with the current with no plan in mind does not constitute fishing but it takes much experience before you can expect to understand water movement in even the most elementary manner. Although it is necessary to row or motor to the spot you intend fishing from, this must be done with great care for you may be passing over the very drift you wish to use. Use an outboard with respect and only when necessary for it is so easy to disturb the fish with the vibrations and they may stay disturbed for the rest of the day. Once over the spot of your choice, set your line and allow the boat to drift with the wind, using an oar only to steady up where necessary. The less splashing around when the line is in the water the better.

With normal, wet fly fishing there is no need to stand up all the time, in fact, if you can cultivate a long cast while sitting down, you will break the skyline even less, but you *will* need a really good long cast. You will also need a long line on the reel. Unlike the river, there is plenty of space for a fish to run and consequently you may fish with a lighter line.

On a boat, the fish runs itself out, you do not need to stop him running, the sheer weight of the line will do the job in the end. With a spinning outfit, you may find the multiplier a better tool to use as a very long line may be kept in reserve; you should never spin with less than 200 yds. A lake is best fished from a boat in a good strong breeze, this hides you (and the boat) to some extent, especially if the water is clear. After casting, it is important to keep in touch with the fly all the time and this means right up to the moment you lift the fly from the water. Many fish do not take until the fly is just leaving the water and in deep water it takes quite a while to reach the

216

surface. Trout are especially slow in rising from any depth. In wind-swept water your flies should be fairly bright. All lake flies tend to be colourful, although when one considers the natural fly life of a lake, olives, midges etc., this is rather surprising. Some lake and reservoir flies are shown in fig. 89 and plate 22.

Fig. 89. Lake and Reservoir Flies

Large	Medium	Small
Black lure (jungle)	Squirrell & Orange	*Thalia special*
Badger lure	Polystickle brown	Teal group
Sweeny Todd lure	Polystickle green	Mallard group
Worm fly	Polystickle orange	Alexandra
General	Shrimp	March brown
Bumble puppy	Chief Needabeh	Rogue
Matuka	White Marabou	Peter Ross

Wet flies should be fished a foot or so from the surface to begin with. They can be allowed to fish a little deeper on each run until the correct level is reached. Long casts can be accomplished with a little less effort in a boat as coils of loose line may be left on the wooded floor boards. This eliminates the extra drag of the spool for the line to overcome and can lengthen a cast appreciably if the line is made to shoot well.

If fish are rising, and it is not always easy to determine this on a rippling surface due to the waves which flood the boil, a dry fly may be better than a sunken one, but do make sure it is the mouth of the fish which breaks the surface and not the dorsal fin or even the tail as he dives again. If it is the tail, your fish is probably nymphing and taking the fly just as it emerges and struggles to the surface. One difference between river and lake fishing is that no fish has a specific direction to point at. In the river you know he will face upstream under normal circumstances but in a lake he may point anywhere. He is therefore cruising and may take the fly from any angle. If you can see the fish heading for the fly it takes superhuman self-control not to strike until you are sure he has taken and turned away before striking. With the dry fly line as long as you can manage (far easier in a boat than on shore), there is a danger of slapping the water with the false cast, so take care not to have too great an arc and, please, watch the boatman; he may not mind you flicking his hat into the water but he will certainly miss the flies in the brim very badly indeed and you may well follow the hat to its doom.

When seeking sea trout by boat, the usual methods are wet fly or dapping. At night, the attractors and deceivers are sometimes successful, but keep within a fishing depth of between five and twenty feet. If fishing well down, use a long rod and a fairly short cast with a size 10 hook to begin with and do not expect the usual fast take off a river sea trout, it is often very slow, especially when fishing really deep. Cast into the direction of the drift, this will allow the fly to sink well. If fishing the early months, use a larger cast and a size 7 hook. If it is very windy, an even heavier hook may be better.

Salmon are best fished by spinner from a boat. A fly may be successful but this often means trolling and not everyone likes to troll. The fly rod can be taken along for fun and may even catch fish. Of course, two or even three flies may be used from a boat but keep the fish, any fish, well away from the boat once hooked – especially if it is a rubber dinghy! If a fish looks like going under the boat, use the net handle, not the oar, to frighten him off. Nymphing sometimes picks up a salmon and in the cold, in the spring, or in bright weather conditions, a 'nymph' may do well. The most popular salmon 'nymph' is of course, the shrimp or prawn fly with the general practitioner in close attendance. In shallow waters, provided there are plenty of rock lies and a good current from an incoming stream, the salmon may even take a fly trailed across the surface film of the water but this is almost dapping and is explained later.

Trolling
This method of catching fish is often associated with the so called 'he-men' of angling, the shark fishermen, who are lashed safely to their seats while a piece of fish meat is tossed over the stern. The motor then speeds away and the bait is trailed along its wake. Although the idea is roughly the same, there can be a little more skill used in a lake when seeking trout but this is usually more attributable to the boatman than the fisherman. A long line – up to fifty yards, is sent out and the boat is steered into the wind. The bait may be natural, a spinner or even a team of flies. It is an inshore way of fishing but a deep troll across the centre of a big lake with a half pound of fish on the hook

218

may surprise even the locals for this is often the only way of catching the fabulous Ferox. Anglers of Loch Leven or Loch Awe are often seen doing just that and many a big brownie has astonished everyone around in reply so perhaps there is a little more skill in trolling than first seems. The difficulty most newcomers suffer is knowing which way the current is going *before* rowing to the beginning of a drift and it is not always easy to tell how the boat is moving on a big water from the centre.

Fig. 90 The Author seeking rainbows in a Scottish Loch.

Dapping

This rather interesting sport is really a branch of fishing all of its own. It may be conducted from the bank or from a boat, on a river or on a lake; in fact, it is more a way of fishing than a specific site method. Dapping means, roughly, skidding or bouncing a large, fluffy fly across the surface film of water using the principle of surface tension to prevent it gripping the water or, more likely, the water gripping the fly. It probably developed as an angling method from the practice of hooking live daddy-long-legs, or crane flies, onto a hook and dangling them over the

219

water surface. Other insects, such as the sedge or great gnat were also used in this way until eventually the fly makers tried a few successful models and the sport was under way. Soon, a special line was developed; this was called a blow line and is basically a light, wind carried line, which never goes into the water – until a fish takes it there. It is a light, floss, silk line and blows around in the breeze like a nylon flag. It really only works in a good breeze though and, of course, it must be in the right direction. To do the job properly, a special rod is needed although a long fly rod will suffice. It should be around 14–16 ft with a trace of about 12 ft. Casting should be effortless and not too long, so the rod needs to be pretty light if fishing for long periods and in a boat, a rod rest is not unknown. Shakespeare Noris makes an excellent telescopic dapping rod.

The leader should have a long taper and two flies may be used at once. They must be at least 6 ft apart and well dressed to prevent sinking. If a fish is caught, the fly is useless for the rest of the day so change both flies after a take, whether you land the fish or not. As explained, the fly must only skim the surface and, until you become proficient, stick to a single fly. The cast is made high and in a sweeping arc to present the fly end on. It may be snatched off the surface a few seconds after landing or be permitted to skate around on the water surface until the line slips or the fly looks in danger of sinking. It is not as difficult as it sounds but do not have too much line out at first. The method may be used on the bay of a river estuary, or exit to a lake and is usually cast across the stream and allowed to drag round to the quiet water before being lifted. At no time should the line touch the water.

Rainbow Trout

As specific lake dwellers, the rainbow deserves a corner to itself in this book. It is an interesting fish, as explained below. It is an American export and can be distinguished from a brown trout by the slightly blue back and the more numerous, smaller spots on the body. It grows faster than the brownie and is a voracious feeder. It is also a very savage fighter and is like a bull terrier when hooked. It rates pound for pound, very close to the sea trout for sheer courage and sporting qualities. It also tastes very nice indeed. Never go to a rainbow lake for a week without a smoker.

The rainbow can cope with higher temperatures than a

220

brownie and although the brownie will sink when temperatures reach 12°C the rainbow will be quite happy in the shallows up to 15°C.

Although the rainbow spawns in the spring, it will often become egg bound due to lack of spawning grounds and most lakes are therefore stocked artificially. Due to this spawning problem, the rainbow is not usually fit much before June or July. If food is in short supply the rainbow will feed on aquatic plants so always try weed beds as a last resort – and sometimes as a first.

Like brown trout, the rainbow prefers to lie near a lee shore (the bank the wind is blowing towards at any one moment). If the wind is variant and changes about, the fish will move into deeper waters. Although a wind is wanted to hide the blemishes we cannot overcome ourselves, a strong wind is not good nor is a blustery day. A glaring sun doesn't produce good fishing either – a cloudy day is nearly always much better. If the water level of the lake is rising there is usually good fishing to be had.

In the shallows and banks sides, where rainbows usually congregate, feeding is on an upwind pattern. They will seek rocky areas, especially where shelves of differing depths occur, and gravel beds between 5 and 10 ft below the surface.

When fishing for rainbow from the shore, which is very often the best way, you must be prepared to cast a long way or wade out to at least thigh level. Do not cast directly with the direction of a wind, cast slightly across it and fish the waters between 5 and 10 ft deep. Rainbows prefer a little cover and will lie in or near highly oxygenated weed beds in the summer. If fishing these weedy areas use only one fly and fish it with a sink and draw motion.

Boat fishing for rainbow trout differs little from any other form of boat fishing. Do not cast directly downwind, cast a little to the left or right of the wind and prevent a curved line, which would give the same 'non-fishing' drag of a fast current. If the water is calm, you will need to take extra care. Brightness also calls for great care. In a wind you may take all sorts of liberties as the rippled surface hides all but noise. If using a sink and draw method, work the fly faster in quiet waters and do not give the fish too good an inspection or he will see the blemishes. Bright flies should be 'bobbed' even faster but if a strong wind or coloured water is the measure of the day, bob very slowly and give the fish a chance to see the lure.

If you hook a rainbow he will fight like one possessed right up to the last minute, so try to get him around to the windward side of the boat and preferably by the flat ended stern. If he is to the leeward side, the boat will drift onto him and he may well seek the safety of its shadow.

Lastly, the rainbow trout eats roughly twice the amount of food per pound of body weight than a brown trout and is *always* hungry. It will eat almost anything and plenty of rainbows have been found with sticks, stones and bottle tops in their stomachs. The lesson is plain – use any bait you wish, but use it properly and with care, *know* you are going to catch a fish and you probably will.

Evening on a Lake

The so called 'evening rise' on a lake is very well known. But it is seldom known when this 'rise' will occur. Fish tend to go deeper when the sun is strong enough to light up the feeding patches low down (or bad enough to render shore line hugging dangerous), but as the sun sinks, they tend to come back to the shallows. If the sunset is a vague, misty affair with plenty of diffusion to cut down glare, the fish will come in earlier, but a bright, clear sky will cause a late rise. If there are plenty of mountains to the west, the sun will obviously sink earlier than it would on a flat, open landscape. It is the shadow of the surrounding hills which denote sunset to the fish, not the clock.

Evening fishing is consequently a bankside method, either from a boat or from the shore. Wet flies are most definitely better, but this depends on the moon. If the night is brightly moon-lit, the fish will tend to feed on the bottom, seeking out larvae, grubs and other insects which come out to feed themselves at night. Moon-lit nights are seldom very good and you must fish them as you would normally fish during the day. Mind your shadow, don't splash oars and fish with great care. On a *really* dark night the fish will have come right into the bank seeking the shallow aquatic insect life found only there, but remember that fish can see quite well in the dark and the silence of night tends to exaggerate the sound of your movements.

After the 'evening rise', which may last for only five minutes or for a whole hour (or not come at all), there is normally a lull of an hour or so as the fish digest the fruits of their labours and the flies are given a chance to gather in flocks again. The fly then comes back as a fishing method up to midnight or thereabouts, when everything stops until dawn begins to finger into the sky.

For surface fly fishing, the large gnat type insects are best – skidded around in dapping fashion. When fishing deep, fish slowly and never use more than one fly at night, there is far too much risk involved in using more.

Mark the bank with white stones just like a river plan and, if boating on a large lake, do take a compass along – you never know. Do not carry loads of unnecessary gear at night, it will get lost or trodden on and probably won't be used anyway. Such gear as spare reels or scales, fold-up seats and waders are all very well, but not at night. You would do better to carry an extra heavy coat and a hip flask! On the subject of scales it may be worth scribbling a few fish sizes on the side of the boat next to the ruler, which is usually screwed to the seat. Fig. 93 gives an appropriate fish size to weight ratio but a good equation is:

Fig. 91 A morning's catch on the Spey.

Fig. 92. Measurement formula

$$\text{Weight} = \frac{(L + \frac{L}{3}) \times G \times G}{1000}$$

or Weight equals length times length over three times girth squared over one thousand.

Fig. 93. Length to weight ratios

SALMON		TROUT	
inches long	weight (lbs)	inches long	weight
30	12	9	5 oz.
31	13	10	8 oz.
32	14	12	12 oz.
33	15	15	1 lb. 8 oz
36	20	18	2 lb. 8 oz.
40	25	20	3 lb. 8 oz.
44	36	24	6 lb.
48	48	30	12 lb.

The measurements in fig. 93 are, of course, only meant as a rough guide. A kelt will not weigh anything like the same as a fresh fish per inch length and some fish are much fatter than others but it does give an approximation until you get your fish home. You may even pick up a dram if guessing weights come up on the way!

223

10 Whence
the Salmon

This chapter covers such a wide range of fishing aspects, it was almost impossible to give it a title at all. The one it now has really *does* mean 'whence the salmon in all terms of reference. Where, for example, do the best fish come from? Where can you find the beauties so commonly referred to in the text? Where are the fish going to? What is their future as Man pollutes the world? What are the enemies of our game fish and how can they be controlled? We discuss hotels and salmon diseases, trout hatcheries, cooking and bus fares, costly water stretches and national appeals, how can such a range of topics be classified under one title? This chapter is, then, a conglomeration of all the bits and pieces left over, but they are important bits and pieces, as you will see.

WHERE TO FISH

It is always difficult to decide on a fishing trip. Apart from weekend jaunts, such trips are usually combined with the annual holiday and must therefore show at least some semblance of one if the wife and kids are to tag along. A trip to Scotland or Ireland, even specifically for fishing purposes, could hardly be unacceptable even to the most discerning holiday-maker for the sheer scenery of the highlands or a shimmering lough is enough to raise pimples on anyones geese or, to quote Arthur Oglesby, 'make one wish to turn base over apex with joy'. Whether you are fishing on holiday or not, the added satisfaction of nice surroundings is hardly to be scoffed at, yet not everyone likes to climb steep hills to reach forest burns or to sit in freezing weather by the side of a windswept lake. You must organise your holiday, or wife, to suit all events. But, to the fisherman, there are plenty of opportunities for everyone to enjoy themselves on a fishing trip if care is taken to plan it properly.

o

SCOTLAND

Some of the worlds finest salmon fishing is to be had in this magic land and the Scottish Tourist Board of 2, Rutland Place, Edinburgh EH1 2YU will be happy to help you plan a tour as will the Highlands and Islands Development Board of Inverness, Scotland. This board produces a whole series of books on fishing in appropriate areas and every possible piece of information for the angler is to be found in them.

There are just thousands of lochs and rivers in Scotland and very few do not contain fish. The problem is to suggest a few without casting aspersions on the rest. For this reason I am only listing the better known spots because I do not know the others very well, and not because they aren't good. Fishing can be excellent one year and terrible the next so fish where you will, the chances are even.

Scotland has a great interest in its fishermen tourists and all the information one could ask for is forthcoming. For this reason I have listed Scottish fishing in great detail.

The Highland counties of Scotland are currently undergoing surveys backed by the Scottish Tourist Board. This will result in a thorough list of guides eventually and you will be able to plan your trip from one large book. There are already quite a few. As a general rule the Scottish river trout choices are terrific and varied, perhaps the best trouting rivers being the Tweed, Tay, Don, Deveron and Spey. It can vary though and you would be well advised to make local enquiries once there before setting about serious fishing. Sea trout fishing is probably better in Scotland than in any other country in the world. Loch Stack, Loch Maree and Loch Hope offer fabulous sport but do take a local boatman with you on these waters. Costs incidentally of such luxury fishing may exceed £5 per day but don't forget the hire of the boat and the boatman is included. Salmon fishing can be divided into three categories; the casual salmon angler on association (£1 a day) waters; the hotel salmon fishers, who are given fairly good salmon waters as part of their enticement to the hotel; and really serious 'salmon only' men who pay fabulous sums for really good beats on such rivers as the Tay, the Spey, the Tweed and the Dee. This is salmon fishing at its very best. However, the hotel beats are not to be scoffed at, the rivers Thurso, Naver, Inver, Awe and

Dee offer pretty big salmon at the right time and it is usually well within the reach of the average pocket. The best salmon are found in spring and the best rivers for this time of year are well to the north and east of Scotland. From the river Naver in the north to the Tweed in the south, spring fishing is at its best. Most of the west coast waters do not pick up until May. The Don, the Girvan, the Cree or the Nith may offer fish from March onwards.

Summer salmon fishing is often taken over by the West coast spate rivers. Grilse tend to run upstream in July and August but the Tweed and the Nith are Autumn waters.

For sea trout the North-west waters are best between June and September for day loch fishing or night river fishing. Trout lochs are best after June. Some excellent waters have been privately developed and the most prominent success stories can be told at the lake of Menteith and loch Lindores. The Linlithgow offers rich brown trout water. Loch Shin and Lochinver are excellent waters too.

In Scotland there is a close season for netting lasting 168 days. This close season is from August or September until March. Rods are not allowed between October (in some cases November) and February. These seasons are shown in fig. 94. The trout close season is from October 7 to March 14 but many clubs extend this period to give fish a better chance. Trout cannot be sold after September 1st or before April 1st and never under 8 ins in length.

Fig. 95 Salmon netting.

Fig. 94. Scottish Close Season

Nets	Rods	Water
1 Sept.–15 Feb.	1 Nov.–15 Feb.	Add
27 Aug.–10 Feb.	1 Nov.–10 Feb.	Ailort
27 Aug.–10 Feb.	1 Nov.–10 Feb.	Aline
27 Aug.–10 Feb.	1 Nov.–10 Feb.	Alness
10 Sept.–24 Feb.	1 Nov.–9 Feb.	Annan
27 Aug.–10 Feb.	1 Nov.–10 Feb.	Applecross
27 Aug.–10 Feb.	1 Nov.–10 Feb.	Arnisdale (Loch Hourn)
27 Aug.–10 Feb.	16 Oct.–10 Feb.	Awe
27 Aug.–10 Feb.	1 Nov.–10 Feb.	Ayr
27 Aug.–10 Feb.	1 Nov.–10 Feb.	Baa and Goladoir
27 Aug.–10 Feb.	1 Nov.–10 Feb.	Badachro and Kerry (Gairloch)
27 Aug.–10 Feb.	1 Nov.–10 Feb.	Balgay and Shieldaig
27 Aug.–10 Feb.	16 Oct–10 Feb.	Beauly
27 Aug.–10 Feb.	1 Nov.–10 Feb.	Barriedale
10 Sept.–24 Feb.	1 Nov.–24 Feb.	Bervie

Nets	Rods	Water
27 Aug.–10 Feb.	1 Nov.–10 Feb.	Bladnoch
27 Aug.–10 Feb.	1 Nov.–10 Feb.	Broom
27 Aug.–10 Feb.	16 Oct.–31 Jan.	Brora
10 Sept.–24 Feb.	1 Nov.–24 Feb.	Carradale
27 Aug.–10 Feb.	1 Nov.–10 Feb.	Carron
10 Sept.–24 Feb.	1 Nov.–24 Feb.	Clayburn (East Harris)
27 Aug.–10 Feb.	1 Nov.–10 Feb.	Clyde and Leven
27 Aug.–10 Feb.	1 Oct.–25 Jan.	Conon
14 Sept.–28 Feb.	1 Oct.–28 Feb.	Cree
27 Aug.–10 Feb.	17 Oct–10 Feb.	Creed or Stornoway and Laxay, Lewis
27 Aug.–10 Feb.	1 Nov.–10 Feb.	Creran (Loch Creran)
27 Aug.–10 Feb.	1 Nov.–10 Feb.	Croe and Shiel
27 Aug.–10 Feb.	1 Oct.–31 Jan.	Dee (Aberdeenshire)
27 Aug.–10 Feb.	1 Nov.–10 Feb.	Dee (Kirkcudbrightshire)
27 Aug.–10 Feb.	1 Nov.–10 Feb.	Deveron
27 Aug.–10 Feb.	1 Nov.–10 Feb.	Don
27 Aug.–10 Feb.	1 Nov.–10 Feb.	Doon
1 Sept.–15 Feb.	16 Oct–15 Feb.	Drummachloy or Glenmore (Bute)
27 Aug.–10 Feb.	16 Oct–10 Feb.	Dunbeath
21 Aug.– 4 Feb.	1 Nov.–31 Jan.	Earn
1 Sept.–15 Feb.	1 Nov.–15 Feb.	Echaig
1 Sept.–15 Feb.	1 Nov.–15 Feb.	Esk, North
1 Sept.–15 Feb.	1 Nov.–15 Feb.	Esk, South
27 Aug.–10 Feb.	1 Nov.–10 Feb.	Ewe
10 Sept.–24 Feb.	1 Nov.–24 Feb.	Fincastle (W. Harris)
27 Aug.–10 Feb.	1 Oct.–10 Feb.	Findhorn
10 Sept.–24 Feb.	1 Nov.–24 Feb.	Fleet (Kirkcudbright)
10 Sept.–24 Feb.	1 Nov.–24 Feb.	Fleet (Sutherland)
27 Aug.–10 Feb.	1 Nov.–10 Feb.	Forss
27 Aug.–10 Feb.	1 Nov.–31 Jan.	Forth
1 Sept.–15 Feb.	1 Nov.–15 Feb.	Fyne, Shira and Aray (Loch Fyne)
27 Aug.–10 Feb.	1 Nov.–24 Feb.	Girvan
27 Aug.–10 Feb.	1 Nov.–10 Feb.	Glenelg
27 Aug.–10 Feb.	1 Nov.–10 Feb.	Gour
27 Aug.–10 Feb.	1 Nov.–10 Feb.	Greiss, Laxdale or Thunga
27 Aug.–10 Feb.	1 Nov.–10 Feb.	Grudie or Dionard
27 Aug.–10 Feb.	1 Nov.–10 Feb.	Gruinard and Little Guinard
27 Aug.–10 Feb.	1 Oct.–11 Jan.	Halladale, Strathy, Naver and Borgie
27 Aug.–10 Feb.	1 Oct.–10 Jan.	Helmsdale
27 Aug.–10 Feb.	1 Oct.–11 Jan.	Hope and Polla or Strathbeg
10 Sept.–24 Feb.	1 Nov.–24 Feb.	Hownmore
27 Aug.–10 Feb.	1 Nov.–10 Feb.	Inchard
10 Sept.–24 Feb.	1 Nov.–24 Feb.	Inner (in Jura)
27 Aug.–10 Feb.	1 Nov.–10 Feb.	Inver
27 Aug.–10 Feb.	1 Nov.–24 Feb.	Iorsa (in Arran)
27 Aug.–10 Feb.	1 Nov.–24 Feb.	Irvine and Garnock
27 Aug.–10 Feb.	1 Nov.–10 Feb.	Kannaird
27 Aug.–10 Feb.	1 Nov.–10 Feb.	Kilchoan
27 Aug.–10 Feb.	1 Nov.–10 Feb.	Kinloch (Kyle or Tongue)

Nets	Rods	Water
27 Aug.–10 Feb.	1 Nov.–10 Feb.	Kirkaig
27 Aug.–10 Feb.	1 Nov.–10 Feb.	Kishorn
27 Aug.–10 Feb.	1 Oct.–10 Jan.	Kyle of Southerland
10 Sept.–24 Feb.	1 Nov.–24 Feb.	Laggan and Sorn (Islay)
27 Aug.–10 Feb.	1 Nov.–10 Feb.	Laxford
27 Aug.–10 Feb.	1 Nov.–10 Feb.	Leven
27 Aug.–10 Feb.	1 Nov.–10 Feb.	Little Loch Broom
27 Aug.–10 Feb.	1 Nov.–10 Feb.	Loch Duich
27 Aug.–10 Feb.	1 Nov.–10 Feb.	Loch Luing
27 Aug.–10 Feb.	17 Oct.–10 Feb.	Loch Roag
27 Aug.–10 Feb.	1 Nov.–10 Feb.	Lochy
27 Aug.–10 Feb.	16 Oct.–10 Feb.	Lossie
10 Sept.–24 Feb.	1 Nov.–24 Feb.	Luce
27 Aug.–10 Feb.	1 Nov.–10 Feb.	Lussa (Island of Mull)
27 Aug.–10 Feb.	1 Nov.–10 Feb.	Moidart
27 Aug.–10 Feb.	1 Nov.–10 Feb.	Morar
10 Sept.–24 Feb.	1 Nov.–24 Feb.	Mullanagaren, Horasary and Lochnaciste (North Uist)
27 Aug.–10 Feb.	1 Oct.–10 Feb.	Nairn
27 Aug.–10 Feb.	1 Nov.–10 Feb.	Nell, Feochan and Euchar
27 Aug.–10 Feb.	16 Oct.–14 Jan.	Ness
10 Sept.–24 Feb.	1 Dec.–24 Feb.	Nith
10 Sept.–24 Feb.	1 Nov.–24 Feb.	Orkney Isles
27 Aug.–10 Feb.	1 Nov.–10 Feb.	Ormsary (Loch Killisport), Loch Head and Stornoway
27 Aug.–10 Feb.	1 Nov.–10 Feb.	Pennygowan or Glenforsa & Aros
27 Aug.–10 Feb.	1 Nov.–10 Feb.	Resort
1 Sept.–15 Feb.	1 Nov.–15 Feb.	Ruel
27 Aug.–10 Feb.	1 Nov.–10 Feb.	Sanda
27 Aug.–10 Feb.	1 Nov.–10 Feb.	Scaddle
10 Sept.–24 Feb.	1 Nov.–24 Feb.	Shetland Isles
27 Aug.–10 Feb.	1 Nov.–10 Feb.	Shiel
27 Aug.–10 Feb.	1 Nov.–10 Feb.	Sligachan
27 Aug.–10 Feb.	1 Nov.–10 Feb.	Snizort
27 Aug.–10 Feb.	1 Oct.–10 Feb.	Spey
10 Sept.–24 Feb.	1 Nov.–24 Feb.	Stinchar
21 Aug.– 4 Feb.	16 Oct.–14 Jan.	Tay
27 Aug.–10 Feb.	6 Oct.–10 Jan.	Thurso
27 Aug.–10 Feb.	1 Nov.–10 Feb.	Torridon
15 Sept.–14 Feb.	1 Dec.–31 Jan.	Tweed
10 Sept.–24 Feb.	1 Nov.– 9 Feb.	Ugie
27 Aug.–10 Feb.	1 Nov.–10 Feb.	Ullapool
10 Sept.–24 Feb.	30 Nov.–24 Feb.	Urr
27 Aug.–10 Feb.	1 Nov.–10 Feb.	Wick
10 Sept.–24 Feb.	1 Nov.–24 Feb.	Ythan

Where to fish in Scotland

ABERDEENSHIRE

RIVER DEE: Salmon, permit obtainable from Cambus O'May Hotel, near Ballater. Fly only 15 April – 15 June.

Fig. 96 Landing a salmon on the Tweed.

(courtesy of the Scottish Tourist Board)

Fig. 97 In the net – a fine salmon.

(courtesy of the Scottish Tourist Board)

Fly and artificial spinner baits at other times. Season: 1 February – 30 September. Best: April, May, June and September.

RIVER DON (KEMMAY FISHINGS): Salmon, brown trout. Permit obtainable from F. J. Milton, Kemnay House, Kemnay, AB5 9LH. Season: 11 February – 11 October.

RIVER DON (INVERURIE): Salmon, brown trout. Permit obtainable from Town House, Inverurie, AB5 9SN. Salmon season: 11 February – 31 October. Trout, 15 March – 6 October. Best salmon: February – June and September – October; Trout, May – August.

RIVER DON (LOWER PARKHILL BEAT, NORTH BANK ONLY): Salmon, brown trout. Permit obtainable from: J. S. Sharpe (Fishing Tackle Ltd.), 35 Belmonst St., Aberdeen. Salmon best season: March – October; trout, April – September.

ANGUS

ESK RIVER (NORTH): Sea trout, brown trout. Permit obtainable from Joseph Johnston & Sons Ltd., 3, American St., Montrose. Free details of restrictions on request. Season: February – October. Best season: April, July and August.

ESK RIVER (SOUTH): Salmon, sea trout, brown trout. Permit obtainable from: Kirriemuir Angling Club: Dykehead Post Office or Clova Hotel. No spinning after 31 May. No permits issued on Thursdays and Saturdays. Season: 16 February – 31 October; best: April – July.

ARGYLL

RIVER AWE: Salmon, sea trout, trout. Permit obtainable from: Loch Awe Hotel, Loch Awe. Best season for Salmon: late May to September.

LOCH AWE: Brown trout, Salmon. Permit obtainable from: Portsonachan Hotel, by Dalmally. Fishing free. Boat £1 per day. No salmon fishing on Sunday. Season runs from March 15 – October 15, with the best trout fishing from March – June and from September – October. The best salmon period is July and August.

AYRSHIRE

RIVER AYR: Brown trout, sea trout and salmon are found. Permit may be obtained from Sorn Angling Club: John

Quinn, 11 Firpark, Sorn, Mauchline; Local Esso and Shell petrol stations. Spinning is not permitted until June 1. The season for trout fishing runs from March 15 – October 6. Salmon and sea trout fishing is from March 15 – October 31.

RIVER AYR: Salmon, sea trout and brown trout are found here. Permits may be obtained from the Auchinleck Angling Association: J. McColm, Secretary, 21 Milne Ave., Auchinleck. Only brown trout fishing is permitted on Sunday. The season for Salmon and sea trout fishing runs from March 15 – October 15. Brown trout fishing runs from March 15 – September 15. Best salmon and sea trout fishing is from August – October.

BANFFSHIRE

RIVER AVON: Salmon, grilse, sea trout and brown trout. Permit: Richmond Arms Hotel, Tomintoul.

RIVER AVON: Salmon, grilse, sea trout and brown trout. Permit: Delnashaugh Hotel, Balindalloch. Ground baiting and prawning is forbidden. The season is from February 11 – September 30 and the best fish are found in May, July, August and September. A very friendly place.

RIVERS AVON AND LIVET: Salmon, sea trout, grilse and brown trout. Permit: Peter Grant, Gordon Arms Hotel, Tomintoul; a real fishing hotel. The season is from February – September 30 and is best in May, June and September.

RIVER SPEY: 3 miles of salmon, sea trout and brown trout. Permits: Craigellachie Hotel, Craigellachie. The season is from February 11 – September 30 and is best between April and June.

BERWICKSHIRE

THE TWEED: Salmon and sea trout. Permit: Tillmouth park Hotel, Cornhill-on-Tweed, Coldstream. Boats are available. The season is from February 1 – November 30 and is best between March and April.

BUTE

BLACKWATER, KILMORY, SLIDDERY AND ROSA WATERS: Sea trout and brown trout. Permit: Arran Angling Association, W. R. Ure, Royal Bank of Scotland, Whiting

Fig. 98 Tailing a salmon.
(courtesy of the Scottish Tourist Board)

231

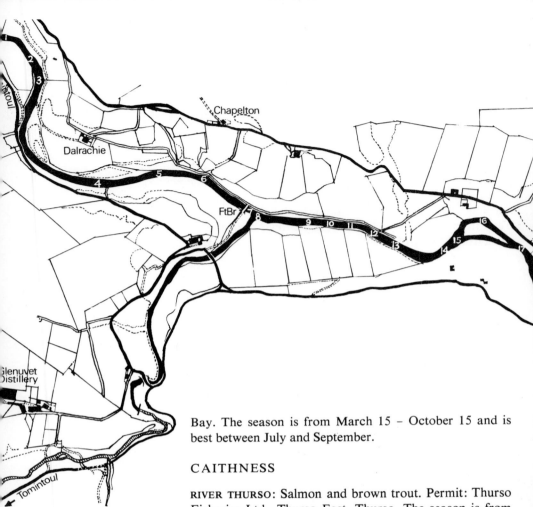

Bay. The season is from March 15 – October 15 and is best between July and September.

CAITHNESS

RIVER THURSO: Salmon and brown trout. Permit: Thurso Fisheries Ltd., Thurso East, Thurso. The season is from January 11 – October 5 and is best in April, May, July and September.

RIVER WICK: Salmon and sea trout. Permit: Wick Angling Association, 16 Back Bridge Street, Wick. The season for salmon is from February 11 – October 15 and is best during August and September.

DUMFRIESSHIRE

RIVER ANNAN (NEWBIE ESTATES): Salmon, sea trout and brown trout. Permit: T. Nelson, Newbie Mill, Annan. Only fly fishing is permitted, except when water is above the white line at Balabank Bridge, when spinning is permitted. Worm fishing is only allowed in floodwater conditions. The season is from February 25 – November

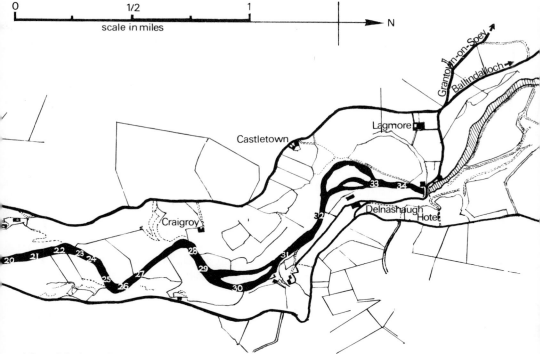

15 and is best for salmon fishing during February, April and October. The best sea trout are found in June and September.

Fig. 99 The fine Delnashaugh water in Scotland.

RIVER NIGH AND CAIRN WATER (ABOVE DUMFRIES): Salmon, sea trout and brown trout. Permit: Dumfries and Galloway Angling Association: Messrs. McMillan, 6 Friars' Vennel, Dumfries. The season for salmon and sea trout fishing is from February 25 – November 30. Brown trout are found between March 15 and October 6. Best salmon and trout are found during August and September.

CASTLE MILK WATER (ST. MUNGO PARISH, EXCLUDING BROCKLERIGG WATER): Salmon, sea trout and brown trout. Permit: Castle Milk estates office, Lockerbie. Only fly fishing is permitted and boats are prohibited. The season is from February 25 – November 15 and is best between August and October.

RIVER ESK AND LIDDLE RIVER: Salmon and sea trout. Permit: Bailiff, Tel: Canonbie 279 or Esk and Liddle Fisheries Association: R. J. B. Jill, Solicitor, Langholm, Secretary. No day tickets. Spinning until April 14; thereafter the spinning is only permitted when the water is above markers at Willow Pool, Canonbie Bridge and Skippers Bridge and markers on River Liddle. Season for salmon fishing is from February 1 – October 31, sea trout fishing from April 1 – September 30, brown trout fishing from April 15 – September 30. Best salmon can be found during Autumn and best sea trout are found during June and July.

RIVER ESK AND LIDDLE (UPPER WATERS): Salmon, sea trout and brown trout. Permit: Esk and Liddle Fisheries Association. Day tickets are not available. Spinning is permitted until April 14 and thereafter only when water is above markers. Sunday fishing is not allowed. The season for salmon fishing is from February 1 – October 31, sea trout fishing season is from April 1 – September 30, and brown trout season is from April 15 – September 30. Best salmon are found during Autumn and best sea trout are obtained in June and July.

RIVER ESK (LANGHOLM TICKET): Salmon, sea trout and brown trout. Permit: Esk and Liddle Fisheries Association. No day tickets are available it costs £3 per week or £12 for the season. Spinning is permitted until April 14; and thereafter only when water is above markers. Sunday fishing is not allowed. The season for salmon fishing is from February 1 – October 31, for sea trout fishing is from April 1 – October 31, for brown trout fishing is from April 15 – September 30. Best salmon are found during Autumn and best sea trout are obtained in June and July.

RIVER ESK (WESTERKIRK TICKET): Salmon, sea trout and brown trout. Permit: Esk and Liddle Fisheries Association. Fishing is £1 per week or £4 for the season. Day tickets are not available. Spinning and Sunday fishing is prohibited. The season for fishing is from April 15 – September 30.

DUNBARTONSHIRE

RIVER LEVEN: Salmon, sea trout and brown trout. Permit: Loch Lomond Angling Improvement Association: Messrs. Harvey and Lumsden, C. A., 86, St. Vincent St., Glasgow C2. Membership is limited and there is a waiting list with a fee of £5. The season for salmon and sea trout fishing is from February 11 – October 31. Brown trout are found between March 15 and October 6.

234

LOCH LOMOND: Salmon, sea trout and brown trout. Permit: Loch Lomond Angling Improvement Association. Membership is now limited and there is a waiting list with an entrance fee of £5. The season for salmon fishing is from February 11 – October 31, and for brown trout fishing from March 15 – October 6.

FIFE

RIVER EDEN AND CARES BURN: Salmon, sea trout and brown trout. Permit: Eden Angling Association: J. Fyffe, 67, Braehead, Cupar. The season for fishing is from March 15 – October 6. Best trout are found during April, May and June. Best sea trout are obtained in August and September.

INVERNESSHIRE

RIVER FINDHORN: Salmon and brown trout. Permit: Freeburn Hotel, Tomatin. The season for salmon fishing is from February to September and for trout, April to September.

LOCH GARTEN: Brown trout. Permit: G. G. Mortimer, High Street, Grantown-on-Spey who also provides permits for Loch Vaa, Loch Dallas and part of the River Spey. The season is from March 15 – September 30.

RIVER NESS: Salmon and sea trout. Permit: Inverness Angling Club, J. Fraser, 33 Hawthorn Drive, Inverness. The fishing season is from January 15 – October 15, best season being from July to October.

LOCH NESS: Salmon, brown trout and sea trout plus an occasional monster. Permit: Foyers Hotel, Loch Ness. Boat, outboard and gillies are available. The fishing season is from March 15 – September 25, being best during May, June and September.

RIVER SPEY: Salmon, sea trout and brown trout. Permit: The Boat Hotel, Boat of Garten. The season is from March 11 – September 30 for trout and best salmon and trout are found between April and June.

RIVER SPEY (LEFT BANK, FROM SPEY DAM TO KINGUSSIE) Two miles of right bank below Ruthven Bridge at Kingussie, and two miles of right bank at Inshriach below

235

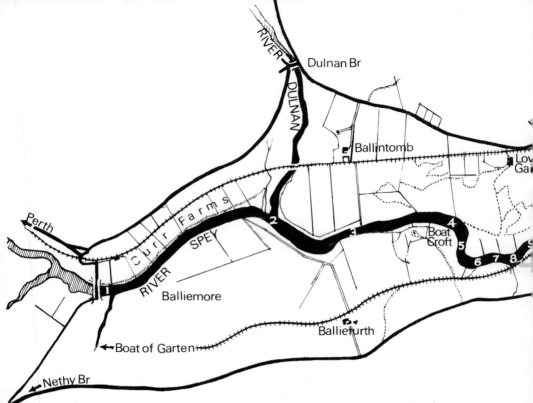

Fig. 100 The Strathspey Angling Association water on the River Spey.

Kingussie: Trout, salmon and occasional sea trout. Permit: Mrs. J. Walker, Secretary Badenoch Angling Association, Mains of Balavil. Spinning is only allowed when fly fishing is impracticable. The season is from April 1 – September 30 being best during May and June.

RIVER SPEY (BOTH SIDES, $4\frac{1}{2}$ MILE STRETCH) Trout and salmon. Permit: Abernethy Angling Improvement Association, John McInnes, 'Balnafoich', Boat of Garten. Permits, issued only to visitors who are resident in the area on business or holiday, on application. The fishing season is from February 11 – September 30.

KINROSS-SHIRE

LOCH LEVEN: Trout. Permit: Kinross Estate Co. Kinross Estate Office, Kinross. Boats are available with outboard motors. The season for fishing is from April to September.

KIRKCUDBRIGHTSHIRE

WATER OF FLEET: Sea trout, occasional salmon and grilse. Permit: Cally Estate Office, Gatehouse-of-Fleet. Spinning is only allowed above first marker when water covers red line on marker posts otherwise only fly fishing is per-

236

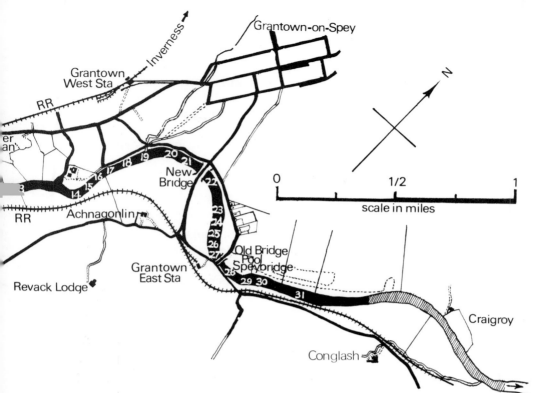

mitted. The season for fishing is from June 1 – October 31. Best sea trout are found during June to September and salmon and grilse are obtained in August, September and October.

RIVER KEN: Salmon and trout. Permit: New Galloway Angling Association: J. S. Bertram, Secretary, High Street, New Galloway. Spinning and bait fishing is not permitted before May 1. Maggot is not allowed. The season for trout fishing is from April 1 – September 30; for salmon and sea trout fishing from April 1 – October 31 being best during May, June and September.

LOCH KEN: Salmon, sea trout and brown trout. Permit: Milton Park Hotel, Dalry, Castle Douglas. Fishing is free to residents and boats are available.

WATER URR: Salmon, sea trout, brown trout and grilse. Permit: Delbeattie Angling Association: David Forbes Strachan, Secretary, Barrhill Rd., Dalbeattie. Spinning is only allowed when markers are covered. Day permits are not available. The season for fishing is from February 25 – November 30 being best in April, May, July, August, September and October.

LANARKSHIRE

RIVER CLYDE (ROBERTON TO THANKERTON): Brown trout. Permit: Lamington and District Angling Improvement Association: P. D. McAndrew, Old Station House, Symington, Biggar. The season for fishing is from March 15 – October 6. Best trout are found in September.

MORAY

LOCH DALLAS: Brown trout. Permit: The Smokers' and Sports shop, 90 High Street, Forres.

RIVER DULNAIN: (Both banks from Inverlaidnan Bridge, approximately 2 miles above Carrbridge village to mouth): Salmon, sea trout and brown trout. Permit: Strathspey Angling Improvement Association: G. G. Mortimer, High Street, Grantown-On-Spey. The season for salmon and sea trout fishing is from February 11 – September 30, and for brown trout from March 15 – September 30.

RIVER FINDHORN: Salmon and sea trout Permit: J. Geddes, Tolbooth Street, Forres. Day tickets are not available and permits are only issued to visitors who stay in the parishes of Forres and Rafford. The season for fishing is from February 11 – September 30 being best during Spring and Autumn.

RIVER SPEY (approximately 7 miles, both banks, from the bridge at Broomhill to the end of Long Pool approximately 1 mile below the old Spey bridge): Salmon, sea trout and brown trout. Permit: Strathspey Angling Improvement Association; also G. G. Mortimer, High Street, Grantown-On-Spey. The season for salmon and sea trout fishing is from February 11 – September 30; for brown trout from March 15 – September 30.

NAIRNSHIRE

RIVER NAIRN: Salmon and trout. Permit: Mr. Pat Fraser, High St., Nairn.

ORKNEY

The principal lochs – Boardhouse, Harray, Hundland, Stenness and Swannay are free for sea trout fishing. Access to lochs is readily granted by farmers in vicinity, many of whom hire boats. Other good trout lochs are

238

Bosquoy, Isbister near Twatt, Isbister in Rendall, Kirbister, Wasdale and Peerie Water. Good sea trout fishing is during spring and autumn in bays and inlets all round the shores. The Orkney Trout fishing Association (Secretary: Mr. R. Windwick, 36, Quoybanks Crescent, Kirkwall, Orkney) will gladly advise visitors. Annual subscription to the Association is 50 new pence.

PEEBLESSHIRE

THE TWEED (PEEBLES TOWN WATER): Salmon, brown trout. Permit: Ian Fraser, Tackle Dealer, 1, Bridgegate. No thread-line fishing for trout and no weights, wirecast or bubble floats. Spinning for salmon, maximum hook size 4; from February 15 – November 30 only fly fishing is permitted, maximum hook size 8. From February 1 – February 15 and September 15 – November 30. Single, double and treble hooks and swivels restricted to maximum size 4. The season for salmon fishing is from February 21 – November 30 being best in February, March and September to November. Trout are found between March 15 and October 6 being best between April and September.

THE TWEED (UPPER RIVER) (About 15 miles of river from mouth of Lyne Water upwards): Brown trout. Permit: Messrs. Blackwood & Smith, W. S. Peebles. Only fly fishing is allowed during April and September. Bubble float fishing is prohibited and spinning and minnow fishing is not allowed throughout the season. Fishing season starts on April 1 until September 30, best being in April, May and June.

THE TWEED (16 miles of river, Peebles Town Water and a few small reserved parts excepted): Brown trout. Permit: County of Peebles Angling Improvement Association: James Allan, 31, Edderston Road, Peebles. Spinning is not allowed and bait fishing is prohibited in April and September. Permits also cover Lyne. The season for fishing starts on April 1 until September 30. Best trout are found during April and May and good evening fishing in summer.

THE TWEED (From Wire Bridge Pool 1 mile Peebles to Scrogbank below Walkerburn): Salmon. Permit: Peeblesshire Salmon Fishing Association: Blackwood & Smith, W. S., 39 High St. Peebles, or Hardy Brothers (Alnwick) Ltd., 37a George St., Edinburgh. Double and treble hooks

239

Fig. 101 The River Tweed at dawn.

(courtesy of the Scottish Tourist Board)

are restricted to maximum size 4, single hooks maximum size 4, and swivels to maximum size 4. With fly, weights including loaded flies are forbidden. The season for fishing is from February 21 – November 30. (Minnows are allowed from March 15 – September 14.) The best salmon is found in February, March, October and November.

PERTHSHIRE

RIVER EARN: Salmon, brown trout and sea trout. Permit: St. Fillans and Loch Earn Angling Association: H. Malcolm, Dirnaheishe, St. Fillans. (Diving minnows are not allowed.) The season for salmon fishing is from March 15 until October 15. For trout from April 1 – September 3. Best salmon and sea trout are found in September, October and best trout in April, May, June and August.

240

RIVER EARN (CRIEFF AND DISTRICT): Salmon, sea trout and brown trout. Permit: Crieff Angling Club, per Messrs. Wm. Cook and Son, Tackle Dealers, High St., Crieff. Daily permits are limited. Prawn, diving minnows and bubble floats are not allowed, and worms and gaffs are not permitted before May 1. The season for fishing is from February 1 – October 15. Best salmon is found in April, September, October and best sea trout are obtained in June, July and August.

LOCH EARN: Salmon and brown trout. Permit: St. Fillans and Loch Earn Angling Association: H. Malcolm, Dirnaheishe, St. Fillans. Diving minnows are not allowed. The season for salmon fishing is from March 15 – October 15 best being in September and October. Trout fishing season is from April 1 – September 3, and best trout are obtained in April, May, June and August.

RIVER FORTH (Stretches from Gartmore Bridge upstream): Brown trout, some salmon and sea trout. Permit: Covenanters' Inn, Aberfoyle. The season for salmon and sea trout is from February 1 – October 31; and for brown trout between March 15 and October 6.

RIVER FORTH ($6\frac{1}{2}$ miles down stream from Gartmore Bridge to Buchlyvie): Brown trout, salmon and sea trout. Permit: A. E. Billett, Glenhead, Gartmore, Tackle Shops, Glasgow. The season for salmon and sea trout starts on February 1 until October 31 and for brown trout March 15 until October 6.

LOCH MARLEE: Salmon and trout. Permit: Angus Hotel, Blairgowrie (non-residents may also obtain permit at the hotel or at the local tackle shop). Boats are available. Only fly fishing is allowed for salmon. The season for salmon fishing is from March 15 – October 15 being best during August and September; the trout season starts on March 15 until October 3 and best trout can be obtained in May.

RIVER TAY (Within boundaries of City of Perth): Salmon, sea trout and brown trout. Permit: City Chamberlain, 1, High St., Perth. Maximum 20 permits per day. The season for salmon and sea trout starts on January 15 until October 15, best being in January, June, September and October.

RIVER TAY: Salmon and trout. Permit: Logierait Hotel, Ballinluig. Boats and gillies are available. The season is from Janaury 15 –October 15.

RIVER TAY: Salmon. Permit: Dun Aluinn Hotel, Aberfeldy. The season is from January 15 – October 15.

RIVER TAY: Salmon and trout. Permit: The Kenmore Hotel, Kenmore. Fishing is free for the hotel guests. The season starts on January 15 until October 15.

RIVER TAY: Salmon and trout. Permit: Weem Hotel, Weem (by Aberfeldy).

RIVER TAY: Salmon. Permit: Messrs. P. D. Malloch, Tackle Manufacturers, Scott St., Perth. Occasionally an odd day's fishing may be available.

LOCH TAY: Salmon and trout. Permit: The Kenmore Hotel, Kenmore. Fishing is free to hotel guests.

LOCH TAY: Salmon and trout. Permit: Bridge of Lochay Hotel, Killin. Fishing is free to residents. Boat available. The season is from March 15 – October, being best in May.

LOCH TAY: Salmon and trout. Permit: The Clachaig Hotel, Killin. (Non-residents may also obtain permits). Sunday fishing is not permitted. The season is from January 15 until October 16.

RIVER TUMMEL: Salmon and brown trout. Permit: Pine Trees Hotel, Pitlochry. (Non-residents may also obtain permits from the hotel). The season is from January 15 until October 15, best being in April, May, June and September. Plenty of coarse fishing is available in the neighbourhood and Angus Hamilton of the Pine Trees is a very amiable and helpful host, quite willing to show you around.

ROSS AND CROMARTY

RIVER BLACKWATER: Salmon and trout. Permit: Craigdarroch Hotel, Contin (by Strathpeffer). The season starts on April 1 until September.

RIVER BLACKWATER: Salmon. Permit: Strathgarve Lodge, Garve. The best fishing season is during June and August.

RIVER BLACKWATER (UPPER BEAT): North of Scotland Hydro-Electric Board: Salmon and brown trout. Permit: Loch Achonachie Angling Club: D. MacRitchie, 'Scarasdal', Strathpeffer. Only fly fishing and spinning is permitted; worming is not allowed. The season is from June 1 – September 30.

LOCH MAREE: Salmon, sea trout and brown trout. Permit: Loch Maree Hotel, Loch Maree. Boats are available. The season is from April to October 15, being best for salmon during April and June and best for sea trout in July and October.

LOCH MAREE: Salmon and sea trout. Permit: Gairloch Hotel, Gairloch, by Achnasheen. Only fly fishing is permitted. The season is from mid-April until mid-October, being best during May, June, July and September.

LOCH MAREE: Salmon and sea trout. Permit: Pool House Hotel, Poolewe (open on April 1 until October 31). Only fly fishing is allowed. The season is from February 11 – October 31, best being July until October inclusive.

ROXBURGHSHIRE

THE TWEED: Salmon, sea trout and trout. Permit: George and Abbotsford Hotel, Melrose.

THE TWEED (Melrose): Brown trout. Permit: Melrose and District Angling Association: J. Broomfield, Secretary, 'Ravensbourne', Douglas Rd., Melrose. Spinning is not allowed and day permits are not available on Saturdays. The season is from April 1 – October 6. Best being during day times in April, May and September (fly fishing); good evening fishing rises in other months.

SHETLAND

More than 100 lochs, burns, sea lochs and sea-shores on numerous inlets all around Shetland are controlled by the Shetland Anglers' Association: Secretary, Andrew Miller, 3, Gladstone Terrace. Lerwick: Sea trout and brown trout. Permit: Mr. C. Jamieson, Bank of Scotland, Commercial St., Lerwick. Fly fishing only, except on Loch of Girlsta and certain of the lochs of the Villa and Burrastow Estates (West Mainland) where spinning is allowed. Boats are available on Asta, Tingwall and other lochs. Sunday fishing is discouraged. The season for sea trout is from February 25 – October 31. Best sea trout are found during February until April, and during July until October. The season for brown trout fishing starts on March 15 until October 6, being best between May and August.

STIRLINGSHIRE

RIVER AVON: Brown trout. Permit: Slamannan Angling and Protective Association: W. Sloan, 3 Aitken Drive, Slamannan, Falkirk. Sunday fishing is permitted. The fishing season is from March 15 – October 6, being best in May and June.

RIVER FORTH: Salmon, sea trout and brown trout. Permit: Town Clerk, Municipal Buildings, Stirling. Old age pensioners in the burgh are allowed to fish free of charge. The season is from February 1 until October 15.

RIVER FORTH ($6\frac{1}{2}$ miles downstream from Gartmore Bridge to Buchlyvie): Brown trout, salmon and sea trout. Permit: A. E. Billett, Glenhead, Gartmore, Tackle Shops, Glasgow. The season for salmon and sea trout is from March 15 until October 6.

LOCH LOMOND: Salmon, sea trout and trout. Permit: Buchanan Arms Hotel, Drymen, (free to hotel guests).

LOCH LOMOND: Salmon and sea trout. Permit: Rowardennan Hotel, Rowardennan. (Fishing is free of charge to the residents.) Loch Lomond is also very famous for coarse fishes of considerable size.

LEWIS (OUTER HEBRIDES)

LOCH CLACHAN: Salmon and sea trout. Permit: The Factor, Stornoway Trust, Estate Office, Stornoway.

RIVER CREED: Salmon and sea trout. Permit: The Factor, Stornoway Trust, Estate Office, Stornoway.

SOUTH UIST AND BENBECULA

LOCH A' BHURSTA, Nan Clach Corr, Nan Clachan, Bee (East and West), Shell, Dun Mhor, A'Phuirt Ruaidh and Caslub: Brown trout are found in all lochs, and a few lochs contain sea trout and occasional salmon can be obtained. Permit: Creagorry P.O. For general information about these waters you may apply to R. T. Sutton, Hon. Secretary, South Uist Angling Club, 13 Liniclate, Benbecula, South Uist. Evening bookings are not available. The season for sea trout and salmon is from February 1 – October 31, and the season for brown trout is between March 15 and September 30.

SKYE (INNER HEBRIDES)

LOCH BERNISDALE: Brown trout. Permit: Skeabost House Hotel.

ISLE OF SKYE (when not being fished by hotel guests). Only fly fishing and spinning is allowed. The season is from March 14 – October 7, being best between July and September.

Some Scottish Angling Clubs

The Scottish Anglers' Association.
Duncan J. McGregor, 117 Hanover St., Edinburgh 2. Tel: 031-664 1740.

Scottish National Angling Clubs Association
Alastair S. Nicoll, P.O. Box 84, 51 Meadowside, Dundee, DD1 9PQ. Tel: (9382) 21081.

Fig. 102 Netting a fish at Kelso.
(courtesy of the Scottish Tourist Board)

245

Scottish National Federation of Angling Clubs.
F. McGuckin, 61 Glamis Rd., Dundee.

Shetland Anglers' Association.
Andrew Miller, 3 Gladstone Terrace, Lerwick, Shetland. Tel: Lerwick 929

Stonehaven and District Angling Association.
Hugh C. Dallas, 33 Cameron St., Stonehaven, Kincardineshire.

Other Information

Tomintoul is the highest village in the Highlands. It sits in beautiful countryside and is a fine central point to set up a fishing base. The hotels all have first class fishing beats and there are plenty of good waters all around. The Gordon Arms has particularly good salmon and sea trout stretches on the Avon; the town water is fair and the Seafield Estate manages water on the Spey from Grantown to Ballindaloch. At Ballindaloch is the lovely Delnashaugh with six Avon beats (See fig. 99). Four rods per beat are allowed and worming is in order on the first three but not on the last. Ground baiting and prawning is prohibited on all beats. Spinning is allowed between July 1 and September 30 only when the river is in spate. The season is from February 12 – September 30.

Parkmoor House at Dufftown is a lovely converted Victorian Mansion House. It is set in the woodlands, only minutes from the whisky capital of Scotland. Shooting, pony trekking and fishing are the theme and some of the best beats on the Spey are available to guests. There are 3,500 acres of pheasant shooting, flight ponds and roe stalking plus 'walked up' grouse; lochs and rivers within a 50 mile radius can be arranged.

For excellent rainbows, Loch Vaa (40 acres) with two boats; Loch Dallas (8 acres) with one boat and Avielochan (14 acres) can be thoroughly recommended.

The Seafield Estate is probably one of the best salmon fishing areas in Scotland. Bookings are not easy of course and there is always difficulty in getting onto these waters. Permits and gillies are obtained from the Estate Office, the Square, Grantown-on-Spey.

The area offers plenty of recreation besides fishing (to keep the family happy). For example, it boasts the highest restaurant in Britain, the Ptarmigan, at 3,656 ft above sea level. This fabulous beauty spot is the main attraction for skiers in the Spey valley. In the winter, the Cairngorm Festival takes place and the chair lifts are quite an experience. At beautiful Aviemore is a fishing centre and a ski school complete with artificial slopes. Then there is the weather service for fishermen and tourists (041-248 3451).

If you would like more details of Scottish games and sports drop a line to: The Scottish Council for Physical Recreation, 4 Queensferry St., Edinburgh 2.

Fishing Courses

There are several really good fishing courses in Scotland. At Aviemore, for example, Philip Elwood and his wife abound in energy and game-fishing knowledge. They supply the equipment, casting platforms, fishing bait, boats etc. and jolly good company thrown in.

For really special angling courses, the River Tay upper scone fishing takes some beating. These courses are held on one of the finest salmon fishing beats in the whole of the United Kingdom, including the famous Pitlochry Pool and 19 other named pools. The water has a consistently high record of catches. In 1969 the total number of salmon caught was 514, the best week being 49 which was during the autumn run. In 1970 the total catch was 451 salmon, with a record of 50 salmon being caught in one week during the spring run.

The charges include the use of two fishing huts, boats with an outboard motor, the services of two gillies, two instructors, use of Hardy Tackle and hotel accommodation.

Fishing from the bank, boat fishing and casting tuition is organised on a rota system by the chief instructor, Mr. Ian Blagburn, World Championship Caster and well known angler, in order to give all pupils a fair chance of all facilities and ensure that they have the opportunity of catching salmon to take home. Mr. J. L. Hardy, Hardy's Marketing Director, World Casting Champion and renowned angler, visits the course during the week.

Spring Course:
Commences Sunday evening   7 March (approx)
Terminates Saturday evening   13 March (approx)

Autumn Course:
Commences Sunday evening   5 September (approx)
Terminates Saturday evening   11 September (approx)

Accommodation is in a hotel near Perth, which is only 7 miles from the fishing. Discussions and lectures are held in the evenings.

There is a limit of 10 pupils per course. Both weeks have been selected for the consistently high record of catches.

All salmon caught are the property of persons attending the course.

Going further North to the Isle of Skye, the Dunvegan Hotel provides good fishing especially for beginners as there is a great variety of water. Dunvegan Hotel has exclusive rights on trout and sea trout lochs and rivers in the vicinity of the hotel, and also issues permits for two very important salmon rivers. The wholly unspoiled beauty of the Isle of Skye makes fishing in the Dunvegan area a most satisfying experience. The courses are run as friendly house parties, and attract many novices as well as experienced fishermen. The tuition is given by Mr. Ian Blagburn of Hardy Brothers, World Championship Caster and well known angler. It is suggested that the beginners do not purchase equipment prior to the course, as Mr. Blagburn will advise on the suitability of rods for each pupil.

There are two courses: September 18 – September 25, and September 25 – October 2.

'Palace Angling Week' fishing holidays are well known in the Highlands. A 7 mile stretch of the Spey is offered along with the casting and fishing course. Hotel accommodation, lectures and film shows; demonstrations of many angling skills and excellent casting tuition comes within the all-in charge of around £30 a week and private beats can be obtained if required. Equipment hire is possible. The courses run from mid-April to the end of May and application should be made to: The Palace Hotel, Grantown-on-Spey, Banffshire.

WALES

'Towy and Teifi, Usk and Wye, Dowey and Dysynni, Conway and Clwyd ... the map of Wales is bright with rivers.' Clive Gammon.

Wales is also bright with salmon, trout and sea trout and there are plenty of free rivers to fish also. For reasonably priced commercial waters; over 20 miles of the Teifi salmon and trout association water cost only £2 a week.

Like Scotland, there are plenty of jolly good hotel

waters in Wales. Then there is the North Welsh Dee and other lovely rivers like the Clwyd. A late river is the fabulous Usk (where the usk grub – the most versatile fly in the world – comes from).

There are seven river authorities in Wales and all waters, be they streams, rivers or lakes, come under one or other of the following:

Gwynedd River Authority: Highfield, Caernarvon. Tel: 2247.

Dee and Clwyd River Authority, 2 Vicars Lane, Chester. Tel: 45004.

Severn River Authority, Portland House, Church St., Malvern, Worcs. Tel: 61511.

Wye River Authority, 4 St. John St., Hereford. Tel: 6313.

Usk River Authority, The Croft, Goldcroft Common, Caerleon, Newport, Mon. Tel: 399.

Glamorgan River Authority, Termains House, Coychurch Rd., Bridgend, Glam. Tel: 2217.

South-West Wales River Authority, Penyfai House, Penyfai Lane, Llanelli, Carms. Tel: 4291.

It is necessary to obtain a licence of the respective authority (usually from a local shop). You will also need a fishing permit from the landowner or fishing club. This is also obtainable locally as a rule.

Fig. 103. Welsh River Authority Licence Fees

River Authority.	Salmon & Sea trout			Trout	
	£ p	£ p	£ p	£ p	£ p
Gwynedd	4.00	1.25	0.50	0.75	0.50
Dee/Clwyd	4.00	1.50	0.50	0.50	0.25
Severn	4.25		0.50	0.50	0.25
Wye	6.50	2.00	0.75	0.50	0.25
Usk	6.50	1.50		1.00	0.50
Glamorgan	1.50			0.50	
South-West Wales	4.50	1.75		4.50	1.75
PERIOD	SEASON	WEEK	DAY	SEASON	WEEK

Wales, in common with Scotland, has a close season. The main waters are shown in fig. 104 although slight changes may occur here and there.

Fig. 104. The Welsh Seasons

River Authority	Salmon	Sea trout	Trout
START OF SEASON			
Gwynedd, Dee			
& Clwyd	1 April	1 April	1 March
Dee	1 March	1 March	1 March
Clwyd	15 March	18 March	1 March
Bala Lake	1 March	1 March	15 January
Severn	2 February	15 March	15 March
Wye	26 January	1 March	1 March
Usk	15 February	15 March	15 March
Glamorgan	2 March	1 April	1 March
SOUTH WALES			
R. Western			
Cleddau	1 February	10 March	10 March
R. Rheidol	10 March	10 March	15 April
Others	10 March	10 March	10 March
END OF SEASON			
Gwynedd Dee			
& Clwyd	17 October	17 October	30 September
R. Dee	15 October	30 September	30 September
R. Clwyd	15 October	15 October	30 September
Bala Lake	15 October	30 September	14 August
Severn	15 September	15 September	15 September
Wye below			
Llanwrthwl Br.	30 September	30 September	30 September
Above			
Llanwrthwl Br.	25 October	30 September	30 September
Usk above			
Talybont on Usk	15 October	30 September	30 September
Below			
Talibont on Usk	30 September	30 September	30 September
Glamorgan	31 October	16 October	30 September
South-West			
Wales	7 October	7 October	30 September

Where to Fish in Wales

BALA LAKE AND RIVER DEE: Salmon, sea trout and trout. Permit: W. E. Pugh, High St.

RIVER GLASLYN: (8 mile stretch both banks) Licence from Hotel, Permit: Glaslyn Angling Association. Boats on Lake Dinas, only 2 miles away both of which are free to guests. A motor boat is available at a nominal charge. Trout are found here.

RIVER CAMMARCH: Salmon and trout. 500 yds of one bank for salmon. Permit: Inn, Tackle Shop; Builth Wells.

RIVER SEVERN ($3\frac{1}{2}$ miles of both banks): Salmon and trout. Permit: Hotel for the season.

RIVER LLUGWY ($1\frac{1}{2}$ miles on one bank only). Salmon and trout. Permit and licence: Hotel.

RIVER ALWEN (at Betws Gwerfil Goch, 1 mile stretch): Salmon and trout. Licence: Local Council Office.

RIVER USK (adjacent, 1 mile stretch at Gliffaes and $1\frac{1}{4}$ mile stretch above Abergavenny.): Salmon and trout. Licence: Hotel.

RIVER DOVEY ($\frac{1}{2}$ mile stretch on both banks): Salmon and trout. Licence and permit: Hotel.

Fig. 105 A Welsh stream, teeming with trout.

RIVER DOVEY ($3\frac{1}{4}$ mile stretch below the village): Salmon and trout. Licence: Local Shop; Permit: Hotel. Maximum five rods at a time.

RIVER WINON ($1\frac{1}{2}$ miles on both banks): Salmon and trout. Licence: Dolgellau.

RIVER MAWDDACH ($1\frac{1}{4}$ mile one bank only): Salmon and trout. Licence and Permit: Hotel.

RIVER MAWDDACH (3 miles one bank): Salmon and trout. Licence and Permit: Hotel.

RIVER CEIRIOG ($\frac{1}{2}$ mile, River Dee, 5 miles stretch on both banks): Salmon and trout. Licence and Permit: Hotel; free fishing to residents.

RIVER DEE ($1\frac{3}{4}$ mile stretch one bank only): Salmon and trout. Permit: River Board; Licence: Corwen.

RIVER TEIFI (2 miles on both banks): Salmon and trout. Permit: Hotel.

RIVER CEIRIOG: ($1\frac{1}{2}$ mile stretch on both banks): Trout. Licence and Permit: Hotel; free to residents.

RIVER TYWI (Approximately 100 yds stretch on one bank): Salmon and trout. Llandovery Association Waters are within 3 miles radius. Licence: W. A. Thomas, 30 High St., Llandovery.

RIVER BRAN (100 yds stretch on both banks): Salmon and trout. Licence: River Board.

RIVER DEE ($1\frac{1}{4}$ mile stretch on both banks): Permit: Hotel; Licence: W. E. Pugh, 49 High St., Bala.

251

RIVER TEIFI (1½ mile stretch on one bank only): Salmon and trout. Permit: Hotel: Licence: Llanfihangel-ar-Arth Post Office.

RIVERS IRFON, CAMMARCH AND DULAIS (Total 7 miles on one bank): Salmon and trout. Permit and Licence: Hotel.

RIVER IRFON (4 mile stretch, 2 trout brooks totalling 3½ miles; stocked lake; small reservoir, River Wye 8 miles away, 3 beats): Salmon and trout. Licence of River Authority: Hotel.

RIVER WYE (7½ mile stretch up-stream and down-stream): Salmon and trout. Permit: Hotel; Licence: Water Bailiff in Llangurig.

RIVER DEE (100 yds on both banks): Salmon and trout. Permit: Hotel; Licence: Tackle shop, Chapel St., Llangollen.

RIVER YSTWYTH on Garden Boundary, (10 mile stretch both banks): Salmon and trout. Permit: Y. Glyn, Llanilar. Licence: Garage in the village.

RIVER GLASLYN (8 mile stretch both banks): Salmon and trout. Permit: Glaslyn Angling Association; Licence: Hotel.

RIVER VYRNWY (1 mile stretch on both banks): Trout. Permit: Hotel; River Board Licence: Oswestry, 10 miles away.

RIVER VYRNWY (¾ mile stretch on one bank only): Trout. Permit: Hotel; River Board Licence: Oswestry.

RIVER VYRNWY (Many miles of fishing available to the Hotel): Permit: Hotel; River Board Licence.

RIVER TEIFI (In Hotel grounds, 650 yds on one bank only): Salmon and trout. Permit and licence: Hotel.

RIVER DWYRYD (2 mile stretch on both banks). Also various lakes in the vicinity can be fished for trout on payment of small fee to the local angling clubs. Permit and licence: Hotel.

RIVER TROTHY (Within hotel grounds, 750 yds stretch on one bank only): Trout. Permit: Hotel; Licence: Monmouth.

RIVER GLASLYN (½ mile stretch on one bank only): Salmon and trout. Permit: Hotel; Licence: Local Post Office.

RIVER GWRYD (3 mile stretch on one bank only): Trout. Permit and Licence: Hotel.

RIVER CWMDU AND RIVER TAWE ($\frac{1}{2}$ mile stretch on one bank only, but miles of Association Water on River Tawe.): Trout only Permit on River Cwmdu is free of charge to hotel guests. Permit for Association Water; near Pontardawe: Morris, The Square, Pontardawe.

RIVER COTHI ($4\frac{1}{2}$ mile stretch on both banks): Salmon and trout. Permit and Licence: Hotel.

RIVER WYE ($4\frac{1}{2}$ mile stretch): River Elan (1 mile stretch): Elan Valley Lakes (1,200 acres): LLYNGWYN LAKE, 6 miles away: Salmon and trout. Licence and Permit: Hotel.

RIVER ELAN (1 mile stretch on both banks): Permit: Hotel; Licence: E. R. Davies, Chemist, West St., Rhayader.

RIVER USK ($1\frac{1}{2}$ mile stretch on one bank only): Salmon and trout. Permit and Licence: Hotel.

RIVER AND ANGIDY PONDS: Salmon and trout. Permits and Licences: Guest House.

RIVER USK (One bank only): Salmon and trout. Permit and Licence: M. Sweet, The Tackle Shop.

For sea trout or salmon estuary fishing, Holyhead tidal predictions are published Nationally so we have quoted a comparison for most coastal towns in fig. 106.

Fig. 106. Tidal Differences on Holyhead

Nearest town	hrs	mins		Nearest town	hrs	mins	
Rhyl	Add	0	34	Fishguard	Sub.	3	15
Colwyn Bay	Add	0	18	St. Davids	Sub.	4	13
Llandudno	Add	0	30	Pembroke Dock	Sub.	3	57
Menai Bridge	Add	0	29	Haverfordwest	Sub.	3	42
Port Dinorwick	Sub.	0	20	Milford Haven	Sub.	4	18
Caernarvon	Sub.	0	30	Tenby	Sub.	4	32
Porth Dinllaen	Sub.	0	58	Carmarthen	Sub.	4	08
Pwilheli	Sub.	2	24	Llanelli	Sub.	4	21
Portmadoc	Sub.	2	14	Rhosili	Sub.	4	24
Barmouth	Sub.	2	15	Swansea	Sub.	4	12
Aberdovey	Sub.	2	22	Porthcawl	Sub.	4	18
Aberystwyth	Sub.	2	40	Barry	Sub.	3	54
New Quay	Sub.	2	47	Cardiff	Sub.	3	36
Cardigan	Sub.	3	13	Penarth	Sub.	3	36
Newport, Mon.	Sub.	3	39				

Fly Fishing Courses

The Central Council For Physical Recreation have a series of three courses in fly fishing during the year.

COURSE NO. 1. Aberystwyth, Nant y Moch Reservoirs, Ystwyth and Pheidol rivers. Easter week, residential fly fishing course at the University College of Aberystwyth buildings.

COURSE NO. 2. Merthyr, Dolygaer Reservoirs. A series of week-end courses operate from April to September.

COURSE NO. 3. Usk, Monmouthshire. A week-end fly fishing course on local waters to be held in the first week of June.

For full information send a post-card to The Central Council for Physical Recreation, 47 Cathedral Rd., Cardiff. Tel. 31546.

ENGLAND

The sheer quantity of English waters and the number of anglers who specialise in specific rivers would make a short list of fishing aspects rather ludicrous in this book. There is an angling club in almost every village, a tackle shop or two in every town and each tiny area has a special book giving full local details for that area. For this reason we suggest you write to the local Town Hall of the area you are interested in; they will send you all the details, complete with maps.

IRELAND

There are over 2,000 miles of coastline around Ireland and water arrives at the emerald isle from the Gulf of Mexico. The gulf stream, as explained in chapter four, supplies salmon and sea trout with food and this undoubtedly accounts for some of the fine salmon fishing in Ireland.

A huge limestone plain runs through the centre of Ireland and deep, slow rivers, 30 mile trout loughs and thousands of smaller lakes fill the hills of Monachan and North Cavan in consequence.

From Donegal to Kerry, and from the Irish Sea to Connemara, the angler will find a panorama of aquatic beauty; with sparkling fresh salmon, acrobatic sea trout or superweight brown trout. He would not be disappointed were he to kep a line into any of Ireland's fresh waterways.

Salmon

Salmon are to be found in all large Irish rivers and in many of the smaller ones too. Of course, the really good waters are carefully preserved and let to anglers along with gillies. Hotels have their share of good waters and the Irish Angling Clubs have rights too. Many of the Irish loughs, such as Lough Corrib, Lough Conn, Lough Fern (Donegal), the Killarney lakes and Lough Currang at Waterville, are completely free for fishing purposes. There are plenty of free salmon rivers too but always check before casting.

For Ireland you need a rod licence to fish for salmon. It is not necessary to buy a season rod licence (a weekly permit costs only £1) but the most you need pay is £14 for a full season in all waters.

The salmon fishing season starts on January 1 in some areas such as Liffey and Garvogne, but February 1 is the most popular opening date. Some even wait until May before lifting the ban but this is exceptional. The first river to close for the season is the Slaney on August 31, followed by the Boyne on September 15, but in general the season ends on September 30 with a few western waters hanging on another two weeks.

The best fishing comes in spring for most rivers, March and April being favourite.The average Irish spring salmon weighs around 10–12 lbs and plenty of twenty pounders put in appearances. Some of the best spring runs are seen on the Boyne, the Slaney, the Nore, the Suir and the Munster Black water. There are often huge grilse runs (5 lb fish) from May onwards although the autumn has its grilse run too. The best salmon fishing in summer is found in the Kerry, Connemara and Donegal Lake and river systems.

Sea Trout (Called White Trout in Ireland)

The best sea trout in the whole of Ireland are found in the smaller lakes and rivers of coastal regions. West Cork, Kerry, Connemara and Donegal abound in sea trout waters and the best time to seek them is from July to September.

Although beautiful, few Irish sea trout exceed 2 lbs, but a 2 lb. sea trout is quite a handful, especially if fresh run (and considering their soft mouths).

Sea trout areas are very carefully controlled. Lough Currane, Waterville and Caragh Lake, Kerry are free but most hotels and Angling Associations will offer good sport for a small fee. Coastal areas are also free but do check this before fishing. Estuary fishing is, of course, free but make sure the land you fish from is not privately owned water.

A salmon rod licence is needed for sea trout fishing and this seems fair enough as most sea trout waters hold salmon too.

Brown Trout

The 'Brownie' is found in almost every water in Ireland. They vary in size, with the smaller fish occuring in the coastal areas of Cork, Kerry, Connemara and Donegal; and the larger (up to 8 lbs) fish, which frequent the clear limestone lakes of Sheelin, Denravaragh, Owel, Ennell, Corra and Arrow. The more acid waters of Carrib, Mask, Connard and Dera tend to be middling, size-wise, but they also house the fabulous Ferox or cannibal trout. Monsters of 30 lbs or more may be whipped out by a good trolling expert and a suitable bait.

Wet fly fishing on the big lakes is common during March, April, May and September. The dry fly comes into its own from May to June and of course, on still summer evenings. Blow line dapping, described in chapter nine, is a distinctly Irish form of fishing. Dry flies on the limestone streams attract the bigger trout in April, May and June. The most prominent rivers are the Robe, the Black River, the Fergus, the Maigue, and the little Brosna. Lakes Carrib, Mask, Corra, Conn Arrow, Derg and Killarney offer free trout fishing.

Many of these lakes and rivers are controlled by the Inland Fisheries Trust, a state organisation, which works with the co-operation of many angling clubs. Trust membership is open to all at £1 per annum. A rod licence is not needed for brown trout fishing.

Rainbow Trout

Poorer waters have been stocked with the rainbows but you would best assure yourself of good rainbow waters by contacting the Irish Tourist Board.

Where to Fish in Ireland

COUNTY GALWAY

BALLINAHINCH: Salmon, sea trout and brown trout are found on lakes and rivers of the Ballinahinch system. Best season for salmon fishing is in June and Autumn. Permit: Ballinahinch Castle Hotel, Ballinafad, Co. Galway.

LOUGH CORRIB: Free fishing for salmon and brown trout. Centres: Oughterard, Headford, Greenfield, Galway City, Clonbur and Doorus Cornamona; all in County Galway, Cong, Co. Mayo.

GOWLA FISHERY (Rivers and Lakes): Best season July 1 – October 12.

GOWLA WATERS: Four beats on river ($3\frac{1}{2}$ miles on both banks); three boats on Gowla Lake; one boat on Mannio's Lake, also fishing on lake above Lough Gowla.

INVER WATERS: One boat on Lough Invermore; two boats on Lough Curreel; one boat each on Lough Shanaket, Cushmeg and Emlaugh; one boat on Lough Luggeen.

BALLINAHINCH UPPER WATERS: Two boats on Athry Lakes; one boat on Lough Emlaugh. Permit: The Zetland Hotel, Cashel Bay, Cashel, Connemara, Co. Galway.

SCREEBE FISHERY: Salmon and sea trout (rivers and lakes). Permit: The Manager, Screebe Fisheries, Screebe House, Co. Galway.

COSTELLOE FISHERY: Salmon and sea trout (rivers and lakes). Permit: The Manager, Costelloe Lodge, Con nemara, Co. Galway.

COUNTY MAYO

LOUGH MASK: Free fishing for brown trout. Centres: Tourmakeady, Ballinrobe, Cong; all in Co. Mayo; Clonbur in Co. Galway.

LOUGHS CONN AND CULLEN: Free fishing for salmon and brown trout. Centres: Crossmolina, Foxford, Pontoon, Ballina; all in Co. Mayo.

LOUGH TALT: Free fishing for trout. Centre: Ballina, Co. Mayo.

LOUGH CARRA: Centres: Ballinrobe, Castlebar, Claremorris; all in Co. Mayo.

COUNTY KERRY

GLENCAR: (Carrah rivers and lakes). Spring fishing

February – April. June and July is for grilse and sea trout fishing. Permit: Glencar Hotel, Glencar, Co. Kerry.

WATERVILLE: (Rivers and Lakes): Salmon fishing is best in spring; sea trout and brown trout are found in summer months.

WATERVILLE RIVER: Excellent salmon fishing on this famous pool. Maximum two rods. Spinning is not allowed after April.

RIVER INNY: The best season for salmon fishing is from July – October; for sea trout from April – June.

RIVER CUMMERAGH: Three beats, excellent for salmon fishing from March onwards and very good for sea trout in Autumn. Gillies (with boats) are also available.

RIVER LAUNE (Muckross Trust): The season for salmon fishing is from March to July and for sea trout, summer and autumn. Permit: Mr. Henneberry, Tralee and District Anglers' Association, The Manor House, Tralee, Co. Kerry. Centre: Killarney.

RIVER ESK: Permit: Mr. P. J. MacDermot, 'Cluain Mhuire', Woodlawn, Killarney.

COUNTY DONEGAL

OWENAE RIVER (Part): The season for spring fishing is from April – June, and for grilse, June and July. Lower reaches of the Owenae River from estuary to Brian's Pool (2 miles approximately) offer salmon and sea trout fishing; 15 pools, both banks. Fly, spinning and worming is allowed. A whole stretch of Owentocker River, with salmon, sea trout and brown trout (12 miles approximately) is available. All the lakes in the Conyngham Estate (12 in all) offer brown trout. Fishing is free and boats are available. The season for salmon and sea trout fishing is from April 1 until the end of September. For brown trout, fishing is from February 15 until the end of September. Permit: Mr. John McGill, Ardara Anglers' Association, Ardara, Co. Donegal.

RIVER BUNDROWES AND LOUGH MELVIN: Salmon and trout. Best fishing season is from April – June for Lough Melvin, and mid-February to the end of April for Bundrowes River. Permit: The Hamilton Hotel, Bundoran, Co. Donegal.

COUNTIES KILKENNY, LAOIS AND WEXFORD

RIVER NORE: Salmon and brown trout. Centres: Kilkenny, Thomastown, both in Co. Kilkenny; Mountrath in Co. Laois; New Ross in Co. Wexford. Permit: Mr. P. A. Troy, Hon. Secretary, Kilkenny Anglers' Association, College Rd., Kilkenny.

COUNTY TIPPERARY

RIVER SUIR: Salmon and trout. The spring fishing season is from February – May; June and July for grilse; excellent dry-fly fishing for trout. Centre: Cahir. Permit: Mr. J. F. McCarthy, Secretary, Cahir and District Anglers' Association, The Mall, Cahir, Co. Tipperary.

COUNTIES CORK AND WATERFORD

RIVER BLACKWATER: Season: Good run of spring fish (February, March, April and May). Grilse (July); Autumn fish (September).

RIVER BRIDE: (Main tributary): Brown trout, grilse and sea trout. Permit: Mr. S. Martin, Portmahon House, 77 Strand Rd. Sandymount, Dublin.

Brown Trout Fishing
(Fly and nymph) April – September.

RIVERS:
River Maigue – Adare, Co. Limerick.
River Fergus – Corofin; Ennis, Co. Clare.
Black River – Headford, Co. Galway.
Robe River – Ballinrobe, Co. Mayo.
River Suir – Thurles, Co. Tipperary.
River Lee (Middle reaches) – Macroom, Co. Cork.
Little Brosna River – Roscrea, Co. Tipperary; Birr, Co. Offaly.

LAKES:
Lough Sheelin – Cavan – Westmeath.
Lough Darravaragh – Westmeath.
Lough Ennel – Westmeath.
Lough Arrow – Sligo.
Lough Carra – Mayo.
Lough Inchiquin – Clare.

All members of the salmon family are found in Northern Ireland, and it is exceedingly difficult to know where to start. In the Foyle district for example the Mourne, the Derg, the Strule, the Glenelly, the Owenkillew, the Roe and the Faughan spread over 200 miles of salmon and sea trout waters. The Lough Neagh river network connects to Britain's largest freshwater lake. The spring salmon and grilse run leads to the Maine, the Moyola and the Blackwater fill with fish by June. The Lower Bann is privately owned and really good beats are to be found at Portna, Movanagher and Cornroe. Lough Neagh is a good resting point as the fish run on to the Moyola and the Blackwater.

Brown trout are so prolific in Lough Neagh that commercial netting takes place. Nymph and fly fishing has shown really good results but, strangely, trolling has not produced many fish. It seems rather unusual that no organised fishing has picked up here, yet there are no boats or clubs as one would expect, so bank fishing is the way but, with so many fish around, this will probably soon change.

The Ministry of Agriculture are stocking many of the lakes with rainbows and much farming is planned. Fly or spinners are allowed on Ministry waters such as: Castlewillan Lakes, the Navar Forest Lakes; Achork, Glencreawan and Meenameen; Mill Lough, Bellanaleck, Killyfole and so on. A 17 lb. brownie was picked out of Lower Lough Erne and Lough Melvin nearby does well too. Salmon fishing is as low as £1 per day in the Foyle system.

In the Foyle system no licence is needed for brown trout but a licence is necessary for salmon and sea trout. This costs £1 for a week or £3 for the season. The conservancy Board area charges are £2.25 for the season or £1.50 for fifteen days. The two boards interlock and a combined licence can be gained by endorsement. The Department of Fisheries of the Ministry of Agriculture has developed a number of trout fisheries. Their charges are: £3 per season or £1.50 for a 15 day general permit. It is necessary to hold a game fishing licence *and* a ministry permit. The Ministry angling guide is supplied free by the Ministry at: 2–4 Queen St., Belfast, BT1 6EP.

The Close Seasons for Northern Ireland are:

CONSERVANCY BOARD AREA: Lough Melvin, October 16 – January 31; Lough Erne System, October 16 – February 25; all other waters November 1 – February 25.

FOYLE AREA: River Foyle (Tidal) and Finn in Co. Donegal, September 16 – March 31; Rivers Mourne, Berg, Strule, Glenelly, Owenkillew and tributaries, Faughan, Roe and Bennett, October 21 – March 31.

Licence addresses are: The Fisheries Conservancy Board for Northern Ireland, 30 High St., Portadown, Co. Armagh.

Foyles Fisheries Commission, 8 Victoria Rd., Londonderry.

County Fermanagh has taken a great interest in the game fisherman and has become quite famous for its early salmon. From February 1 the waters are open.

Lough Melvin is best for salmon and Lough Erne for trout. Plenty of double figure trout have emerged from the latter. The Naver Forest Lake; Mill Lough at Ballanaleck offers terrific rainbows (over 5 lbs) and Mill Lough, Killyfole, offers cheap brown trout fishing (25p). Casting platforms have been erected all through the county.

The best rainbow trout waters are at Castledillon, Gentleowens, Brantree, Roughan, Tullinawood and Darkley. You may send details of any noteworthy fish to: The Fisheries Board, 2–4 Queen St., Belfast, BT1 6EP.

Where to Fish in Northern Ireland

SHAW'S LAKE, Markethill, (40 acres): Brown trout with a few rainbows. The season is from March – October 31. Restrictions: Six fish with a maximum takeable size of 10 ins. Fly fishing only. Permit: Norman Brown, Shaw's Lake.

CASTLEDILLON LAKE. Armagh (52 acres): Rainbow trout. The season is from June 1 – October 31. Restrictions: six fish with a minimum size of 10 ins. Fly and spinning with bait fishing is permitted after August 1. Permit: Armagh and W. V. Troughton's Service Station, Armagh Rd., Portadown.

GENTLE, OWENS, TULLYNAWOOD, DARKLEY AND AUGHNAGURGAN LAKES, (Gentle Owens 23 acres; Tullynawood, 93 acres; Darkley, 18 acres, Aughnagurgan, 15 acres): Rainbow trout. The season is from March 1 – October 31. Gentle Owens opens June 1. Restrictions: Six fish with a minimum takeable size of 10 ins. Darkley and Aughnagurgan – all legal methods; Tullynawood, fly fishing only; Gentle Owens – fly and spinning. Permit: Fisheries Conservancy Board Game fishing rod licence.

BRANTRY LOUGH, Benburb (60 acres): Rainbow trout. The season is from June 1 – October 31. Restrictions: Six fish with a minimum takeable size of 10 ins. Fly fishing only. Permit: Mrs. E. McAnnallen, Tullygiven, Eglish, Dun. Licence: Fisheries Conservancy Board Game fishing rod licence.

ROUGHAN LAKE, Coalisland (48 acres): Rainbow trout. The season starts from June 1 – October 31. Restrictions: Six fish with a minimum takeable size of 10 ins. All legal methods. Licence: Fisheries Conservancy Board Game fishing rod licence; Permit: E. Oliver, The Bungalow Filling Station, Coalisland.

Tags: For research purposes a percentage of the re-stocked fish have been tagged and anglers are requested to forward any tags found on fish caught together with a scale sample and full details of the fish to the Laboratory, The Cutts, Coleraine.

LOUGHBRICLAND, Banbridge (66 acres): Brown trout. Season: March 1 – October 1. Restrictions: Six fish with the minimum takeable size of 10 ins. Fly fishing only, Licence: Fisheries Conservatory Board; Permit: E. Hammond Lake View Service Station, Loughbricland.

Note: Avoid the North and South tips when wading.

CASTLEWELLAN LAKE, Castlewellan (103 acres): Brown and rainbow trout. Season: March 1 – October 31. Restrictions: Six fish minimum takeable size of 10 ins. Fly, spinning with bait fishing permitted after August 1. Licence: Fisheries Conservancy Board. Permit: The Forest Office beside the car park, in Castlewellan, Forest Park.

SPELGA RESERVOIR, Hilltown (148 acres), Brown trout. The season starts on March 1 and ends October 31. Restrictions: Six fish with a minimum takeable size of 8 ins. No Sunday fishing. Fly or spinning only. A licence of the Fisheries Conservancy Board is needed and a permit is obtainable from B. Spiers, Main St. Hilltown. For hygienic reasons, as well as safety reasons, wading is not permitted and no fishing is allowed from the dam.

KILLYLAND RESERVOIR, Larne (50 acres). Brown trout. The season is from March 1 – October 31. There are some restrictions: Six fish with a minimum takeable size of 9 ins. All fishing methods are allowed if legal. Licence: Fisheries Conservancy Board. Permit: Messrs. R. and A. Farquar, Glenwherry Service Stn., Ballymena.

RIVER MAIN. Under an agreement with the Ministry, the Main Angling Club have agreed to issue up to 12 daily permits to people wanting to fish on their stretch of the river, which covers (with few exceptions) about 4 miles of fishing from both banks of the river from a point a few hundred yards above Cullybackey to just above Dunminning Bridge. Daily permits: Gaston's Supermarket, Cullybackey.

LOUGHS BRADAN AND LEE. (Bradan, 60 acres. Lee 37 acres.) Brown trout. Season: April 1 – October 20. Restrictions: Six fish with a minimum takeable size of 9 ins. Fly or spinner with worming at Lough Lee. No fishing is allowed from the car park weir. No licence is needed but a permit is. It can be obtained from Messrs. Flanagans 17–18, Sedan Avenue, Omagh.

MOOR LOUGH AND LOUGH ASH, Donemana (Ash, 38 acres; Moor, 40 acres.) Brown trout. Season: April 1 – October 20. Restrictions: Six fish with a minimum takeable size of 9 ins by any legal method. Permit: Ministry of Agriculture from W. Smythe's Burmah Service Stn. Tags should be returned to the Foyle Fishery.

UPPER AND LOWER LOUGH ERNE, Enniskillen. (37,800 acres.) Salmon and Brown trout. Season: March 1 – October 15. All trout under 12 ins must be returned to the water. A Fisheries Conservancy licence is needed for Salmon fishing. Permits are available from Post Offices and local tackle dealers. Return tags to the Ministry.

LOUGH NAVAR FOREST LAKES, Enniskillen (14 miles – 10, 46 and 47 acres.) Brown and rainbow trout. Season: March 1 – October 15. Restrictions: Six fish with a minimum taking size of 8 ins. Fly, spinning or worming. There are three mountain lakes: Achork (10 acres) Meenameen (46 acres) and Glencreawan (47 acres). These lakes situated in a forest area are close to a scenic drive. They are well stocked with brown trout and rainbow trout. The fish are numerous and average about 10 ozs although a rainbow trout weighing 5 lbs was taken from Glencreawan in 1969. Achork and Meenameen hold many hard fighting brown trout of $\frac{3}{4}$ lb – 1 lb. and over. Fishing is only allowed from the shores which are rocky and clean. A number of good fishing stands have been provided. Permits can be obtained from Lough Navar Forest Office.

MILL LOUGH (Bellanaleck) Enniskillen (100 acres): Rainbow and brown trout. The season is from March 1 – October 15. Restrictions: Six fish with a minimum size of 10 ins is allowed. Fly and spinning. Bait fishing is allowed from August 1. A Fisheries Conservancy licence is needed. Permits can be obtained from: Mr. G. A. Cathcart, local shop in Bellanaleck.

MILL LOUGH (Eillifole, 56 acres): Brown and rainbow trout. The season is from March 1 – October 15. Restrictions: Six fish with a minimum takeable size of 10 ins. Fly and spinning only. Licence: Fisheries Conservancy Board. Permit: M. J. Mulligan's Shop and Service Station at Dernawilt crossroads.

THE ATLANTIC SALMON RESEARCH TRUST

BY

VICE-ADMIRAL SIR HUGH MACKENZIE,

K.C., D.S.O., D.S.C.

How can salmon be sustained in the second half of the 20th century in the face of the pressures exerted on the species and its natural habitat by Man? There is no simple answer to the question, but a vital factor is 'Conservation', in the broad sense that where the pattern or balance of nature is changed or destroyed by Man, then Man must supply, in some degree, the positive counter measures needed to make good what may be lost and to help restore the balance.

The Duke of Edinburgh's message to an international conference organised in 1969 by the Atlantic Salmon Research Trust to discuss fishing for salmon on the high seas reinforces the point:

'One of the very first things which primitive Man discovered as he turned to cultivation and the domestication of animals, was that seed must be kept back for sowing and a breeding stock must be maintained for his flocks and herds to survive.

264

'The present day fishing industries of the world do not appear to have learnt the fundamental lesson.

'I hope the Atlantic Salmon Conference will help to wake up the fishing industries and National Governments to the facts of life. I hope it will help to make it clear that a wild population cannot be exploited indefinitely and that if our rudimentary form of world government cannot sort out this relatively simple problem there is not much hope for the future of the world.'

High seas fishing – mainly by drift-nets in the N. W. Atlantic off the West coast of Greenland and by long-lines in the N. E. Atlantic off the coast of Norway – remains a major issue which overshadows all that is being done towards the better management of our salmon resources; its scale can be seen from fig. 107, which depicts the annual total catch of salmon-producing countries (i.e. home-water catches) and the growth of high seas fishing: as fish caught by the latter are almost exclusively salmon (i.e. fish that have spent two or more winters at sea since migrating as smolts), catches of grilse have been excluded.

As already made plain in this book the salmon has to face many threats: over-exploitation by Man remains possibly the most serious, whether this be on the high seas, along the coasts whilst homing to its native haunts, or in these, the rivers of its birth. The antidote is Conservation, and this requires a sure foundation of research, education and an informed public.

The Trust

The Trust has been formed to combat the many and increasing threats to the survival of salmon and sea trout. The scale of this problem is outlined below, but its solution is the direct concern of all who are interested in salmon or sea trout – whether as netsmen, anglers, dealers, tackle-makers or owners of fishings, or as 'Conservationists'.

The Problem

In many North Atlantic rivers, salmon have been a diminishing species since the Industrial Revolution; in this country intensified industrialisation, pollution, abstraction and dam-building, coupled with new exploitations, for example, by high seas fishing, have increased the risk that the remaining stocks may cease to be commercial and

Fig. 107

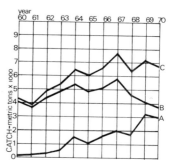

265

recreational assets; only concerted measures, quickly taken, can check this risk.

Salmon hatch and spend, as parr, the first years of their lives in rivers before going down to the sea as smolts; once in the sea they grow rapidly and in the course of the next three years they return to the rivers from which they came, to spawn and complete the cycle. Spawned fish, or kelts, if they survive, will again go down to the sea and a few kelts return to spawn again. If this cycle is seriously interrupted at any point, whether in river, estuary or the sea, by obstacles, pollution, disease or over-cropping, the results can be disastrous to the species. Sea trout have a similar life cycle and are subject to similar hazards. They are therefore included in the aims of the Trust.

The difficulties in maintaining such a valuable natural resource as salmon and sea trout are being tackled in various ways by Government Departments. Statutory Authorities, industry, private enterprise; some Universities, particularly Liverpool, play a major role. There are bodies with similar objectives in Canada, the U.S.A. and Europe. Experience has shown that given proper conservation salmon can recover their former abundance; there have also been remarkable changes in salmon populations which appear to be unrelated to human activities. A better understanding of the whole ecology governing the species and more efficient management could lead not only to the restoration of stocks now at low ebb but eventually perhaps, to fisheries more productive than have ever been known before.

But notwithstanding, for example, the part played in this country by the Salmon Research Group of the Natural Environment Research Council and, internationally, by the Anadromous and Catadromous Fish Committee of the International Council for the Exploration of the Sea, there is no overall co-ordination of all of this work: the subject is common to all, yet there is no central organisation from which information can be made readily available to all. When so many people in so many countries have such a deep interest in protecting such a valuable natural asset this state of affairs must be remedied.

Programme
To achieve its aims the Trust has adopted the following programme:

266

a To collate and co-ordinate the efforts of all bodies in all countries concerned with conservation of Atlantic salmon and sea trout; to collect all available relevant statistics; to make the resulting information known wherever it can be useful.

b To promote and encourage research projects for the regeneration and maintenance of salmon and sea trout stocks. A case in point is work being undertaken by the Salmon Research Trust of Ireland.

c To provide training facilities for those engaged in the management of salmon fisheries; to encourage the sound training and proper employment of scientists specialising in salmon and sea trout by financing travelling fellowships in co-operation with Universities.

d To assist River Authorities, Fishery Boards and other appropriate Authorities, if requested by them, in surveying and improving their river systems so as to increase productivity.

e To be represented at conferences; to organise others in case of need to achieve total cover of work related to salmon; to sponsor visits to countries where salmon research work is being conducted; to collaborate with the International Atlantic Salmon Foundation, registered in the United States.

Cost

The gross total cost of such a programme, spanning seven years, is estimated at half a million pounds, which is thus the target for the Appeal. The extent to which work can be done will depend entirely on the response to the Appeal.

Progress hitherto has been made possible by the support of the Dulverton Trust, Associated Fisheries Ltd., the International Atlantic Salmon Foundation, and more recently by the response of individuals and other organisations; but there is still a long way to go.

Whilst approaches to major units in industry and commerce form a normal part of appeal procedure, the main effort is concentrated on organising throughout the United Kingdom a personal approach to local interests and to individuals who are potential supporters. This involves setting up voluntary regional committees, broadly county by county in England and on major river systems in Scotland and Wales. By individual members of each committee enlisting further support, and so on down the line, forming additional sub-committees where and if necessary it is hoped the Appeal will snowball until all interested within any particular locality will have had their attention drawn to it and have been invited to subscribe. To prime this pump the area committees can be provided by the Trust's headquarters with lists of potential subscribers in their area, including, i.e., firms, tackle dealers, fishing hotels, individuals.

Setting up such an organisation – from Land's End to John O'Groats – takes time; but where already effective there has been a rapid rise in the volume of subscriptions received.

Overshadowing any practical research work, which the Trust may wish to support, there hangs the issue of high seas fishing for salmon; while the Trust as a registered charity cannot engage in the political arguments, it continues to collect factual information bearing directly on the problem, presenting this wherever most appropriate, and it attaches great importance to research programmes directed towards providing the scientific evidence needed to elucidate conclusively the effects of high seas fishing on home-water catches. Additionally, it is necessary to give priority to more fundamental research and to education. With the advice of the Scientific Advisory Panel, augmented by representatives from the Ministry of Agriculture, Fisheries and Food, the Department of Agriculture and Fisheries for Scotland, and the Natural Environment Research Council, the Trust has decided to make a start, in formal association with the Salmon Research Trust of Ireland, on the first two priorities, the benefits of which will be made widely available:

1: A research project to investigate rearing smolts in one year instead of two, by the use of warmed water.
2: Training courses in hatchery management and techniques, including tagging and rearing of young salmon to the smolt stage.

In addition, the Trust has had generous offers of facilities for research of the river Brora in Southerland, the Grimersta in Lewis, and the Kilmarie in Skye: Scientific surveys of all three are being arranged in conjunction with the Department of Agriculture and Fisheries for Scotland and with the University of Liverpool, to establish how best to make immediate use of these exciting prospects. Meantime, the Trust continues to co-ordinate its programme with that being developed by the International Atlantic

Salmon Foundation, which includes, for example, a survey of the economic factors involved in salmon fisheries, on the high seas and in home-waters.

The Trust receives neither grant nor subsidy. It is dependant entirely on voluntary help and is appealing, therefore, for the total cost of its programme.

Further information can be obtained from:
The Director,
Atlantic Salmon Research Trust Ltd.,
29, South St., Farnham, Surrey.
Tel: FARNHAM 24400.

Well, you should now have a pretty good idea of how to set about catching a salmon or trout. We end this book with a perfectly true story of a short fishing expedition in the summer of 1971.

George Mortimer and I arrived at the waterside of an excellent Spey beat around noon. Within half an hour I had landed a nice 10 lb hen, but that was all. After a while George took the gillie off to lunch, and the rest of the party fished through. The gillie, on his return, decided one member of the party, an eminent University lecturer, wasn't casting a good line. So he proceeded to show him how. The first attempt resulted in a large splash and a wet gillie. Eyebrows raised at this but the gillie insisted on doing it again, so he did – with an even louder splash. Well, gillies don't fall into rivers very often – not twice anyway. So George, who had given up proposing to an aboriginal (who happened to be with the party), 'tutted' a few times and said he had better take the gillie home. Booze *was* mentioned, but only in whispers.

That evening a hushed telephone message told me of a fearful car crash; George was in hospital and the car was wrecked.

I arrived at the hospital in great anguish. George looked up tearfully and through trembling white lips whispered, 'It is in the boot!' 'What is in the boot?' I asked. 'Your bloody salmon!' bellowed George 'I can't sleep from worrying over it'.

And sure enough, the salmon *was* in the boot; intact – and very tasty it was too. George has the lumps and bumps of that car crash to this day but neither he nor the gillie are any the worse for it – and they did save the salmon. . . .

Index